W9-AMX-716

Southern Literary Studies
Louis D. Rubin, Jr., Editor

DOMESTIC NOVELISTS
IN THE OLD SOUTH

DOMESTIC NOVELISTS IN THE OLD SOUTH

Defenders of Southern Culture

Elizabeth Moss

LOUISIANA STATE UNIVERSITY PRESS
Baton Rouge and London

Designer: G. Phoebe
Typeface: Janson Text
Typesetter: G & S Typesetters, Inc.
Printer and binder: Thomson-Shore, Inc.

Library of Congress Cataloging-in-Publication Data
Moss, Elizabeth, 1959–
    Domestic novelists in the Old South : defenders of Southern
culture / Elizabeth Moss.
        p.   cm. — (Southern literary studies)
    Includes bibliographical references (p.   ) and index.
    ISBN 0-8071-1730-7 (cloth : alk. paper)
    1. Domestic fiction, American—Southern States—History and
criticism.   2. Women and literature—Southern States—History—19th
century.   3. American fiction—Women authors—History and criticism.
4. American fiction—19th century—History and criticism.
5. Southern States in literature.   6. Family in literature.   7. Home
in literature.   I. Title.   II. Series.
PS373.D57M67   1992
813'.3099287—dc20
                                                                        91-40827
                                                                        CIP

The author is grateful to the University of Virginia Library for permission to quote from letters of Augusta Evans and Caroline Hentz in the following collections: the Augusta Evans Wilson Collection (#8293) and the Barrett Author Collection (#9040), both in Clifton Waller Barrett Library, Manuscripts Division, Special Collections Department, University of Virginia Library. The author is also grateful to the following repositories for permission to quote from the collections and documents noted: the Museums of the City of Mobile, for letters of Augusta Evans Wilson; the South Carolina Historical Society, for the Caroline Howard Gilman Papers; the South Caroliniana Library, University of South Carolina, for the Samuel Gilman Papers; Woodruff Library, Emory University, for the Mildred Seydell Papers; Perkins Library, Duke University, for the Mary Virginia Terhune Papers; and the Southern Historical Collection, University of North Carolina at Chapel Hill, for the Rachel Heustis Papers and the Hentz Family Papers.

For Steve
who always believed

Contents

Acknowledgments

Many people have helped make this book possible, and I am pleased to have an opportunity to acknowledge my appreciation publicly. First, I would like to thank Rowland Berthoff for never questioning my decision to study an obscure group of southern women writers. His intellectual rigor and editorial eye improved the quality of my argument and my manuscript, and his patience and good humor made the process enjoyable. I am grateful, too, to Mark Leff, whose scholarly example serves as constant inspiration; his friendship and generosity provided vital sustenance throughout this project. Wayne Fields made a history student welcome in the English department; his appreciation of the antebellum South and enthusiasm for the interrelationship between literature and history kept my work interesting and in perspective. Barbara Carson introduced me to southern women writers and taught me to appreciate their place in American culture; at a later stage, she subjected my work to careful scrutiny and rid my prose of many infelicities. Gary Williams persuaded me to study southern history in the first place and helped teach me how to write and think; any evidence of these processes contained herein redound to his credit. I would also like to thank the Mr. and Mrs. Spencer T. Olin Foundation and Washington University in St. Louis for substantial financial assistance.

Three people deserve especial mention: Elizabeth Fox-Genovese and Drew Gilpin Faust made time to read this manuscript at a crucial stage and offered many helpful suggestions for its improvement. William Perry Fidler answered many questions, made manuscripts from his private collection available, and checked my work against his for inconsistencies.

Friends and family played an equally important role in seeing this work to completion. Patricia Nelson and Holly Bode cheerfully provided

Acknowledgments

books and more books; Melanie Cameron lent her computer—and her ear—without complaint; Jane White discussed the complexities of southern womanhood ad infinitum; Zahra Yousefi kept me moving ahead when everything argued against it. Arlina and Calvin Moss traveled across the South in search of domestic novelists on more than one occasion; their enthusiasm and lavish support got this project off the ground and kept it going. Finally, Steve Reich has accommodated the unique demands of southern women writers for almost a decade. The dedication to this volume only begins to suggest my debt to him.

DOMESTIC NOVELISTS
IN THE OLD SOUTH

Introduction

The Domestic Novel in the South

*F*rom her modest frame house in
Charleston, South Carolina, Caroline Gilman watched the gathering clouds
of civil war with a degree of skepticism. By 1860 the southern novelist had
weathered a long series of secession scares; she had every reason to believe
that the most recent call for southern independence would go unheeded.
As late as December 16, four days before the state legislature withdrew
South Carolina from the Union, Gilman optimistically wrote her children, "We trust the danger from abroad is over." Should the proposed
secession ordinance pass, however, Gilman admitted to "a good deal of
alarm about the Forts. If they are not surrendered to our people . . . the
slaughter must be dreadful." [1]

It fell to Gilman's granddaughter Nina Glover to notify relatives in
Massachusetts of the Palmetto State's secession. Gilman could not find
the strength to write; in an uncharacteristic display of nerves, she spent
December 21 planting asters in the Unitarian church cemetery, taking
comfort in her proximity to her husband's grave. "She says there is a great
deal for her to do there, and we are glad of it," Nina Glover wrote in
explanation of her grandmother's silence, "because she reads the newspapers so much." Still, the retreat to the churchyard failed to refresh Gilman's sagging spirits. In solitary communion with nature she was forced
to confront the reality she had so long denied: in spite of her tireless
promotion of sectional conciliation, civil war was inevitable. [2]

Gilman was the oldest of five popular antebellum southern women
writers who dedicated their careers to the discussion and, more often, the
defense of southern culture. Beginning in approximately 1833 and con-

---

1. Caroline Howard Gilman to her children, December 16, 1860, in Caroline Howard Gilman Papers, South Carolina Historical Society, Charleston.
2. Nina Glover to Mrs. C. J. Bowen, December 21, 1860, *ibid.*

tinuing through 1866, Caroline Gilman (1794–1888), Caroline Hentz (1800–1856), Maria McIntosh (1803–1878), Mary Virginia Terhune (1830–1922), and Augusta Evans (1835–1909) regaled Americans with tales of saintly mistresses, chivalrous masters, and loyal servants, using their prose to respond to northern and sometimes southern criticism and to acquaint their audience with what they believed was the "true" South. Portraying the South as an ordered, harmonious society governed by the aristocratic code of noblesse oblige, the five systematically countered charges of southern depravity leveled by antislavery advocates, arguing that the peculiar institution was but part of a larger system of reciprocal relationships that made southern society the moral superior of the individualistic North. Writing about the world they knew and, in many cases, specifying the source of their information, they mounted a domestic defense of their native or adopted region, thus laying the foundation for the romanticized version of southern history that captured American imagination during the late nineteenth and early twentieth centuries.[3]

Yet for all their enthusiasm, the writers did not exempt the South and its people from criticism; on the contrary, they subjected their region to careful scrutiny, finding much fault with the behavior of the planter class, particularly that of planter women. Although the five expressed confidence in the essential goodness of southerners throughout the antebellum era, their prose was rife with examples of the profligacy of the southern elite, a development they attributed to the influence of wealth and leisure. Openly acknowledging the importance of home influence in securing the future of southern civilization, the five writers offered their own extended critique of the ornamental feminine ideal that dominated antebellum dis-

3. The evolution of the plantation myth is discussed in Francis Pendleton Gaines, *The Southern Plantation: A Study in the Development and the Accuracy of a Tradition* (1924; rpr. Gloucester, Mass., 1962). See also Mary Ann Wimsatt, "Antebellum Fiction," in *The History of Southern Literature*, ed. Louis D. Rubin, Jr., *et al.* (Baton Rouge, 1985), 92–107; Lucinda H. Mackethan, "Plantation Fiction, 1865–1900," *ibid.*, 209–18; Elizabeth Muhlenfeld, "The Civil War and Authorship," *ibid.*, 178–87. For a description of stock characters, see Ritchie D. Watson, Jr., *The Cavalier in Virginia Fiction* (Baton Rouge, 1985); Kathryn Lee Seidel, *The Southern Belle in the American Novel* (Tampa, 1985); Rollin G. Osterweis, *The Myth of the Lost Cause, 1865–1900* (Hamden, Conn., 1973); Robert Lively, *Fiction Fights the Civil War: An Unfinished Chapter in the Literary History of the American People* (Chapel Hill, 1957); and Joyce Appleby, "Reconciliation and the Northern Novelists, 1865–1880," *Civil War History*, X (1964), 117–29.

cussions of femininity. Paradoxically, their fiction provided female readers with means and motivation to transcend the bounds of culturally prescribed womanhood but at the same time articulated grave doubts as to southern femininity's potential for rehabilitation.

The southern writers waged their ideological warfare through domestic fiction, a popular nineteenth-century literary form written exclusively by women for women. Grounded in the female moralist tradition of late-eighteenth-century England, the domestic novel was introduced in New England in 1822 and developed indigenously in response to economic and demographic changes under way in the Northeast. Typically chronicling the trials and tribulations of an intelligent, emotional, and exceedingly virtuous female temporarily forced to make her way alone, the domestic novel as formulated in the American North explored the problems and possibilities of domesticity, using stilted language and convoluted plots to emphasize the importance of home and community. That the fundamental plot of domestic novels seldom varied, at least on a superficial level, that the heroines and their troubles were, at first glance, strikingly similar, and that the saccharine tales inevitably saw feminine virtue rewarded through marriage and motherhood did not deter the genre's loyal readership. By the middle 1850s, domestic novels accounted for the majority of best-selling fiction, leading Nathaniel Hawthorne to complain that "a d——d mob of scribbling women" posed a serious threat to his livelihood. Although the southern domestic novelists never sold books by the hundreds of thousands, as Hawthorne claimed, they commanded a respectable following. Caroline Hentz, for example, sold 93,000 copies of her novels over three years, and Augusta Evans claimed late in her career that her assorted works had sold over 425,000 copies, "irrespective of foreign sales."[4]

The phenomenal popularity of domestic fiction was facilitated by the transformation of American publishing from a precarious undertaking to a sophisticated enterprise. Before 1820, literature was primarily the prov-

4. Nathaniel Hawthorne to William D. Ticknor, January, 1855, in Caroline Ticknor, *Hawthorne and His Publisher* (Boston, 1913), 141–42; James D. Hart, *The Popular Book: A History of America's Literary Taste* (New York, 1950), 97; Augusta Evans Wilson to Mildred Rutherford, October 12, [no year given], in Mildred Seydell Papers, Woodruff Library, Emory University. See also Nina Baym, *Woman's Fiction: A Guide to Novels by and About Women in America, 1820–1870* (Ithaca, 1978), 22–50; Fred Lewis Pattee, *The Feminine Fifties* (New York, 1940); and Alexander Cowie, *The Rise of the American Novel* (New York, 1951).

ince of gentlemen able to capitalize and market their endeavors with no thought to financial reward; with a few notable exceptions, women writers were conspicuously silent. By the third decade of the nineteenth century, however, a series of developments made publishing particularly attractive to the less financially secure. Technological innovations and improved transportation made it possible for books to be printed and distributed inexpensively and efficiently; copyright laws helped protect authors from literary pirates; an ever-increasing number of literate Americans made writing commercially feasible. A significant shift in readers' tastes toward fiction, combined with the introduction of modern advertising and marketing techniques, had particular implications for would-be women writers: the largest group of new readers were women with the economic wherewithal to demand literature tailored to their specific interests. With publishers anxious to gain a foothold in what suddenly had become a volatile market, aspiring female litterateurs were presented with an unprecedented opportunity to achieve fame and fortune. Caroline Gilman, Caroline Hentz, Maria McIntosh, Mary Virginia Terhune, and Augusta Evans were key figures in the making of the modern best-seller.[5]

From Gilman's early efforts to find an audience in the 1830s to Augusta Evans's reputed ability thirty years later to command $15,000 for a manuscript sight unseen, the individual and collective careers of the five southern domestic novelists illustrate the changing position of women in the literary marketplace and lend insight into the public and private concerns of the first and second generations of professional women writers. For Gilman, Hentz, and Terhune, who were married and mothers of small children, writing involved considerable strain as they struggled to balance their primary domestic responsibilities with the demands of their muse.

5. William Charvat, *Literary Publishing in America, 1790–1850* (Philadelphia, 1959); Hellmut Lehman-Haupt with Lawrence C. Wroth and Rollo Silver, *The Book in America: A History of the Making and Selling of Books in the United States* (New York, 1951); Mary Kelley, *Private Woman, Public Stage: Literary Domesticity in Nineteenth-Century America* (New York, 1984), 6–27; Mary Ryan, *The Empire of the Mother: American Writing About Domesticity, 1830–1860* (New York, 1982), 12–18; Helen Papashvily, *All the Happy Endings: A Study of the Domestic Novel in America, the Women Who Wrote It, the Women Who Read It, in the Nineteenth Century* (New York, 1956), 35–45; Herbert Ross Brown, *The Sentimental Novel in America, 1789–1860* (Durham, 1940). Susan Geary discusses the development of modern advertising techniques in "The Domestic Novel as a Commercial Commodity: Making a Best Seller in the 1850s," *Papers of the Bibliographical Society of America*, LXX (1976), 365–93.

For McIntosh, who remained single, and Evans, who married relatively late and remained childless, publication entailed stresses of a different sort. As career women at a time and in a region that defined adult femininity exclusively in terms of marriage and motherhood, McIntosh and Evans were constantly aware that they had rejected their biological destiny. All five writers regularly confronted the inherent irony of their profession: champions of domesticity, they nevertheless led lives that bore little resemblance to the one they recommended to their female audience.[6]

Although there was considerable variation in the individual incomes of the southern domestic novelists, all five depended on their writing for a portion of their respective household economies. Caroline Gilman's earnings in the late 1830s and 1840s supplemented her clergyman husband's modest salary; the depressed national economy reduced her royalties, but consistent sales paid for a small domestic staff and a summer house on Sullivan's Island. Caroline Hentz's novels were her family's sole support; after her husband succumbed to illness in the early 1850s, Hentz "turn[ed] her brains to gold" and published sixteen volumes during the last seven years of her life. Maria McIntosh's successful juvenile series and several domestic novels made her less dependent on her family and friends; while she never regained the fortune she lost in the panic of 1837, fees from her popular fiction provided her with a degree of financial autonomy. Mary Virginia Terhune, also a clergyman's wife, came to take her substantial royalties for granted. Her first novel made "several hundreds on the first edition," and she remained a commercial force for the rest of her life. Augusta Evans's early fiction bought her family a new house and the first economic security they had known. Over time Evans's economic need became less urgent—in 1868 she married a wealthy railroad executive, Lorenzo Wilson—but though her productivity slowed, she continued to command substantial fees as Augusta Evans Wilson. One publisher claimed that Evans—or "Mrs. Wilson," as post–Civil War popular culture ultimately named her—made over $100,000 in her lifetime.[7]

6. See Kelley, *Private Woman*, 7; and Anne Goodwyn Jones, *Tomorrow Is Another Day: The Woman Writer in the South, 1859–1936* (Baton Rouge, 1981), 4–5.
7. On Gilman see Samuel Gilman to Louisa Loring, November 8, 1838, in Samuel Gilman Papers, South Caroliniana Library, University of South Carolina; Daniel Walker Howe, "A Massachusetts Yankee in Senator Calhoun's Court: Samuel Gilman in South Carolina," *New England Quarterly*, XLIV (1971), 197–220; and Kelley, *Private Woman*, 14. On

The lasting influence of these five writers is suggested by successive generations of southern women readers. It is not coincidental that Anna Maria Green from Milledgeville, Georgia, decided to study Latin after reading an Augusta Evans novel nor that Elizabeth Lyle Saxon, a pupil of Caroline Hentz's, later participated in Progressive reform and wrote extensively on women's issues. Neither is it surprising that the writers Ellen Glasgow and Mary Johnston, who themselves rebelled against what they perceived as the oppressive bonds of contemporary southern womanhood, invoked domestic fiction in their literary definition of the South's "new woman." Glasgow's Virginia Pendleton, for example, mother of a modern female, read domestic novels in her youth, while Johnston's Hagar Ashendyne, a new woman in her own right, once played with a doll named after Evans' Vashti. Domestic novels awakened these fictional characters to the problems and possibilities of southern womanhood much the same way the domestic novelists themselves inspired southern women in reality.[8] By leading lives above reproach, by demonstrating beyond all question that intellectual women could fulfill their domestic responsibilities in addition to their professional obligations, Gilman, Hentz, McIntosh, Terhune, and Evans invited readers to transcend the culturally prescribed bonds of womanhood and take an active role in southern history. That Green, Saxon, Glasgow, Johnston, and a host of others met the challenge of southern domestic fiction and "overstep[ped] the bounds of authorized

---

Hentz see Caroline Lee Hentz to Abraham Hart, March 7, 1851, in Simon Gratz Collection, Historical Society of Pennsylvania, Philadelphia. On McIntosh see Kelley, *Private Woman*, 33–35, 145–48, 257–58; Baym, *Woman's Fiction*, 86–109; Julia K. Colles, *Authors and Writers Associated with Morristown* (Morristown, N.J., 1895); Julia Deane Freeman [Mary Forrest], *Women of the South Distinguished in Literature* (New York, 1860), 163–70; and John S. Hart, *The Female Prose Writers of America* (Philadelphia, 1852), 63–69. On Terhune see Mary Virginia Terhune to Virginia Eppes Dance, June 5, 1852, in Mary Virginia Terhune Papers, Perkins Library, Duke University; and Mary Virginia Terhune [Marion Harland], *Marion Harland's Autobiography: The Story of a Long Life* (New York, 1910), 363. On Evans see William P. Fidler, *Augusta Evans Wilson, 1835–1909* (Tuscaloosa, 1951); and Hart, *The Female Prose Writers of America*, 120.

8. See Anne Firor Scott, *The Southern Lady: From Pedestal to Politics, 1830–1930* (Chicago, 1970), 14, 174; Ellen Glasgow, *Virginia* (1913; rpr. Garden City, 1929); and Mary Johnston, *Hagar* (Boston, 1913). See also Jones, *Tomorrow Is Another Day*, 183–270.

'feminized pursuits'" testified to the force of the southern domestic novelists' example.[9]

Of even greater significance was the southern domestic novelists' original contribution to the proslavery ideology that galvanized the antebellum South. From Caroline Gilman's and Caroline Hentz's early explorations of the roots of southern distinctiveness in the 1830s and Maria McIntosh's exhaustive studies in the 1840s and early 1850s of the trials of southerners moved North, to Mary Virginia Terhune's and Augusta Evans's diatribes against northern religion and reform in the middle and late 1850s, southern domestic fiction documented the evolution of a uniquely feminine system of belief that reflected both its authors' personal experiences and their changing perceptions of northern and southern relations. In general, Gilman, Hentz, and McIntosh, who were born at the turn of the nineteenth century and lived in both northern and southern states, were more optimistic in their assessment of contemporary politics; they were convinced that with proper education, northerners and southerners could learn to coexist. Children of the early Republic, these three early domestic novelists had grown up on tales of the American Revolution and believed implicitly that the shared sense of purpose characteristic of the immediate postrevolutionary era could be regained. For this reason, Gilman, Hentz, and McIntosh largely resisted the temptation to chastise the North openly, voicing their resentment instead through certain ambiguities in their fiction and more directly in their private correspondence. In contrast, Terhune and Evans, who were born and came of age in the turbulent 1830s and 1840s, were openly critical of the North and its people. A generation further removed from the Revolution, the later writers were familiar only with a long history of national division, and their education and experience told them that this was the natural state of affairs. Accordingly, Terhune's and Evans' fiction was overtly condemnatory; their work held out little hope for national reconciliation, and in at least one novel Evans implied that civil war was inevitable.

This is not to say that Gilman, Hentz, and McIntosh were less politically astute than Terhune and Evans nor that the younger writers were

9. Mary Virginia Terhune [Marion Harland], "The Domestic Infelicity of Literary Women," *Arena*, II (1890), 318.

more bellicose than their predecessors; it is simply to suggest that the individual and collective life experiences of the southern domestic novelists were critical to the formation of their intensely political literary vision. Although the five writers agreed on the fundamental superiority of the South and its inhabitants, they were divided—primarily along generational lines—as to how best to assert that superiority and, further, to what end. For Gilman, Hentz, and McIntosh, who launched their careers in the 1830s and 1840s, instruction of northerners and southerners in the ways of their opposites was enough; for Terhune and Evans, who began to publish in the 1850s, the strategy of intersectional education, at least the sort of education proposed by their elders, was made obsolete by contemporary northern attitudes. The later writers found the explicit castigation of all things northern far more appealing, although tellingly they justified their moral outrage as a pedagogical technique. This variety within the essential similarity of southern domestic fiction underscores its potential to illuminate the elusive mind of the South; the continued popularity of southern domestic fiction across four decades and two generations suggests that southern domestic novels and novelists played a critical part in framing the so-called "Negro question" and familiarizing American women with its ramifications.

All five novelists owned slaves at some point in their lives, although, with the exception of Maria McIntosh, never more than a few at any given time; they were, however, closely connected with the small segment of the southern population who controlled the peculiar institution. Caroline Hentz, for example, spent the better part of thirty years educating the daughters of the Deep South's planter elite; she was intimately acquainted with the idiosyncrasies of the ruling class. Maria McIntosh was born into one of the wealthiest and most prominent families in Georgia; until she lost her fortune in the panic of 1837, she enjoyed the rarefied life her novels described. Augusta Evans, too, had expectations of power and position. Her aunt, Mrs. Seaborne Jones, owned one of the largest plantations in Georgia, and though Evans was denied her inheritance as a result of her father's poor business sense, she remained keenly aware of the social privilege that should have been hers.[10] All five writers, in fact, identified

---

10. Contemporary biographical sources include Hart, *Female Prose Writers*; Freeman, *Women of the South*; James C. Derby, *Fifty Years Among Authors, Books, and Publishers* (New

9

their interests with the southern aristocracy regardless of their financial circumstances or, even more significantly, place of birth. Harriet Martineau once observed that Caroline Gilman had so thoroughly absorbed the elite ideology during her residence in South Carolina that, at least in Martineau's estimation, she had surrendered all claim to her distinguished New England heritage. Gilman "observed to me in the slave-market at Charleston," Martineau wrote, "that her doctrine was that one race must be subordinate to the other, and that if the black should ever have the upper hand, she should not object to standing on that table and being sold to the highest bidder." Martineau did not doubt Gilman's sincerity.[11]

A wealth of experience and observation informed the southern domestic novelists' propaganda. Well traveled and better educated than most southern or northern women, these five writers had viewed slavery in a variety of contexts; their defense of the peculiar institution had the apparent ring of truth. Gilman, for instance, spent part of her girlhood at her brother's Savannah plantation before taking up permanent residence in Charleston; Hentz lived in North Carolina, Kentucky, Ohio, Alabama, and Georgia before settling in northern Florida; Evans had moved from Georgia to Texas and back to her beloved Alabama by the time she was fifteen. Furthermore, in four out of five cases the southern domestic novelists were directly familiar with free society and its limitations. Gilman and Hentz were born and reared in Massachusetts; McIntosh moved to New York from Georgia upon her parents' death; Mary Virginia Terhune, who was born in Virginia, had taken at least one lengthy tour of the North before marrying a northerner and relocating in New Jersey. Even Augusta Evans could claim some knowledge of the North from her avid reading of northern books and periodicals and correspondence with southern travelers. This firsthand information permitted the southern domestic novelists to generalize about the circumstances of slavery throughout the South

<hr>

York, 1884); James Wood Davidson, *The Living Writers of the South* (New York, 1869); Sarah J. Hale, *Woman's Record; or, Sketches of All Distinguished Women from the Beginning Until* A.D. *1850* (New York, 1853); and Sarah K. Bolton, *Successful Women* (Boston, 1888).

11. Harriet Martineau, *Harriet Martineau's Autobiography*, ed. Maria Chapman (Boston, 1877), I, 34. See also Howe, "A Massachusetts Yankee"; and Jan Bakker, "Caroline Gilman and the Issue of Slavery in the *Rose* Magazine, 1832–1839," *Southern Studies*, XXIV (1985), 273–83.

and social conditions in the North with a degree of accuracy, enhancing their credibility with northern and southern readers alike.[12]

But the southern domestic novelists did more than reiterate the ideology of the ruling class; they developed a compelling, if not altogether convincing, defense of slavery in terms of southern culture that reflected their perceptions of southern society and women's place within it. While some portions of the domestic defense of southern culture obviously were derivative—Hentz, for example, borrowed freely from Thomas Dew and Josiah Nott, among others, in *The Planter's Northern Bride* (1854)—its emphasis on the regenerative powers of the southern home and family as mediated through the aristocratic southern female set it apart from the mainstream.[13] Planter women, southern domestic fiction contended, had the privilege and the obligation to serve as the center of their immediate and extended community; they could not shirk their responsibilities if that community were to endure. That the community extolled in southern domestic fiction resembled nothing less than a well-ordered household was clearly deliberate. Male apologists could concentrate on the prerogatives of the master, the five novelists implied. They themselves were concerned with the redemptive potential of the plantation mistress, and in the hands of the southern domestic novelists, that symbol of southern culture largely assumed responsibility for the salvation of southern civilization. Through the development of her physical, intellectual, and moral faculties, the discharge of her feminine responsibilities, and the proper use of her "influence," the novelists argued, the aristocratic southern female could protect her community from northern encroachment; conversely, by succumbing to the myriad temptations that the writers associated exclusively with northern society, that same woman could precipitate regional decline.[·]

12. Harriet Beecher Stowe, in contrast, claimed only a passing acquaintance with the peculiar institution. See Thomas G. Gossett, *"Uncle Tom's Cabin" and American Culture* (Dallas, 1985), 611–62.

13. See Caroline Hentz, *The Planter's Northern Bride*, ed. Rhoda Ellison (1854; rpr. Chapel Hill, 1970), vii–xxii. Compare with Thomas Dew, "Abolition of Negro Slavery," *American Quarterly Review*, XII (1832), 189–265, and Josiah Nott, *Two Lectures on the Natural History of the Caucasian and Negro Races* (Mobile, 1844). Both articles can be found in *The Ideology of Slavery: Proslavery Thought in the Antebellum South, 1830–1860*, ed. Drew Gilpin Faust (Baton Rouge, 1981). See also Faust, *A Sacred Circle: The Dilemma of the Intellectual in the Old South, 1840–1860* (Baltimore, 1977).

Introduction

Although it is impossible to measure the impact of southern domestic fiction in winning proslavery supporters, certainly the five domestic novelists reached a broader audience than male apologists. Southern domes tic fiction, which was published with rare exceptions in the North, flourished above and below the Mason-Dixon Line; clearly Gilman, Hentz, McIntosh, Terhune, and Evans struck a responsive chord in the North despite their exploration of southern themes. Hentz's *Linda; or, The Young Pilot of the Belle Creole* (1850) went through thirteen editions in three years; Terhune wrote three of the best-selling books of 1858: *Alone* (1854), *The Hidden Path* (1855), and *Moss-side* (1857). Even Evans's overtly propagandistic *Macaria* (1864), which was published at the height of the Civil War, sold so well in the North that by the war's end Evans had amassed a small fortune in royalties.[14] Furthermore, because the domestic novelists publicly foreswore political commentary, their fiction with its deeply embedded prosouthern message was more likely to be read than that written by more overt critics of the northern regime.[15] And their extreme popularity provided them with a ready audience should they decide to promulgate their southern loyalties openly. When Maria McIntosh decided to respond publicly to the outrage of *Uncle Tom's Cabin*, she had no trouble finding space for her views in a New York paper; in fact, her lengthy argument was reprinted in pamphlet form. Likewise, Augusta Evans was able to monopolize the features page of the Mobile *Daily Advertiser* for several weeks for her series on northern and southern literature, providing northern readers with ample time to comment upon her ideas.[16]

14. See Geary, "The Domestic Novel"; *American Publisher's Circular*, XIV (August, 1859), 391; Derby, *Fifty Years Among Authors*; and William P. Fidler, "Augusta Evans Wilson as Confederate Propagandist," *Alabama Review*, II (1949), 32–44. See also Arthur B. Maurice, "Best Sellers of Yesterday: I—Augusta Jane Evans' *St. Elmo*," *Bookman*, XXXI (1910), 35–42; Hamilton W. Mabie, "The Most Popular Novels in America," *Forum*, XVI (1893), 505–15; Ernest Elmo Calkins, "Named for a Best-Seller," *Saturday Review of Literature*, XXI (1939), 3–4, 14–17.

15. Drew Gilpin Faust's explanation for the success of the nationalist ideology of the Confederacy is instructive in this context. See Faust, *The Creation of Confederate Nationalism: Ideology and Identity in the Civil War South* (Baton Rouge, 1989), 32.

16. Maria McIntosh, *A Letter on the Address of the Women of England to Their Sisters of America in Relation to Slavery* (New York, 1853), 25–26; Augusta Evans, "Northern Litera-

In spite of their literary and historical significance, however, the lives and works of these five novelists have received scant scholarly attention. As domestic writers, they typically take subordinate positions to the more colorful northerners Sara Parton (1811–1872), Catharine Sedgwick (1789–1867), E. D. E. N. Southworth (1819–1899), Harriet Beecher Stowe (1811–1896), and Susan Warner (1819–1885).[17] As southern propagandists, Gilman, Hentz, McIntosh, Terhune, and Evans are almost wholly unrecognized. Historians who explore female advocacy of slavery focus on "serious" writers such as Louisa McCord and Mary Chesnut. Domestic novelists are overlooked.[18] Part of the problem stems from scholarly per-

---

ture," Mobile *Daily Advertiser*, October 11 and 16, 1859; Evans, "Southern Literature," Mobile *Daily Advertiser*, October 30, November 6, 1859. See also Fidler, "Confederate Propagandist."

17. Representative articles include Joanne Dobson, "*The Hidden Hand*: Subversion of Cultural Ideology in Three Mid-Nineteenth-Century Women's Novels," *American Quarterly*, XXXVIII (1986), 223–42; Mary Kelley, "The Literary Domestics: Private Woman on a Public Stage," in *Ideas in America's Culture: From Republic to Mass Society*, ed. Hamilton Cravens (Ames, Iowa, 1982), 83–102; Mary Kelley, "The Sentimentalists: Promise and Betrayal in the Home," *Signs*, IV (1979), 434–46; Jane Tompkins, "Sentimental Power: *Uncle Tom's Cabin* and the Politics of Literary History," in *The New Feminist Criticism: Essays on Women, Literature, and Theory*, ed. Elaine Showalter (New York, 1985), 81–104; Beverly R. Voloshin, "The Limits of Domesticity: The Female *Bildungsroman* in America, 1820–1870," *Women's Studies*, X (1984), 283–302. Reprints of domestic novels reflect a northern bias as well. See, for example, Maria Cummins, *The Lamplighter*, ed. Nina Baym (1854; rpr. New Brunswick, 1988); Sara Parton [Fanny Fern], *Ruth Hall*, ed. Joyce W. Warren (1854; rpr. New Brunswick, 1986); Catharine Sedgwick, *Hope Leslie*, ed. Mary Kelley (1822; rpr. New Brunswick, 1987); E. D. E. N. Southworth, *The Hidden Hand*, ed. Joanne Dobson (1859; rpr. New Brunswick, 1988); Susan Warner, *The Wide, Wide World*, ed. Jane Tompkins (1850; rpr. New York, 1987). See also Tompkins, *Sensational Designs: The Cultural Work of American Fiction, 1790–1860* (New York, 1985), 122–85.

18. See, for example, Elizabeth Fox-Genovese, *Within the Plantation Household: Black and White Women of the Old South* (Chapel Hill, 1989), 242–89, 334–71; and Elizabeth Muhlenfeld, *Mary Boykin Chesnut: A Biography* (Baton Rouge, 1981). Although isolated articles and master's theses note the prosouthern content of a given novelist's work, they fail to recognize the didactic thrust of southern domestic fiction in general. Examples include Robert Hilldrup, "Cold War Against the Yankees in the Antebellum Literature of Southern Women," *North Carolina Historical Review*, XXXI (1954), 370–84; Jeanette Tandy, "Pro-Slavery Propaganda in American Fiction of the Fifties," *South Atlantic Quarterly*, XXI (1922), 41–50, 170–78; Lindsey Whichard, "Caroline Lee Hentz, Pro-Slavery Propagandist" (M.A.

sistence in viewing domestic fiction as a national phenomenon; regional and, for that matter, authorial idiosyncrasies are discounted on the grounds that, because the novels were written by women for women, their content is identical. More fundamental difficulties, however, arise from the literature itself, for southern domestic fiction was by design not immediately recognizable as propaganda. Manipulating the key elements of domestic fiction—a naïve young girl, a brooding hero, a family in chaos—southern domestic novels fused the conventional *Bildungsroman*, or story of development, with the rhetoric of proslavery, veiling an explicitly political message in the dense prose and convoluted plots characteristic of the literary genre; employing language and imagery that were, at first glance, identical to those of their northern counterparts, they transformed an apparently innocuous romance into an effective propaganda tool.

In southern domestic fiction, intersectional rivalries initiated by interfering northerners eventually separate lovers, split families, and destroy lives. Imported northern values (temporarily) debase the moral currency of southern society and throw the community into disarray.[19] Even the central character of the southern domestic novel, the ingenuous heroine, differed significantly from her northern sister. Whereas northern heroines usually were orphans, southerners typically had at least one living parent, usually their father. Whereas northerners characteristically traveled from place to place on their respective journeys toward self-knowledge and integration, southerners more often than not remained in a plantation setting. Finally, whereas northerners almost never strayed from the path of righteousness, southerners frequently wandered, choosing obviously unscrupulous male and female companions and rejecting "the sensible in favor of the easy, the vain, and the rich."[20]

Jane Tompkins has argued that popular fiction is of literary signifi-

---

thesis, University of North Carolina, 1951); Alan Berdan, "Caroline Lee Hentz: Northern Defender of Southern Tradition" (M.A. thesis, St. John's University, 1948).

19. Steven Stowe discusses the tendency of the southern aristocracy to "conflate" the personal and the political in *Intimacy and Power in the Old South: Ritual in the Lives of the Planters* (Baltimore, 1987). See also William R. Taylor, *Cavalier and Yankee: The Old South and American National Character* (New York, 1961); and Faust, *A Sacred Circle*.

20. Seidel, *The Southern Belle in the American Novel*, 4; Seidel, "The Southern Belle as an Antebellum Ideal," *Southern Quarterly*, XV (1977), 387–401.

cance because it articulates the concerns of a discrete historical moment; merging with dominant social and intellectual culture, popular novels place contemporary problems in a literary context, using familiar language and images to make a given issue comprehensible to readers. Popular novelists had "designs" on their readers, Tompkins asserts; interested in provoking a specific behavior, they fed readers information accordingly. Certainly, the dynamics of southern domestic fiction are suggestive. The published and unpublished work of Gilman, Hentz, McIntosh, Terhune, and Evans, for example, expresses concern about the physical and mental health of planter-class women, the relationship between women and men and between women and slaves, the boundaries of the southern community, and the general stability of southern society. Clearly, southern domestic novelists perceived themselves and their interests as unique. And while northern domestic fiction indicates that middle- and upper-class writers and readers may have been interested in changing their society through the integration of "feminine" values into larger society, the emphasis in southern fiction on achieving and sustaining social and political equilibrium reveals a profound commitment to the South's existing structure. By extension, the cultural agenda of the southern domestic novel reflected the fundamental conservatism of its readers and writers and their shared belief in the moral superiority of their region; embodying the unique concerns of the slave regime, it struggled to make that world and its values comprehensible to a national audience and, in so doing, brought the ideological underpinnings of the plantation South into sharp relief.[21]

Recent historiography emphasizes the importance of reading and writing in forming the slaveholding female's sense of self and shaping her extremely conservative world view. Elizabeth Fox-Genovese observes that reading helped planter women identify and resolve a variety of issues, providing "models of personal excellence, sources of personal consolation, and standards of personal and social good." To members of a culture that frequently devalued feminine achievement, reading offered crucial rein-

21. Tompkins, *Sensational Designs*, xi–xix, 147–85; Jane Tompkins, "The Reader in History: The Changing Shape of Literary Response," in *Reader-Response Criticism: From Formalism to Post-Structuralism*, ed. Tompkins (Baltimore, 1980), 201–32. See also Janice A. Radway, *Reading the Romance: Women, Patriarchy, and Popular Literature* (Chapel Hill, 1984), especially 86–156.

forcement, reassurance of their significance. Although current studies concentrate on the impact of serious as opposed to popular literature, a distinction that antebellum readers often made themselves, there is indication that domestic novels were of singular importance in the socialization of the female elite. Steven Stowe suggests that by familiarizing women with their unique responsibilities and defining their expectations of womanhood, specifically courtship and marriage, domestic fiction "lent substance to the women's sphere and made it habitable." And while Stowe's evidence is inconclusive, he speculates that southern women interpreted didactic literature differently from the way northerners did. The persistence of marriage to cement families and fortunes within the southern aristocracy at the same time that elite northerners were moving toward a companionate model is but one suggestion that northerners and southerners brought different assumptions to popular women's fiction.[22]

There is every reason to expect significant regional variations within the genre of domestic fiction. The increasing divergence of the North and the South over the course of the antebellum period greatly influenced the social and political agendas of northern and southern women and had direct bearing on the content of popular women's fiction. In the North, for example, the development of a market-based economy with its attendant ideology of bourgeois individualism encouraged the polarization of society into public and private, or male and female, spheres of activity that facilitated female unity across class lines. Upper- and middle-class women, especially those who lived in areas of rapid growth, claimed unity with their working-class sisters and, using the moral authority vested in their separate sphere, organized to improve their immediate and extended communities. Sewing circles, missionary societies, and a variety of organizations calculated to uplift unfortunate mothers and children proliferated throughout the antebellum North; organized abolitionism and the first women's rights movement grew directly from northern female voluntary associations. In the South, however, elite southern women rejected both

22. Fox-Genovese, *Within the Plantation Household*, 242–43; Stowe, *Intimacy and Power*, 67–68, 105–106; Steven Stowe, "City, Country, and the Feminine Voice," in *Intellectual Life in Antebellum Charleston*, ed. Michael O'Brien and David Moltke-Hansen (Knoxville, 1986), 295–324.

the reform impulse and the notion of female solidarity upon which it was predicated. Unlike their northern counterparts, planter women conceived of society as naturally hierarchical; to deny the apparent inequalities of race, class, and gender was to call into question the philosophical basis of southern civilization. For this reason, southern women of privilege typically identified their interests with those of their men. Unlikely to feel any kinship with yeoman or slave women, they failed to use the commonality of the female experience in the South as an impetus for social change.[23]

Until recently, historians have blamed the lack of women's explicit political activity in the antebellum South on the repressive actions of planter men. William R. Taylor, for example, asserts that the terror of abolitionism and militant feminism led southern males to formulate an elaborate pattern of gender roles designed to prevent unrest among the female population. As the nineteenth century unfolded, southern women were accorded greater authority within their region provided that they exercised that authority exclusively within the established boundaries of domesticity. Women were "given the Home on the understanding that [their] benevolence was to stop at the bounds of the family"; in a very real sense, they were "bought off, offered half the loaf in the hope they would not demand more."[24] Catherine Clinton agrees that slave owners' "bunker mentality" impeded southern women from creating the sort of "female culture" that spurred northern women to challenge restrictive social mo-

23. Fox-Genovese, *Within the Plantation Household*, 62, 64. On the polarization of antebellum society see, for example, Nancy Cott, *The Bonds of Womanhood: "Woman's Sphere" in New England, 1780–1835* (New Haven, 1977); Kathryn Kish Sklar, *Catharine Beecher: A Study in American Domesticity* (New Haven, 1973); Barbara Welter, "The Cult of True Womanhood, 1820–1860," in Welter, *Dimity Convictions: The American Woman in the Nineteenth Century* (Athens, Ohio, 1976), 21–41; and Ann Douglas, *The Feminization of American Culture* (New York, 1977). On voluntary associations see Keith Melder, *Beginnings of Sisterhood: The American Woman's Rights Movement, 1800–1850* (New York, 1977); Ellen Carol Dubois, *Feminism and Suffrage: The Emergence of an Independent Women's Movement* (Ithaca, 1978); Blanche Hersh, *The Slavery of Sex: Feminist Abolitionists in Nineteenth-Century America* (Urbana, 1978); and Barbara J. Berg, *The Remembered Gate: Origins of American Feminism* (New York, 1978). On the South's resistance to women's organization see Scott, *The Southern Lady*; Jean Friedman, *The Enclosed Garden: Women and Community in the Evangelical South, 1830–1900* (Chapel Hill, 1985); and John C. Ruoff, "Southern Womanhood, 1865–1920: An Intellectual and Cultural Study" (Ph.D. dissertation, University of Illinois, 1976).

24. Taylor, *Cavalier and Yankee*, 167.

res. The planters' struggle for social and intellectual control led them to deny their women any autonomy; even requests for improved education were suspect. Over time, antebellum plantation mistresses became virtually immobilized to such an extent that the "ideological and practical divergence between females North and South was perhaps even greater than the split between male cultures."[25]

A corollary of this argument is that planter women would have engaged in sweeping social reform had their circumstances been different, that Sarah and Angelina Grimké, the planter's daughters turned feminist and abolitionist spokeswomen, were but the most visible representatives of a majority of elite southern females. Current scholarship, however, suggests that this was not the case: elite southern women willingly supported the hierarchical construct of their society because they reaped considerable benefits from social inequality. Planter women were first and foremost members of a ruling elite; they derived their primary identities from their privileged status and were more likely than planter-class men to uphold the boundaries of caste and class. Although modern sensibilities are offended by the idea that planter-class women willingly participated in sustaining their culture, historians who seek to rehabilitate the plantation mistress by underscoring her oppression and, in more extreme cases, equating her circumstances with those of her female slave choose their evidence selectively. Far more common were the elite southern women who accepted their lot without question, the self-same readers and writers of southern domestic fiction.[26]

In spite of the reexamination of the physical and intellectual experience of planter-class women, scholars have failed to investigate the medium of popular southern women's fiction; this vital resource remains untapped, its wealth of information concerning the personal and political attitudes of planter-class females unincorporated into the ongoing revision of south-

25. Catherine Clinton, *The Plantation Mistress: Women's World in the Old South* (New York, 1982), 13–14. See also Anne Firor Scott, "Women's Perspective on the Patriarchy," *Journal of American History*, LXI (1974), 52–64; and Irving H. Bartlett and C. Glenn Cambor, "The History and Psychodynamics of Southern Womanhood," *Women's Studies*, II (1974), 9–24.

26. Fox-Genovese, *Within the Plantation Household*, 47–48, 338–39; George C. Rable, *Civil Wars: Women and the Crisis of Southern Nationalism* (Urbana, 1989), 1–3.

ern women's history. The abundance of female-oriented fiction written by Gilman, Hentz, McIntosh, Terhune, and Evans indicates that popular literature helped to formalize and codify the elite southern female's conservative world view, familiarizing readers with the issues separating North and South by translating political rhetoric into easily accessible language and images. By projecting an alternative standard for feminine behavior, southern domestic novels encouraged planter-class women to participate in contemporary political discourse while remaining within the bounds of accepted feminine behavior.

The implicit and explicit political content of northern domestic fiction has received careful attention. The northern domestic novel, which developed alongside the organized women's reform movement, grew out of northerners' anxieties toward their rapidly modernizing world; domestic fiction provided a vehicle through which native-born upper- and middle-class women could articulate their growing concerns about the state of contemporary northern society. At times, their observations were extremely personal; in every case, best-selling northern domestic novelists were members of the established New England urban elite, a group most sensitive to status decline. Still, amidst the variety of northern fiction ran a common theme: American society was in danger, and it was incumbent upon women to intervene, to transform that society through the imposition of feminine values upon the larger world. That the evangelical tone of much of northern domestic fiction impelled many northern women to participate in reform activity goes without question; northern domestic writers were nothing less than "preachers of the fictional page," determined to reconstruct society along commonly recognized protofeminist lines.[27]

The published and unpublished work of the southern domestic novelists has received no such scrutiny; while scholars consistently note their puzzlement that nearly half were native or self-identified southerners, they make no effort to factor regional peculiarities into their analysis, much less to work toward an alternative southern model.[28] Only Anne Goodwyn

27. Ryan, *The Empire of the Mother*, 97–142; Kelley, *Private Woman*, 285–315.
28. See Baym, *Woman's Fiction*, 67–71, 86–109, 126–39, 197–207, 278–96; and Kelley, *Private Woman*, 347n. See also Frances B. Cogan, *All-American Girl: The Ideal of Real Womanhood in Mid-Nineteenth-Century America* (Athens, Ga., 1989). Cogan identifies an al-

Jones has worked toward a reading of southern domestic fiction that gives
equal weight to region, class, and gender. Given that the impact of indus-
trialization escaped comment by southern intellectuals until the 1930s
with the advent of the Southern Literary Renaissance, Jones argues that it
is unlikely that popular writers, particularly popular women writers, would
have tackled the subject a century earlier. Furthermore, since antebellum
southern ideology had more to do with race than with the bourgeois values of the North, it is unreasonable to expect southern women writers to
address the issues raised by "materialism and individualism" in the same
way northern writers did. Finally, since the value system of the planter
class was, at least in theory, antithetical to northern ideology, it is only
logical that fiction written by elite southern women would reflect a dis-
tinctly southern slate of concerns.[29]

The lives and work of Gilman, Hentz, McIntosh, Terhune, and Evans
suggest that southern domestic fiction raises its own set of questions. In
the first place, the five best-selling southern novelists evidence none of
that preoccupation with restructuring society pivotal to northern domestic fiction; southern writers merely wanted to improve the existing construct of their region. While northern writers criticized society in general,
blaming the declension of American values variously on men, industry,
and urbanization, southern writers were much more specific. Identifying
their region as America's last best hope, they focused their dissatisfaction
on the North, defining its culture and its people as the mirror image of
their own. Finally, while northern writers were appalled by what they perceived to be the rampant materialism of America and used their fiction to
protest its implications for women, southern writers waxed eloquent about
the nutritive properties of the southern environment. The stratified South
was most conducive to the sort of community that prevented the spread
of materialism, the southern novelists argued; the problem as they saw it
was more how to quarantine the South from pernicious northernism than
how to combat an already entrenched ethic of individualism. That Gilman, Hentz, McIntosh, Terhune, and Evans found an audience above the

---

ternative standard for female behavior in the Northeast and paradoxically uses southern
domestic novels as evidence.

29. Jones, *Tomorrow Is Another Day*, 54–55.

Mason-Dixon Line—a point frequently used to assert the universality of the domestic message—simply emphasizes the need to heed the "text and context" of popular fiction."[30]

The literary roots of the southern domestic novel further distinguish it from the northern prototype. The northern domestic novel grew out of a didactic or homiletic literary model peculiar to New England, but southern domestic fiction, which entered the South over a decade after the Massachusetts writer Catharine Sedgwick inaugurated the best-selling genre, had a heritage all its own.[31] In fact, the southern domestic novel was most clearly influenced by the indigenous tradition of plantation fiction. Although the plantation novel, which flourished from 1832 until the eve of the Civil War, tended to emphasize the heroism of the planter-cavalier rather than the resourcefulness of his lady-wife, a reflection of its primarily male authorship, southern domestic fiction essentially duplicated its setting and cast of characters. Yet the correspondence between plantation and southern domestic fiction extended well beyond these superficial similarities. Both literary forms, for example, tapped into readers' apprehensions about the precarious state of southern affairs, stressing the stability of the South and the instability of the North; both lamented the materialism of the modern day; both designated the home, with woman its custodian, as the bedrock of southern civilization; both projected the South as the bastion of national virtue and the North as the nation's ruin. Most important, both the plantation novel and the southern domestic novel were quickly enlisted in the service of the southern cause as southern writers became increasingly convinced that their culture was under attack from northerners, especially northern abolitionists.[32]

30. Fox-Genovese, *Within the Plantation Household*, 242–43.

31. Ryan, *The Empire of the Mother*, 21; Seidel, *The Southern Belle in the American Novel*, 4.

32. John Pendleton Kennedy is formally credited with inaugurating the plantation tradition in southern literature, which introduced a host of black and white and northern and southern stereotypes into the American imagination. With the publication of *Swallow Barn; or, a Sojourn in the Old Dominion* in 1832, Kennedy laid the groundwork for the defense of southern culture found in subsequent southern domestic fiction. For discussion of the origins of the plantation tradition see Taylor, *Cavalier and Yankee*, 178–92. Francis Pendleton Gaines's *The Southern Plantation* (1924; rpr. Gloucester, Mass., 1962) remains the definitive

The use of popular literature to define—and to justify—regional differences was hardly new; neither was it necessarily of southern origin. William R. Taylor observes that from the early national period onward, American writers routinely contrasted the "commercial" North with the "agrarian" South, paying little attention to the accuracy of the description at any given point. Depicting the South as an aristocratic region governed by honor and duty and the North as a classless society that rewarded talent and hard work, writers from both regions extolled a country that balanced the stability of the Old World against the instability of the New. Citizens took comfort in the knowledge that the static South counterpointed the chaotic North, confident that this particular configuration of national qualities perpetuated the promise of the Revolution. For a time, North and South coexisted harmoniously in both fact and fiction, but with the reopening of the slavery question in the 1830s, political dissension spilled over into popular literature. Forced to defend their peculiar institution against what they perceived as rampant abolitionism, southern writers argued the positive good of slavery in religious, scientific, and economic terms. Books and pamphlets defining the North-South struggle in terms of a battle between evil and good flooded the nation, giving the long-accepted list of regional differences a moral dimension. The plantation novel and the southern domestic novel were two clear manifestations of male and female southern writers' need to protect their region from what they perceived as unrelenting northern aggression.[33]

The similarities in the theory and practice of plantation and southern domestic fiction have led many historians and literary critics to regard the genres as one and the same, yet there are equally valid reasons to differentiate between the two. Bertram Wyatt-Brown observes that the purpose

---

work on plantation fiction. More recently, Mary Ann Wimsatt has surveyed the leading practitioners of the genre in "Antebellum Fiction." See also Watson, *The Cavalier in Virginia Fiction*; and Seidel, *The Southern Belle in the American Novel*.

33. Taylor, *Cavalier and Yankee*, 96–97. Drew Gilpin Faust presents examples of each position in *The Ideology of Slavery*. For an alternative interpretation see Larry Tise, *Proslavery: A History of the Defense of Slavery in America, 1701–1840* (Athens, Ga., 1987). At least one historian believes that southern propagandists wrote to convince other southerners. See Ralph E. Morrow, "The Proslavery Argument Revisited," *Mississippi Valley Historical Review*, XLVII (1961), 79–94.

of plantation fiction was to ensure the proper behavior of slaveholders as well as to provide readers beyond the South with an accurate portrait of southern life. Celebrating the virtues of southern civilization and exploring the distinctive character of the southern people, plantation novels used "stereotypes and artificial plots" to convey their "scarcely subtle themes which exhibited strong pride in slave-state ways." Designed to counteract the negative publicity circulated by antislavery forces, plantation novels were nothing more than "highly legitimate means to legitimate political ends" that held the added attraction of illustrating moral truths in a manner that fused nicely with "traditional [southern] ethics."[34]

While Wyatt-Brown's generalizations are clearly applicable to southern domestic fiction, the published and unpublished writings of Gilman, Hentz, McIntosh, Terhune, and Evans reveal that these authors had a specifically feminine agenda that paralleled rather than intertwined with contemporary male concerns. Although plantation novelists, like domestic novelists, urged a renewed commitment to the values of domesticity and predicated the ability of the South to remain uncontaminated by northern values on the strength of its indigenous institutions, male and female writers had different ideas concerning how best to achieve that end. What role were women to play in "shoring up the long-revered values" of southern society?[35] How fixed was the boundary between public and private activity? What was a proper division of authority within the home and family, and how did that impinge upon the distribution of power within the larger southern community? Although these questions figured prominently in both plantation and southern domestic fiction, the answers plantation writers and domestic writers proposed revealed fundamental differences in the way men and women defined their society and their respective places within it.

From Caroline Hentz's ill-fated *Lovell's Folly* (1833), technically the first southern domestic novel though it was almost immediately withdrawn from publication, to Mary Virginia Terhune's *Sunnybank* (1866), a panegyric to a lost way of life, southern domestic fiction recorded the

34. Bertram Wyatt-Brown, "The Evolution of Heroes' Honor in the Southern Literary Tradition," in *The Evolution of Southern Culture*, ed. Numan V. Bartley (Athens, Ga., 1988), 112–14.

35. *Ibid.*, 114.

experience of planter-class females, providing readers with a blueprint for personal and social regeneration.[36] Written in language and images easily accessible to women above and below the Mason-Dixon Line, the southern domestic novel voiced a variety of implicit and explicit political concerns, familiarizing readers with the implications of national division while at the same time holding out hope for the resolution of intersectional tensions. While the content of individual novels differed according to the precise historical moment and the particular writer's tastes, the motivation behind and message of southern domestic fiction remained the same throughout the antebellum period: southern women of privilege must take an active role in protecting their region from northern encroachment; only through the efforts of the planter class, specifically planter-class women, could the northern threat be averted. The published and unpublished writings of Gilman, Hentz, McIntosh, Terhune, and Evans illustrate the evolving political consciousness of elite southern women and suggest that this segment of the southern population was very much a part of the vital intellectual and political culture of its region.

Although there is considerable variation in individual readings of domestic fiction, generally critics fall into two camps: those who disparage the narrow focus of the domestic novel and emphasize its fundamentally conservative world view and those who stress the breadth of the domestic sphere and therefore read the message of domestic fiction as profoundly radical.[37] Although both positions have some merit, neither adequately addresses the tremendous diversity within the domestic genre nor recognizes that the genre evolved over the course of the antebellum period. The sharp

36. Caroline Hentz's *Lovell's Folly* (Cincinnati, 1833) was withdrawn from circulation almost immediately after publication to prevent suit for libel. Hentz's northern characters were easily recognizable as prominent local citizens. See Papashvily, *All the Happy Endings*, 75–94; and Rhoda Ellison, "Mrs. Hentz and the Green-eyed Monster," *American Quarterly*, XXII (1950), 345–50.

37. Herbert Ross Brown and Alexander Cowie argue that domestic fiction was overwhelmingly conservative. See also Henry Nash Smith, "The Scribbling Women and the Cosmic Success Story," *Critical Inquiry*, I (1974), 47–49; Ann Douglas, Joanne Dobson, Mary Kelley, and Jane Tompkins take the other side. Kathleen Lant summarizes both positions (with respect to domestic fiction) in "Behind a Mask: A Study of Nineteenth-Century American Fiction by Women" (Ph.D. dissertation, University of Oregon, 1982), 86–140.

divisions in literary and historical interpretations of domestic fiction arise in part from scholarly uncertainty as to what constitutes literary merit. Nina Baym comments that literary critics have traditionally defined a "classic" in terms of a given work's ability to explicate some aspect of the American experience but adds that the desirable qualities of "American-ness" have typically reflected only the experience of middle-class white males. Not until the early 1970s did the study of American literature come to embrace "a more varied and fruitful area of investigation," with the result that popular fiction, particularly popular women's fiction, received renewed attention.

Whereas literary traditionalists use the domestic novel as an example of why the canon of American literature should remain unchanged, their opponents argue just the opposite; ironically, with regard to southern do-mestic fiction, both schools have proved equally destructive.[38] Scholars on both sides of the argument gloss over authorial idiosyncrasies and mini-mize regional distinctions in an attempt to establish (or discredit) the worth of domestic fiction, minimizing its literary and historical signifi-cance in the process. The lives and work of the five southern domestic novelists suggest that there is a middle ground, that the interests of a sig-nificant number of women writers were both broader, and in certain cases narrower, than the nationally based interpretation advanced by either school. Certainly Gilman, Hentz, McIntosh, Terhune, and Evans engaged in implicit and explicit political commentary, but their goal was neither to cast off male oppression nor to degrade American letters; they were con-cerned instead with establishing the moral innocence of their native or adopted region and exploring the proper role of women, particularly women of the planter class, in sustaining southern society.

While it is easy to interpret the assertions of feminine independence that characterize domestic fiction as indicative of novelists' dissatisfaction with their place in society, it is not always appropriate. In the case of the southern domestic writers, examination of their public and private writ-ings reveals a profound conservatism. They frequently spoke out against the women's rights movement, regarding it as yet another northern evil,

38. Nina Baym, "Melodramas of Beset Manhood: How Theories of American Fiction Exclude Women Authors," in *The New Feminist Criticism: Essays on Women, Literature, and Theory*, ed. Elaine Showalter (New York, 1985), 63–80.

and they were quick to point out the generative relationship between the phenomenon of women's rights and organized abolitionism. The independence that the five southerners endorsed in their fiction was moral and intellectual; they believed women had the right and the obligation to exercise their consciences and their minds. Furthermore, this unique sort of independence was restricted, typically by choice of the heroine. Southern writers expected women to marry and raise families; although heroines might venture into the working world, they always return to the domestic circle. Both schools clearly misinterpret the defiance of southern domestic heroines. They attempt not to subvert authority but simply to assert their moral autonomy; they run toward, not away from, their feminine destiny.[39]

Just as criticism based on a national survey of the genre confuses the thrust of domestic fiction, it distorts the motivation of its writers. Historians and literary critics offer a variety of explanations about why women wrote, all predicated on the assumption that gender is sufficient explanation for the proliferation of scribbling women in Victorian America. For example, some scholars (male and female) suggest that women wrote to degrade American letters, flooding the literary marketplace with inferior material in an effort to prevent the success of serious (that is, male) writers.[40] Others argue that changes in the household economy led to women's alienation from society; writers used their prose to create the community that male institutions denied them. Still others believe that women wrote to exorcise their anger at their male oppressors.[41]

The body of fiction penned by the five best-selling southern domestic novelists, however, reveals little of the disjunctiveness that these interpretations would suggest; on the contrary, they wrote with authority and confidence. Their fiction emanates a sense of purpose and a self-conscious desire to contribute to the ongoing debate on southern morality, and while tension is present in isolated novels, it is hardly ubiquitous. Judith

39. For alternative readings see Papashvily, *All the Happy Endings*; Dee Garrison, "Immoral Fiction in the Late Victorian Library," *American Quarterly*, XXVIII (1976), 71–89; and Beatrice Hofstadter, "Popular Culture and the Romantic Heroine," *American Scholar*, XXX (1960), 98–116.

40. See, for example, Brown, *The Sentimental Novel*; Cowie, *The Rise of the American Novel*; Douglas, *The Feminization of American Culture*; and Smith, "The Scribbling Women."

41. See, for example, Papashvily, *All the Happy Endings*; Garrison, "Immoral Fiction"; and Hofstadter, "Popular Culture and the Romantic Heroine."

Fetterley's observation that writers frequently use different voices for different novels is particularly pertinent in this context: self-contradiction in one work should not be taken as representative of the author's canon, much less of an entire genre. Some women undoubtedly did agonize over their writing lives, but others did not. The five southern sentimental writers seem to have been more concerned whether their fiction would sell than whether it was proper for them to write it. After all, women had been a significant presence in American literature since the Revolution; of the some two hundred works of fiction published in the United States between 1779 and 1829, over one-third were directed toward women. With the introduction of the domestic novel in 1822, the percentage of literature that addressed the female audience increased to the extent that by the mid-nineteenth century, Fetterley believes, "the woman who picked up her pen . . . may have felt that she was occupying essentially feminine territory."[42]

If some domestic novelists insisted that they were not writers, that they were, as Ann Douglas Wood argues, writing "unconsciously," the southern writers indicate a great degree of awareness about their profession.[43] Both Mary Virginia Terhune and Augusta Evans regularly featured heroines who write for publication. Beulah Benton and Irene Huntingdon, two of Evans's most famous heroines, achieve considerable success as journalists. Terhune and Evans in particular used their writing heroines as opportunities to discuss the problems unique to women writers. Beulah Benton, for example, learns that southern publications depend on voluntary contributions from the public; editors are unwilling to solicit, much less to commission, manuscripts. Evans uses Benton's foray into publishing to discuss why southern publications were generally inferior to those produced in the North and to prescribe measures for developing a regional literature. That some domestic authors preferred to think of themselves as professionals rather than as artists does not necessarily indicate that they suffered from "anxiety of authorship." In fact, in the case of the southern domestic writers their use of the distinction suggests that they

42. Judith Fetterley, ed., *Provisions: A Reader from Nineteenth-Century American Women* (Bloomington, 1985), 6–7.

43. Ann Douglas Wood, "The 'Scribbling Women' and Fanny Fern: Why Women Wrote," *American Quarterly*, XXIII (1971), 3–24.

were satisfied with their work. "I have never thought myself a poet, only a versifier," Caroline Gilman told her biographer. Yet Gilman was not unhappy with this designation; she realized that even though her poetry did not meet her personal standards of excellence, a ready market existed for her efforts. Contemplating the publication of a volume of her verse, she wrote her sister in Massachusetts, "It seems as if the Poems might be worth something. . . . Though below Mrs. Sigourney's, they are as good as Mrs. Gould's & better than Mrs. Follins's. I think they would be acceptable."[44]

Clearly, the southern domestic writers viewed themselves as women with a mission. Conscious of their responsibilities to their region, they tailored their arguments to suit the tastes of their primarily native-born upper- to middle-class female readers, using their knowledge of their market to launch an effective propaganda campaign. Indeed, the southern domestic writers enjoyed such enormous popularity because they perceived themselves as professionals. They were not overwhelmed by the literary market; rather, they manipulated it to serve the interests of the South. Gilman, for instance, wrote the *Recollections of a Housekeeper* (1834), which was reissued in 1852 as *Recollections of a New England Housekeeper*, in tandem with the *Recollections of a Southern Matron* (1838); Hentz frequently sent her heroes and heroines to the North, where they made lifelong friends; McIntosh regularly married northern men to southern women, converting them to the southern cause in the process. All five writers struggled to portray regional characteristics realistically, working from the premise that there was some good everywhere and in everyone. God might have created both regions, McIntosh argued in *The Lofty and the Lowly; or, Good in All and None All-Good* (1853), but the southern domestic novelists believed that it was woman's duty to ensure sectional harmony. To that end, they struggled to reach the broadest possible audience, using their innate intelligence and facility with the written word to win supporters above and below the Mason-Dixon Line.[45]

44. Caroline Howard Gilman to Anna Maria White, December 3, [no year given], in Caroline Howard Gilman Papers.

45. See Caroline Gilman's *Recollections of a Housekeeper* (New York, 1834) under its more familiar title, *Recollections of a New England Housekeeper*, in a later edition (New York, 1852). See also Gilman, *Recollections of a Southern Matron* (1838; rpr. New York, 1852); Maria

Like better-known southern male novelists, they were disturbed by changes in the American landscape. Distressed by the spread of individualism and materialism, they associated these so-called evils of modernization with the North and sought to protect their region from infection through their fiction. The predominantly agricultural South, the five writers argued, fostered communal values; Yankee industry eroded them. It was to call attention to this phenomenon and to propose a means to halt its spread that the southerners launched their propaganda campaign. Southern women wrote to confront conflicting values; the ideas they confronted and the conflict they encountered, however, had more to do with their experience as southerners than as females. Writing with confidence and authority, the five discussed the problems and possibilities of the South knowledgeably, prescribing a specific course of action for southern women in upholding southern institutions. Unconcerned about the propriety of their actions, they believed that their mission sanctioned their behavior.[46]

Bertram Wyatt-Brown has argued that loyalty to an indigenous code of honor distinguished antebellum southerners from northerners. More than "an idealization of conduct," honor defined southerners' collective identity, providing a moral framework for individual and community action. Central to the code of honor were clearly defined gender roles: defiant, aggressive masculine behavior was buttressed by compliant, passive feminine conduct. Under extraordinary circumstances such as war, however, southern women were permitted, if not encouraged, to behave differently, to model themselves after the women of classical civilization who defended their homes and families against the enemy. It was this second dimension of honor that informed the lives and works of the southern

---

McIntosh, *The Lofty and the Lowly; or, Good in All and None All-Good* (New York, 1853), preface.

46. Bertram Wyatt-Brown, *Southern Honor: Ethics and Behavior in the Old South* (New York, 1982), 226–53; Wyatt-Brown, "Honor and Secession," in Wyatt-Brown, *Yankee Saints and Southern Sinners* (Baton Rouge, 1985). See also Kenneth S. Greenberg, *Masters and Statesmen: The Political Culture of American Slavery* (Baltimore, 1985), 3–41, for a discussion of honor in the political arena. Elizabeth Fox-Genovese comments on female honor in the antebellum South in *Within the Plantation Household*, 200–204.

domestic novelists.[47] Barred from the political arena, they nevertheless acted politically, appropriating a uniquely feminine literary genre to launch a propaganda campaign that paralleled the efforts of male apologists in its intensity. Writing in the language of domesticity, they appealed to the women of America, using the images of home and hearth to make a persuasive case for southern culture; their literary crusade spanned some four decades and left a lasting impression on the American imagination. Clearly, the lives and work of Caroline Gilman, Caroline Hentz, Maria McIntosh, Mary Virginia Terhune, and Augusta Evans illuminate the important role domestic novelists and domestic novels played in the ideological warfare of antebellum America.

In Mobile, Alabama, on the eve of the Civil War, Evans shared Gilman's vigil impatiently. Yearning for excitement, the twenty-five-year-old novelist rejoiced when her state seceded on January 11 and linked its destiny with South Carolina, Mississippi, and Florida. "I am an earnest and uncompromising Secessionist," Evans asserted on January 13, adding that if she were permitted to address the Georgia convention on secession, she would "say triumphantly: 'let the star of the Empire blaze along the way to freedom; let us conquer or perish together; delay is ruinous, suicidal; the time has come!'"[48] Evans's youthful enthusiasm blinded her to the truth that Gilman had realized so painfully: the domestic defense of southern culture had run its course; the future of the South was now in the hands of the Confederate army.

47. Wyatt-Brown, *Southern Honor*, 226–53.
48. Augusta Evans to L. Virginia French, January 13, 1861, in *Alabama Historical Quarterly*, III (1941), 65–67.

I

The Sacred Mission

Before Jabez Lamar M. Curry, the Confederate congressman, consented in the summer of 1863 to lecture on southern women and slavery, he consulted his friend and fellow Alabamian Augusta Evans. By 1863, the twenty-eight-year-old Evans, an ardent Confederate, had established herself as the South's leading female novelist. Celebrated for her learning, her charm, and her total commitment to the South, Evans was eminently qualified to discuss the strengths and weaknesses of southern womanhood. Curry could ask for no better adviser.

Evans received Curry's letter in mid-July and immediately proclaimed herself inadequate to the task: "Were I capable . . . I should be proud and happy to render you all possible assistance." It was absolutely absurd, she wrote the congressman, to suppose that she "could suggest an idea which had not been already weighed and canvassed by you, labelled for use, or rejected as vapid and irrelevant." Only because she "fully appreciate[d] the compliment implied" in Curry's "flattering consultation" would she agree to discuss the "most ordinary aspects" of the "contemplated theme." Her elegant handwriting covered both sides of some ten pages of thin white stationery.[1]

Planter women "as a class" fell woefully short of fulfilling their obligations to their region, Evans told Curry. "Enervated, lethargic, incapable of enduring fatigue, and . . . afflicted with chronic lassitude," they lacked the motivation, if not the ability, to care for themselves and their families. Taught from childhood to rely upon the efforts of others, planter-class women never developed the practical and intellectual skills requisite for effective household management. "Having a number of servants always at hand," the novelist observed, "the Southern matron accustoms herself to

---

1. Augusta Evans to J. L. M. Curry, July 15, 1863, in J. L. M. Curry Papers, Library of Congress.

having every office in the household performed by others while she sits passive and inert." With no internal or external inducement to physical or mental activity, she continued, planter-class women typically "fold their listless fingers, and failing in requisite energy, become the victims of chronic vis inertiae."

Ignorance and selfishness rather than a lack of native ability prevented the majority of elite southern women from realizing their potential as "stewards" of southern culture, Evans contended. "In tropical climes," she explained, "women are generally more richly endowed than in colder latitudes . . . nature seems to stamp them . . . noble, perfect instruments for the advancement of Art." With "more leisure for the cultivation of their intellects and the perfection of womanly accomplishments," Evans asserted, southern women of privilege had an unparalleled opportunity to make important contributions to southern society. Yet more often than not, the novelist lamented, the plantation mistress sat "passive and inert . . . an incubus to her Husband, utterly incapable of properly educating and attending to her children," with the result that southern civilization as a whole suffered.

While Evans freely admitted that the limited incentives "southern circles" offered for feminine achievement restricted women's accomplishments, she argued that this was no excuse for indolence; women should pursue knowledge for its own sake. "We have thousands who are graceful, pretty, witty and pleasant," she noted, "but their information is painfully scanty; their judgment defective; their reasoning faculties dwarfed, their aspirations weak and frivolous." Poorly educated, habitually lazy females brought no credit to their region, Evans told Curry, confident that she herself was the exception that proved the rule.

Was the character of southern women prejudicially affected by slavery? "*Entre Nous*, I believe that it is," Evans confided, though she assured Curry that "the evils are not necessarily inherent nor . . . an inevitable sequence of the institution." In fact, Evans attributed many of the afflictions of slaveholding women to nothing more than insufficient exercise. In the North, where white labor was employed, "infinitely more of the household work devolved upon the Mistress," with the result that women enjoyed an overall better standard of health. "She who kneads her own bread, is very rarely troubled with dyspepsia," Evans wrote, "and one who habitually churns her butter, or inadvertently handles her broom, is a stranger to the horrors of asthma, and nervous headaches. In the South where "*brooms, rolling-pins, dashers* and *hoes* have grown obsolete," southern women languished. Clearly, southern women might be exalted by slavery, but "the practical and melancholy results" of her extended observations told Evans that this was not the case.

Evans's candid assessment of slaveholding women highlighted the political agenda of the antebellum southern domestic novel. Identifying the dominant feminine ideal, the Southern Lady, as the primary source of planter women's problems, southern domestic fiction exhorted readers to transcend superficiality and take an active role within their community. By seeking education, taking exercise, marrying prudently, and administering their households responsibly, slaveholding women could strengthen the South's domestic institutions and protect them from northern infection. Arguing that the values of the home were nothing more or less than the values of southern community, the southern domestic novel blurred the boundary between public and private spheres and gave southern women license and motivation to act politically.

To a certain extent southern domestic fiction's preoccupation with the character of southern women was simply part of a general nineteenth-century struggle to come to terms with the apparent disintegration of what Americans called "the Home." Yet the pervasive anxiety over the changing role of the family and its immediate members had particular resonance in the South, where the mere suggestion of domestic instability was perceived as a threat to slavery. Convinced that the status of women was inextricably linked with the future of the peculiar institution, antebellum southerners agonized over woman's proper place, giving and taking away her authority as contemporary politics dictated.[2] But whereas the majority of southern writers used their concern to formulate an ideology of female subordination, Evans and her colleagues moved in the opposite

2. On the changing family in America see, for example, Carl N. Degler, *At Odds: Women and the Family in America from the Revolution to the Present* (New York, 1980); Mary Ryan, *The Cradle of the Middle Class: The Family in Oneida County, N.Y., 1790–1865* (New York, 1981); and Ryan, *The Empire of the Mother.* On the southern family compare Daniel Blake Smith, *Inside the Great House: Planter Family Life in Eighteenth-Century Chesapeake Society* (Ithaca, 1980); Jan Lewis, *The Pursuit of Happiness: Family and Values in Jefferson's Virginia* (New York, 1983); Jane Turner Censer, *North Carolina Planters and Their Children, 1800–1860* (Baton Rouge, 1984); Stowe, *Intimacy and Power*; and Wyatt-Brown, *Southern Honor.*

direction. Using the South's obsession with decline as justification for women's greater participation within the southern community, Augusta Evans, Caroline Gilman, Caroline Hentz, Maria McIntosh, and Mary Virginia Terhune predicated the longevity of plantation culture upon the efforts of middle- and upper-class women and, in so doing, challenged the long-standing ideological connection between women and slaves.[3]

As early as 1835 Thomas Dew, the college professor and proslavery theorist, suggested that the equilibrium of the slave regime hinged upon women's subordination. Asserting that man occupied "the foreground of the picture" by virtue of his "greater physical strength," Dew assigned woman the home, where, suited by temperament and anatomy, she reigned supreme. Where man plunged "into the turmoil and bustle of an active, selfish world," woman was "kept aloof from the . . . storm of active life" and accorded protection much like the black slave. Confined "within the domestic circle," woman was "not familiarized to the out of door dangers and hardships of a cold and suffering world": whereas "courage and boldness" prepared man to enter the fray, "timidity and modesty" demanded that woman avoid it. But while Dew argued on the one hand that women should be nothing more than ornaments of society, he was quick to emphasize the authority that position entailed. Because women were able to "delight and fascinate" with their superficial charms, they could accomplish much. "Grace, modesty and loveliness," uniquely feminine qualities, carried their own power, and because that power was "emblematical of that of divinity," it was obviously superior to that wielded by man. Man was forced to "wind his way through the difficult and intricate mazes of philosophy," using his "intellectual powers" to master his environment, but woman asserted her authority through feminine charm. "Woman we behold dependent and weak," Dew wrote, yet "out of that very weakness and dependence springs an irresistible power."[4]

Twenty years later, the southern apologist George Fitzhugh affirmed Dew's position. Citing the northern women's rights movement as evidence

3. See Taylor, *Cavalier and Yankee*, 145–76. See also Faust, *A Sacred Circle*; and C. Hugh Holman, *The Immoderate Past: The Southern Writer and History* (Athens, Ga., 1976).

4. Thomas Dew, "On the Characteristic Differences Between the Sexes, and on the Position and Influence of Woman in Society," *Southern Literary Messenger*, I (May, 1835), 493–512; (July, 1835), 621–23; (August, 1835), 672–91; Fox-Genovese, *Within the Plantation Household*, 197–200.

that free society was "in a state 'of dissolution and thaw,' of demoralization and transition," Fitzhugh predicated the stability of the South on
the continued subordination of women; yet, like Dew, he asserted that
woman's social and political subjugation provided her great opportunity.
"So long as she is nervous, fickle, capricious, delicate, diffident and dependent, man will worship and adore her," Fitzhugh wrote. "Her weakness is
her strength, and her true art is to cultivate and improve that weakness."
Reiterating Dew's belief that "woman naturally shrinks from public gaze,"
Fitzhugh argued that females—like children and slaves—had one right,
that of protection, which according to Fitzhugh involved "the obligation
to obey." Female obedience to a "husband, a lord and master" precluded
"mal-treatment"; disobedience, however, ensured abuses against which
the law could provide no protection. "True womanly art," Fitzhugh concluded, "will give [woman] an empire and a sway far greater than she
deserves."[5]

The persistence and prominence of prescriptions for ornamental
femininity in antebellum southern culture have led historians to characterize the region's dominant feminine ideal, the Southern Lady, as an extreme manifestation of True Womanhood, a behavioral model advanced
through contemporary periodical literature. The product of male guilt
rather than female aspiration, True Womanhood mandated female pas-
sivity; woman was essentially held hostage in the home to accommodate
man's rampant acquisitiveness. Although current scholarship questions the
accuracy of this description of Victorian femininity with regard to middle-
and working-class women in the North and Midwest, True Womanhood
in some form or other remains popular in discussions of southern women.[6]
Catherine Clinton, for example, believes that southern women accepted
the male-defined Lady-ideal at face value and spent their lives trying to

5. George Fitzhugh, *Sociology for the South; or, The Failure of Free Society* (1854; rpr.
New York, 1965), 213–17. See also Fox-Genovese's discussion of gender roles in *Within the
Plantation Household*, 192–241. For discussion of the deferential nature of southern society
see Clement Eaton, *The Growth of Southern Civilization* (New York, 1961), 1–24; Rosser
Howard Taylor, *Ante-bellum South Carolina: A Social and Cultural History* (Chapel Hill, 1942);
Greenberg, *Masters and Statesmen*; and Wyatt-Brown, *Southern Honor*.

6. Welter, "The Cult of True Womanhood," 21–41. For dissenting positions see, for
example, Joan Jensen, *Loosening the Bonds: Mid-Atlantic Farm Women, 1750–1850* (New Haven, 1986); and Ryan, *Cradle of the Middle Class*.

meet its impossible standards. While Clinton believes that the inordinate responsibilities entailed by an agricultural economy made it difficult for even the wealthiest females to engage in the leisured life-style the Lady-ideal prescribed, she identifies the contradictions between reality and social expectations as a source of tension within the southern women's world. In the North, women were provided with the more attainable model of "the 'notable housewife,' the ideological granddaughter of Cotton Mather's 'daughters of Zion.'" In the South, women had no choice but the repressive ideal of the Southern Lady.[7]

Speculation concerning both the prevalence and the level of acceptance of the Lady-ideal among the South's female population is complicated by the testimony of antebellum southern writers. Contemporary literature written by men and women typically portrayed women according to Thomas Dew's specifications: "lovely and dependent," unsuited to all but the most ornamental pursuits. Early plantation fiction may have accorded women some degree of autonomy, but as the nation descended into civil war and the ideal of the Lady became more firmly entrenched in southern ideology, female characters in novels written by southern men grew increasingly dependent, their list of accomplishments becoming even more superficial.[8] Only southern domestic fiction written by southern women for southern women explored the variety of options available to the female elite. Exposing the Lady-ideal as detrimental to the physical health and emotional well-being of its middle- and upper-class aspirants, southern domestic fiction charted the transformation of weak, self-

7. Clinton, *The Plantation Mistress*, 9; Catherine Clinton, "Caught in the Web of the Big House: Women and Slavery," in *The Web of Southern Social Relations: Women, Family, and Education*, ed. Walter J. Fraser, Jr., R. Frank Saunders, Jr., and Jon L. Wakelyn (Athens, Ga., 1985), 19–34; Scott, *The Southern Lady*; Scott, "Women's Perspective," 52–64; Jones, *Tomorrow Is Another Day*.

8. Taylor, *Cavalier and Yankee*, 174–75; John C. Ruoff, "Frivolity to Consumption; or, Southern Womanhood in Antebellum Literature," *Civil War History*, XVIII (1972), 213–30; Keith L. Bryant, Jr., "The Role and Status of the Female Yeomanry in the Antebellum South: The Literary View," *Southern Quarterly*, XVIII (1980), 73–87; Leslie Kent Anderson, "A Myth of the Southern Lady: Antebellum Proslavery Rhetoric and the Proper Place of Woman," *Sociological Spectrum*, VI (1986), 31–49; Seidel, "The Southern Belle," 387–401. The agricultural press, which reflected the interests of the yeoman class, took exception to this practice. See D. Harland Hagler, "The Ideal Woman in the Antebellum South: Lady or Farmwife?" *Journal of Southern History*, XLVI (1980), 405–17.

centered girls into morally and intellectually autonomous, physically energetic women capable of defending the domestic realm against pernicious northern influences. In emphasizing the potential women held to protect their region through their personal transformation, the southern domestic novelists revealed their self-defined mission: to create nothing less than a generation of female heroines capable of saving their region from northern encroachment.[9]

Certainly, the southern domestic heroine was worthy of emulation. A hybrid of aristocratic grace and middle-class virtue, the domestic heroine combined a keen sense of noblesse oblige with intelligence and physical stamina. Well-educated, resourceful, and self-reliant, she was able to support herself and her family if the situation demanded, putting the lessons she studied diligently in her youth to practical use. Deeply religious and incurably optimistic, the southern heroine never admitted defeat; she simply prayed for guidance and doubled her efforts. Invariably, her endeavors succeeded. She married and assumed the complex role of wife, mother, and plantation administrator. A gracious hostess, competent housewife, and sympathetic mistress, she ministered to the physical and spiritual needs of her white and black families and, in so doing, ensured the moral and social stability of the South.[10]

Yet the southern heroine did not remain the same across time; her personality, achievements, and sphere of influence at any given time reflected current relations between North and South as well as the degree of confidence that individual writers had in her potential to defend her region. Whereas Gilman, Hentz, and McIntosh, the first generation of domestic novelists, argued that exercise and education could transform fragile flower and jaundiced belle alike into women of merit, Terhune and Evans were not as optimistic about the latent heroism of the female

9. On the concept of female heroism see Ellen Moers, *Literary Women: The Great Writers* (New York, 1976); Rachel M. Brownstein, *Becoming a Heroine: Reading About Women in Novels* (New York, 1982); and Carolyn G. Heilbrun, *Writing a Woman's Life* (New York, 1988). See also Elaine Showalter, *A Literature of Their Own: British Women Novelists from Brontë to Lessing* (Princeton, 1977); Patricia Meyer Spacks, *The Female Imagination* (New York, 1976).

10. See Baym, *Woman's Fiction*, 35–39. While this outline is correct as far as it goes, it fails to distinguish between northern and southern domestic heroines; neither does it point up intergenerational differences. See also Seidel, *The Southern Belle in the American Novel*.

planter class. Entering the literary arena in the middle 1850s, some two decades after Gilman, Hentz, and McIntosh had initiated their campaign for female heroism, Terhune and Evans observed that female dissipation continued to plague the South; elite women were not responding to the clarion call of southern domestic fiction to the extent the earlier writers had hoped. Terhune and Evans were forced to consider the possibility that southern heroines were born, not made, that divine intervention rather than comprehensive education was the means through which southern women could transcend the Lady-ideal.

Caroline Howard Gilman felt well qualified to diagnose and prescribe for the ills of planter-class women. A New Englander by birth, she spent part of her adolescence at the Savannah plantation of an older brother, living the fashionable life she vociferously criticized in later years. "We are very dissipated," she wrote her sister in November, 1810. "Even the time I now devote to you is taken from my sleeping hours." The ceaseless whirl of entertaining showed no signs of letting up; the holiday season had descended with full force. But in spite of Gilman's spirited participation in the festivities—she reported that she had danced the whole evening without feeling fatigued—she could not help but disapprove. Her New England heritage made her suspicious of any excessive display. Young Caroline was particularly critical of elite southern women. "The ladies are more trifling than any I have ever seen," she observed. "Their greatest delight is to dress, & their chief pride is to show themselves." The majority of planter-class women, Gilman noted scornfully, "flirt in finery." Gossiping maliciously, they sought to "destroy characters." They accomplished nothing worthwhile, seeking only immediate gratification. "I see nothing remarkable here to attract attention," she declared in disgust, unless it was the affected manner, lack of principle, and sour disposition of the whole of southern womanhood.[11]

Time modified Gilman's negative view of southern femininity. Taking up permanent residence in the South upon her marriage in 1819, she assumed the responsibilities of rearing a family and running a household staffed by slaves. Her struggles to balance the demands of her young chil-

11. Caroline Howard [Gilman] to Anna Maria Howard [White], November 20, 1810, in Caroline Howard Gilman Papers.

dren with those of her profession, along with the opportunity to observe elite southern women at close range, convinced her that her initial impressions of planter-class females were incorrect. Clearly, the lack of education, rather than inherent selfishness, prevented women from properly discharging their domestic duties.[12] Because elite southern women were encouraged toward purely ornamental pursuits by cultural mandate, they were unprepared to assume the burdens of femininity that marriage and motherhood entailed. Certainly, planter-class women had more than enough time to improve themselves and their communities; it was simply that the greater portion of that class were never taught to use their time wisely. When physical exercise was encouraged and proper domestic and academic instruction provided to planter-class women as a whole, the active, morally and intellectually autonomous female would replace the ornamental Lady to the benefit of southern culture.[13]

In her heavily autobiographical *Recollections of a Southern Matron* (1838), Gilman censured the male-defined Lady and her alter ego, the fashionable belle, proposing an alternative standard for female behavior that bore no resemblance to Thomas Dew's ornamental ideal.[14] Cornelia Wilton, only daughter of a South Carolina planter family, exemplifies the strength of mind and body that Gilman commended to the larger female population. In just a few short pages, Cornelia protests inappropriate treatment of slaves, keeps the sabbath holy, prevents a duel, and inspires a degenerate suitor to reform his ways.[15] While Cornelia derives her competence in part from her southern heritage—her ancestors fought heroically in the Revolution—it is her comprehensive academic and domestic

12. Gilman participated in numerous literary and church-related organizations. See Howe, "A Massachusetts Yankee," 197–220; and Bakker, "Caroline Gilman," 273–83. Gilman describes her activities in an unpublished autobiographical essay that apparently served as the basis for John S. Hart's sketch in *The Female Prose Writers*. See Caroline Gilman, Autobiographical Essay (MS in Caroline Howard Gilman Papers, South Carolina Historical Society, Charleston).

13. On the precarious health of southern women see Sally McMillen, *Motherhood in the Old South* (Baton Rouge, 1990); and Clinton, *The Plantation Mistress*, 139–63.

14. Gilman, *Southern Matron*. Hereinafter cited parenthetically by page number in the text.

15. Lant argues that these accomplishments are not as important as Cornelia's realization that southern women wield power through manipulation and deceit. See Lant, "Behind a Mask," 140–64.

education that brings her heroism to the fore. Unlike the majority of her peers, who aspire to the Lady-ideal, Cornelia spends her youth preparing for the burdens of southern womanhood. Studying astronomy, botany, history, and literature in addition to the traditional French, music, and dancing, she receives additional instruction in the variety of domestic skills necessary to run a large estate efficiently.[16] And Cornelia's education is not confined to the classroom; she hunts, fishes, rides, and dances. Physical exertion frees Cornelia from an unhealthy preoccupation with self; it encourages her to become involved with the daily functions of the plantation and, most important, increases her chances of surviving the physical strain associated with marriage and motherhood.[17]

Cornelia's vitality contrasts with the extreme languor of her cousin Anna Allston, who is Gilman's depiction of the Southern Lady. A creature of the affections, Anna lives to please; "her humility, her patience under reproof and her cheerful attention to the wants of others" are her distinguishing characteristics. Incapable of independent thought or action, Anna simply waits for instructions. She takes no interest in the day-to-day affairs of the plantation; fashionably educated, she spends the majority of her time perfecting her ornamental skills, singing, playing the harp, and reciting poetry. For a time Anna is happy; her friends and her family ask no more than that she give a "few simple chords on the pianoforte a charm and tenderness peculiar to her touch." But when Anna's "loveliness and simplicity" beguile a handsome planter into marriage, her physical and intellectual weakness becomes problematic. Unprepared for the responsibilities her position entails, Anna languishes in love. Her heart hangs "like a bud on its stalk"; her fiancé was to her "the sun, breeze and the dew." Anna's excessive dependence bodes poorly for the future of southern civilization. When her groom dies in a mysterious accident several weeks later, she believes that she has no reason to live. Incapable of managing her husband's estate, much less mothering his children, Anna wastes away;

16. For discussion of the planter woman's duties see Clinton, *The Plantation Mistress*, 16–35. Clinton goes so far as to call the planter wife a "slave of slaves." In contrast, Fox-Genovese explores the positive aspects of slaveholding women's lives in *Within the Plantation Household*, 100–45.

17. Clinton explains that the anxiety experienced by planter women facing the physical demands of marriage and motherhood was justified in a region characterized by high female mortality rates. See Clinton, *The Plantation Mistress*, 139–63. See also McMillen, *Motherhood*.

her inability to meet her domestic obligations disturbs her region's social equilibrium (139–40).

If Gilman criticized the excessive dependence of the Southern Lady, she took an equally dim view of the society belle, a popular character in periodical literature who Gilman apparently believed inspired many real-life imitators. Undisciplined, self-indulgent, and devoted to a life of frivolity, the fashionable belle had no redeeming qualities; her lack of principle, false values, and dedication to pleasure made her unusually susceptible to northern infection, and she was therefore of particular danger to southern society. When a man married a belle, Gilman explained, he got nothing more than "a body without a soul and sometimes a dress without a body." Unfit wife for the noble planter, unfit mother to future generations, the belle threatened the longevity of plantation culture (132).[18] Capturing the essence of the fashionable female in the character of Miss Lawton, a vain, foolish young woman who is indiscriminating in her dissipation, Gilman warned readers to shun her example. "Calculating all night, and dressing all day," Miss Lawton flits from party to party, flirting, gambling, and gossiping. Her attractive face and stylish clothing are all she has to offer; bold, stupid, and manipulative, she lacks any trace of substance. Indeed, Miss Lawton's only useful activity is to inspire Cornelia Wilton to "follow fashion no further than fashion follows propriety" (127). Initially impressed with Miss Lawton's glamorous life-style, Cornelia sees the "city belle" for what she is when she hears a male friend remark that he "hates a regular belle more than a green persimmon." Accordingly, she renews her efforts toward productivity.

Clearly, the ornamental Lady and the fashionable belle were not unique to southern society; northern domestic writers found their characters equally disturbing. But while northern observers explained women's shortcomings in terms of corrupted cultural mores on a national scale, southern writers viewed southern women's problems as evidence of northern infection. Gilman's analysis of contemporary southern femininity was essentially an indictment of the urban North, for whereas Cornelia develops her healthy independence in the wholesome environment of the plan-

18. Caroline Hentz paints a grim picture of the fashionable female in "Three Scenes in the Life of a Belle," in Hentz, *Love After Marriage and Other Stories of the Heart* (Philadelphia, 1857).

tation South, Anna Allston and Miss Lawton have been exposed to the degenerate values of the northern city. The city held the power to transform "a fawn-like romping country lassie" into a "polished belle," Gilman asserted, just as it encouraged women to neglect their health and domestic responsibilities (132). Cornelia Wilton's values reflect the staunch independence of the rural South; her infected sisters manifest symptoms of physical and spiritual decay that signaled the decline of southern civilization. As long as southern women obeyed cultural prescriptions for dependence, the South would remain vulnerable to northern values, Gilman argued. When southerners recognized the opportunity women held to regenerate their class and their region and encouraged women to repudiate ornamental womanhood, the region as a whole would become less vulnerable to northern attack. In advancing an alternative standard for elite females, Gilman affirmed her unyielding faith in the redemptive potential of southern women.

Caroline Hentz, another transplanted New Englander, viewed the prospects of southern womanhood with greater sophistication. A teacher for some twenty years at various girls' schools all over the South, Hentz was not overly impressed with the moral or intellectual capacity of her students; nevertheless, she remained convinced that the future of the South depended on the efforts of women from the planter class. Her February 10, 1836, Alabama diary entry records her ambivalence: "It requires more than the patience of a Job, the wisdom of a Solomon, the meekness of a Moses, or the adaptive power of a St. Paul to be sufficient for the duties of our profession." The next day, however, Hentz acknowledged that her own shortcomings might not be responsible for all the failings of her students. "Teachers of childhood & youth," she wrote, were "at the mercy of unreasonable & sometimes unprincipled children." [19] But if Hentz was unable to explain precisely why her particular handful of pupils fell short of her expectations, she had no trouble identifying the source of the problems that afflicted elite southern women as a whole. "From the cradle of infancy to the bridal altar," she argued, southern women of privilege were taught by society "to shine and glitter . . . to devote [their] ir-

19. Caroline Hentz Diary, February 10–11, 1836 (MS in Hentz Family Papers, Southern Historical Collection, University of North Carolina).

redeemable time to the acquisition of the lightest accomplishments—to the costly adornment of [their] person." In view of these social and cultural imperatives, it was no wonder that planter-class women were unable to fill other than the merely superficial role for which their region prepared them. Education and circumstances "bounded" and "compressed" women's minds, Hentz contended; she challenged women to "overstep these limits, and see of what you are capable."[20]

Her frustration in the classroom notwithstanding, Hentz, like Gilman, committed herself to the education of the women of the planter class. Working to familiarize the fragile flowers of the South with their extensive social responsibilities, she, like Gilman, exhorted her audience to repudiate the superficial role society assigned them, arguing that the economic and political circumstances of the contemporary South demanded heroic efforts on the part of its daughters. But while Hentz agreed with Gilman that preoccupation with fashion, concern with the making and spending of money, and increasing disregard for virtuous conduct on the part of the southern elite threatened the safety of southern society, the two disagreed on how women could best defend their region. Gilman argued that southern women should work through their immediate and extended communities to effect change gradually, but Hentz contended that women must act immediately. Gilman implied that women were to respect the patriarchal structure of the southern family and use it to cement the southern community, but Hentz argued that under certain circumstances this was impossible: women were morally obligated to challenge male authority when that authority menaced the home and family.

Political exigencies undoubtedly influenced Hentz's limited endorsement of rebellion. Writing more than a decade after Gilman, Hentz's work reflected the increasingly defensive attitude of southern writers toward slavery. As congressional debate over the disposal of western lands drew focus on the South, writers attempted to offset criticism of the peculiar institution by exaggerating the benevolence of the plantation economy at the North's expense.[21] Hentz, however, approached the sub-

20. Caroline Hentz, "The Sex of the Soul," in Hentz, *The Banished Son and Other Stories of the Heart* (Philadelphia, 1856), 267–68.

21. Taylor, *Cavalier and Yankee*, 145–76. See also Wimsatt, "Antebellum Fiction," 92–107; Faust, *A Sacred Circle*; and Watson, *The Cavalier in Virginia Fiction*.

ject of southern morality with great subtlety. Rather than presenting the South as above reproach, she acknowledged that southern society had its problems, and in a bold departure from the literary mainstream she suggested that only southern women could correct them.

In *Linda; or, The Young Pilot of the Belle Creole* (1850), Hentz introduced one of the most heroic antebellum southern heroines, Linda Walton, to illustrate how middle- and upper-class southern women could single-handedly save their communities. "A noble, independent, yet womanly spirit," Linda has little in common with others of her social class.[22] Unattracted to the superficial pursuits that occupied many planter-class females, Linda is at a loss in fashionable society; she cannot embroider, play the guitar, or sing in foreign languages. Neither does she want to learn. Linda meets her stepmother's attempts to teach her the ornamental arts with tears and recriminations, "drawing her needle through and through the everlasting patchwork, with a look of sad . . . endurance, clouding her late joyous countenance" (31–32). Linda's rejection of the Lady-ideal of ornamental womanhood eventually persuades her father to send her to boarding school in hopes that others can make his daughter conform, but Linda refuses to compromise. Choosing solitude over inappropriate companionship, she earns the nickname "the little parson." Linda's perseverance ultimately is rewarded; her sincere devotion to the "higher principle" transforms school residents into "good, noble women" who have little in common with the male-defined feminine model (88).

Linda's physical and moral strength enables her to sustain her plantation community. While still a child, she saves her nurse, Aunt Judy, from the auction block, running through the night and facing down savage dogs to secure the safety of her beloved retainer. She protects her friends from the unsavory activities of a free black woman, a laundress who sells forbidden goods and smuggles letters for a price, and she defuses the tyranny of her stepbrother, Robert, who abuses his authority as a master. Linda's greatest challenge, however, comes in late adolescence when her father demands that she marry Robert in order to increase the family fortune. She immediately protests: "I wish I were the poorest girl in the southwest, if I must be bought and sold like a negro slave" (104). Running into the

22. Caroline Hentz, *Linda; or, The Young Pilot of the Belle Creole* (Philadelphia, 1850), 116. Hereinafter cited parenthetically by page number in the text.

woods alone and penniless—she leaves behind some 250 slaves—Linda takes up residence with an Indian family. She prefers virtuous poverty to the filial obedience that would hasten the degeneration of the southern aristocracy.

Although Hentz's fiction contained the suggestion of radicalism, her overall message was overwhelmingly conservative. Clearly, Hentz did not endorse the permanent redistribution of power within the southern home; it was only when male decisions threatened the structure of the home and family that women, entrusted with the security of the domestic realm, were bound to intervene. Significantly, Hentz did not leave Linda outside the home, nor did she permit her to remain single. In the end, Linda marries Roland Lee, a sturdy artisan whose morality complements her own. Her marriage ceremony symbolizes the regeneration of the planter class as, encircled by slaves and slaveholders, she plights her troth to an outsider. The infusion of virtue immediately benefits the southern community: Linda's father takes better care of his slaves, the degenerate Robert decides to become a missionary, and a host of Linda's friends renounce ornamental femininity. And Linda's actions secure her community's future: as a wife and mother, Linda will nurture a new generation of moral southerners. In this context, her "rebellion" gains legitimacy. She leaves the home only that it may be strengthened; she censures fashionable society that it may be purified; she seizes temporary power within her family that she may shore up its moral foundations and relinquish her control to one worthy of her respect. Through Linda, an engaging but essentially ordinary southern woman of privilege, Hentz illuminated the process through which southern society could be restored to righteousness, and appealed to the latent heroism of her female readers.[23]

Maria McIntosh amplified Caroline Hentz's message and broadened the domestic heroine's geographic boundaries. Whereas Gilman and Hentz restricted their heroines to the plantation on the grounds that southern women could best defend the South by working through the home and family, McIntosh charged her female characters with the conversion of the

23. For an alternative reading emphasizing the radical aspects of Linda's flight see Garrison, "Immoral Fiction," 71–89.

heathen North. Her heroines directly confronted the evils of society above the Mason-Dixon Line and routinely claimed souls for the South. Arguing that internal reform, although necessary, offered inadequate protection against creeping northern corruption, McIntosh proposed that elite southern women seek out and destroy individualism and materialism at their source before the dreaded northern disease penetrated the southern community.[24]

McIntosh framed her argument in extremely personal terms.[25] The daughter of a wealthy Georgia planter family, she took up residence in the North upon her parents' deaths in 1835. Financial disaster quickly followed; McIntosh lost her fortune in the panic of 1837 and found herself dependent upon her northern relatives. Blaming the corrupt northern banking establishment for her financial ruin, she became convinced that her personal tragedy was merely part of a larger northern plot against the South. Left unchecked, she argued, northern greed would destroy the whole of southern society just as it had almost destroyed her.

In *Two Lives; or, To Seem and To Be* (1846), McIntosh used paired heroines, Grace Elliot and her cousin Isabel Douglass, to illustrate the dangers of northern society. Orphaned daughters of the Georgia aristocracy, Grace and Isabel move North to live with relatives upon the death of Grace's father, who was also Isabel's guardian. Young and vulnerable, the two quickly fall victim to the ambition of their new guardian's wife, Mrs. William Elliot. A frivolous, shallow woman who has devoted her life to the pursuit of pleasure, Mrs. Elliot immediately appropriates Grace's fortune—Isabel has limited funds—to serve her own ends. Having already brought her weak-willed husband to the edge of bankruptcy, she views her southern charges as the means to maintaining her precarious social posi-

---

24. Baym, *Woman's Fiction*, 87. Heroines typically begin their journeys in the South, travel to the North, and then return to the plantation; they do not, however, leave the South voluntarily. See, for example, Maria McIntosh, *Charms and Counter Charms* (New York, 1848), and McIntosh, *The Lofty and the Lowly*.

25. Biographical sources for McIntosh emphasize the correspondence between her life and her work. See Kelley, *Private Woman*, 33–35, 145–48, 257–58; and Baym, *Woman's Fiction*, 86–109. Contemporary accounts include Colles, *Authors and Writers*, 174–76; and Freeman, *Women of the South*, 163–70. John S. Hart tells McIntosh's story in the language of domestic fiction in *The Female Prose Writers*, 63–69.

tion. Before the girls are out of mourning, Mrs. Elliot sets about converting them to ornamental womanhood.[26]

Grace, the richest and, as it turns out, the morally weaker of the two
southerners, proves the most responsive to Mrs. Elliot's advances. Within
a few short months, she is transformed into a mindless belle who no longer
has control of her fortune. As "the southern heiress," she is a drawing card
to many a fashionable event. The years pass, and Grace's character degen-
erates: she waltzes, performs in a play, has an affair with a Frenchman, and
eventually takes up gambling. With Grace's seduction, Mrs. Elliot, the
personification of northern greed, claims another soul for the North.

Grace defends her actions as moral flexibility, the key to survival in
the dissolute North; Isabel rejects that notion. Whereas northern society
erodes Grace's values, it activates Isabel's latent heroism and convinces
her, like McIntosh, to take dramatic steps to halt the unremitting appetite
of the North. When Mrs. Elliot tries to force Isabel to conform to the
negative behavioral model, Isabel leaves, and although social ostracism
and near poverty follow her declaration of independence, she remains true
to her southern principles. Ministering to the less fortunate, imparting
her southern values to receptive northerners, Isabel ventures into the
world outside the Elliots' luxurious home and discovers the multitude of
needy women and children that fashionable northerners are too busy to
consider. By refusing to participate in unwholesome activities, by choosing virtuous poverty over corrupted wealth, Isabel wins respect for herself
and her region and strengthens southern influence above the Mason-
Dixon Line. Conversely, Grace shames southern womanhood and endan-
gers the future of southern civilization (159–61, 174–79, 240–42).

Vindicating the virtue of her class and her region, Isabel faces down
corruption at its source and convinces a substantial number of northerners
that there is another way. In the long run, her most important convert is
her cousin Marion Elliot, who marries a wealthy Virginian and becomes
master of a tidewater plantation, thereby infusing the half-northern Elliot
line with southern virtue. Though Isabel eventually returns to the South,
where she weds a Virginia clergyman, Hubert Falconer, her work is not
completed; in the salutary climate of her plantation, Isabel labors unceas-

26. Maria McIntosh, *Two Lives; or, To Seem and To Be* (1846; rpr. New York, 1865),
26–27, 49–55. Hereinafter cited parenthetically by page number in the text.

ingly to shore up her victories in the North and to protect her region from northern encroachment.

McIntosh's plan of attack was straightforward: southern women of the planter class must prevent the corruption of their region by the North by arresting the disease of individualism at its source. By killing the germs of self-interest before they penetrated the South, southern women of privilege could protect their homeland from infection. By first combating northern influence and then stabilizing the institutions of home and family, planter-class women built up their region's immunity to disease. Elite southern women could no longer trust the fate of southern civilization to politicians, McIntosh warned; they must take matters into their own hands (239–44).

How much faith McIntosh placed in her prescription for a domestic offensive remains unclear. *Two Lives* ends with the death of Grace Elliot upon her return to her Georgia plantation and the adoption of her little girl by Isabel and her husband. That the child has one living parent, a French nobleman, is ignored; apparently her claim to the southern aristocracy takes precedence over membership in the European elite. Grace's deathbed restoration to the South suggests that southern values will eventually prevail if only southerners will stand firm against northern opposition and persuade northerners to seek the truth. Isabel's reclamation of Grace and conversion of her cousin Marion symbolize the potential for the restoration of national equilibrium. Yet in spite of its optimistic ending, McIntosh's novel has its darker side. It is not apparent that Isabel's behavior has a lasting effect on the northern Elliots, nor is it clear that her missionary work does more than temporarily benefit her northern charges. Isabel's marriage to Falconer also is highly problematic. She weds him because he manifests southern values in their purest form; she does not have to claim Falconer for the South, because he is already a southerner and, for that matter, a better southerner than most. Perhaps nearly ten years above the Mason-Dixon Line had convinced McIntosh that reconciliation was impossible, that it could be realized only in domestic fiction.

The tension underlying *Two Lives* contrasts markedly with McIntosh's confident assertion four years later that elite southern women could stem the tide of northern aggression. "Could [the southern woman] but understand all her mission," she commented, "could she induce, or even strive to induce . . . all this, . . . she would prove herself indeed, what one of old named her, the connecting link between man and the angelic world."[27] Writing in the early 1850s, McIntosh seemed to have vanquished her doubts that once her southern sisters were made aware of their extensive duties to their region they would rise to the occasion. With the literary crusade for southern heroines well under way, McIntosh could look with pride upon her own contributions to the cause as both a proponent and an example of the tenets of southern female heroism; clearly, the concerted efforts of the southern domestic novelists would ensure a generation of intelligent, active southern women, capable of defending their homes and families against northern contagion.

But while McIntosh viewed the prospects of southern femininity in 1853 sanguinely, Terhune and Evans did not. Surveying the moral landscape, the younger writers were not pleased with the example set by southern women, nor were they convinced that the literary call to heroism was altogether effective. Whereas first-generation writers contended that planter women, latent heroines all, could realize heroism through exercise and education, second-generation writers argued that this was not necessarily true; in fact, too much education could repress woman's finer instincts and distance her from her domestic responsibilities. In making this break, Terhune and Evans expressed their dismay with their southern constituency and introduced a new variable into the equation for female heroism: God, not woman, was ultimately responsible for creating southern heroines.[28]

Perhaps Terhune and Evans thought that education was an insufficient means to catalyze feminine virtue on a grand scale because they were intimately aware of its limitations. The most sophisticated and well read of the five southern domestic novelists, they were also the only two to suffer a profound spiritual crisis. Children of evangelical parents, they

27. Maria McIntosh, *Woman in America: Her Work and Her Reward* (New York, 1850), 118.

28. See Tompkins' discussion of the impact of evangelicalism on the northern domestic novelist Susan Warner in *Sensational Designs*, 147–85. Kelley notes changes in the literary market between 1830 and 1860 but fails to mention how the first and second generations of literary women integrated their personal and professional experiences into their fiction. See Kelley, *Private Woman*, 3–27.

found it difficult to reconcile the religious beliefs of their youths with philosophical speculation of the middle nineteenth century. Where Gilman found comfort in the cerebral doctrine of the Unitarian church, Terhune and Evans agonized over their immortal souls, caught between their fascination with what Evans labeled "the slough of mis-called philosophy" and the revivalist teachings of the antebellum Deep South. Both women involved friends and family in their respective search for inner peace. Terhune asked her best friend, Virginia Eppes Dance, regularly if she had yet found Christ. Augusta Evans' anguish over orthodox Methodism prompted a lengthy correspondence with a young minister. "Blessed the soul that never began to question and debate regarding its arcana," she declared. Yet for all their spiritual turmoil, Terhune and Evans failed to appreciate that their situations were hardly typical. On the contrary, they used their experiences as a yardstick against which other women could not help but fall short. Convinced like the first generation of southern domestic novelists that the future of the South hinged directly upon the efforts of elite southern women, they were equally certain that the majority of women were unequal to the task.[29]

In *Alone*, Terhune investigated the proper balance between head and heart through her deeply flawed heroine, Ida Ross. Orphaned at fifteen, Ida, an undistinguished daughter of the planter class, goes to live in the city with her father's former associate, Mr. Read, and his incorrigible daughter, Josephine. Unfit moral custodians, the Reads personify the false value system of the North. Although Ida tries to resist their ideology, her desperation to fit into her new family leads her to conform; she practices "deceit, under the name of self-control, heartlessness, . . . veiled distrust and misanthropy." Poorly served at home, Ida receives no better instruction at school; in fact, her fall from grace is hastened by her comprehensive academic education. Taught to accept nothing without positive proof, to rely on her mind rather than her heart, Ida rapidly becomes nothing more than a walking, talking automaton. Although she intuitively realizes

29. On southern women and evangelical religion see Friedman, *The Enclosed Garden.* And see, for example, Mary Virginia Terhune to Virginia Eppes Dance, November 29, 1848, November 4, 1852, in Mary Virginia Terhune Papers, Perkins Library, Duke University. Terhune's unpublished letters to Dance from the mid-1840s through the early 1850s contradict the idyllic youth Terhune describes in *Marion Harland's Autobiography.* See also Augusta Evans to the Reverend Walter Harriss, quoted in Fidler, *Augusta Evans Wilson*, 50, 52.

that this goes against her female nature, she is powerless to change; in her household, "the crying sin was to be 'womanish' . . . [for] 'woman' and 'fool' were synonymous."[30]

Ida's success at school convinces her that only her mind is important; she believes she can learn nothing from the female community and goes so far as to criticize other women who express their emotions spontaneously. Only after a classmate's inability to feel precipitates a duel in which a noble young planter is killed does Ida realize the truth: woman is no more than "a fiend" when she "buries her heart nor mourns above its grave" (230). Running to her plantation, Sunnybank, she sequesters herself in the home of her childhood, confronting her fundamental loneliness and isolation from the human community. Significantly, the successful resolution of Ida's spiritual crisis hinges directly on the endeavors of her slave Uncle Will. "A hale, fine-looking negro; better educated than the generality of his caste, and devotedly pious," Will is the self-appointed minister to the slave population (226). Sensing his mistress's need, he directs her to search her heart and asks for permission to hold Sunday services in the room immediately under hers. Upon hearing Will's fervent prayers, Ida repents her "idolatry, hatred, variance, emulation, wrath [and] envyings," and slowly begins to accept her emotions (230).

Ida's repudiation of pure intellect allows her to embrace her responsibilities as a plantation mistress and to effect positive change within her southern community. Rising from her bed, she surveys the needs of her black and white family. She builds a chapel for Will's congregation and a school for the resident poor whites; she takes in a young woman whose alcoholic father mistreats her, and she finds her employment. Rejoicing in the innumerable opportunities to strengthen the domestic realm, Ida does not return to the Reads' household. She remains at Sunnybank caring for her dependents, and when she marries, she chooses a husband who will share her responsibilities and enable her to do even greater good.

In spite of the happy ending, however, Terhune's overall message was confusing. On the one hand, Ida's growth to heroic womanhood encouraged readers to persist, implying that through personal endeavor and di-

---

30. Mary Virginia Terhune [Marion Harland], *Alone* (Richmond, 1854), 12. Hereinafter cited parenthetically by page number in text.

vine intervention the most jaded female could achieve heroism. Yet the
arbitrary circumstances prompting Ida's metamorphosis suggested that
not every woman could succeed; certainly they could not do it by themselves. Education, the means through which first-generation novelists created female heroes, brings Ida no closer to virtuous womanhood; books
blind her to her feminine duties by teaching her falsely to value intellect
over affection. Heroism comes when she renounces control, when she recognizes that her efforts have been misdirected and asks for God's intervention. Ida essentially has little to do with her own regeneration.[31] As Terhune realized all too clearly, God's will was not always woman's.

"I am suffering tonight with . . . a most woeful depression of spirits,"
Terhune wrote Virginia Eppes Dance in 1848. "I have had much lately to
make me sad, you have no idea how much."[32] Several years later Terhune
was still despondent: "I am oppressed with a sense of my own shortcomings, my thousand failures in duty," she confessed. "Life is too short, and
myself, too weak to perform one tenth of the tasks that I find laid ready to
my hand." In 1852 she asked Dance, "How can I advise others while so
frail and weak myself?" Racked with self-doubt, she declared, "It is a fearful, fearful thing to live!"[33] Although Terhune and Dance eventually
found peace—both women married ministers—Terhune never forgot the
troubled years in her early twenties; each of her heroines undergoes a
period of painful soul-searching. Paradoxically Terhune's own suffering
left her little sympathy for her female audience. Presenting herself as the
embodiment of feminine excellence, Terhune challenged her southern sisters to emulate her example, all the while acknowledging the unlikelihood
that they could succeed.

Evans, who was Terhune's almost exact contemporary, had somewhat
greater justification for the impatience with elite southern women. The
daughter of impoverished aristocrats, Evans enjoyed few of the advantages

31. For an alternative reading, see Baym, *Woman's Fiction*, 200–203. Baym argues that
Terhune associated the principle of community exclusively with women; men were governed
by "the principle of gain." In fact, Terhune's argument is much more complicated. She makes
no distinction on the grounds of gender, portraying men and women as equally vulnerable.
32. Terhune to Dance, November 29, 1848, in Terhune Papers, Duke.
33. Terhune to Dance, November 4, 1852, *ibid.*

and little of the encouragement that Terhune took for granted. Primarily self-taught, she spent much of her childhood on the move as her improvident father searched for employment. The peripatetic life-style took its toll. Evans developed a sense of inferiority and deprivation that stayed with her all her life.[34] Her position on the fringes of southern society made her more critical of aristocratic females than her domestic predecessors. Denied the social circle to which her name entitled her, Evans found the community she craved in the leather-bound volumes that lined a wealthy aunt's library, and in her late teens she channeled her frustration into a lucrative literary career.[35] Decrying "fine-ladyism, this ignoring of labor, to which . . . all should be subjected," she argued that "false-effeminacy and miserable affectation of refinement" became the "unyielding lock on the wheels of social reform."[36]

In *Beulah* (1859), her first successful novel, Evans vented her rage at feminine dependence while at the same time illustrating the dangers of the opposite extreme. Contending that women realized their calling only in the home, she urged readers to prepare themselves physically and intellectually for their role in the coming battle against northern oppression. Increased tensions between North and South already threatened the southern community; women must not let their vanity and selfishness accelerate the decline of southern civilization. True women, Evans asserted, in whatever social or economic positions they might be placed, "should remain imperishable monuments of true female heroism" (171). Through Beulah, the most extremely flawed heroine in southern and, for that matter, domestic literature as a whole, Evans echoed Terhune's arguments that women could be effective stewards of the southern community only when their intellect was balanced by their affections.[37]

34. Jones, *Tomorrow Is Another Day*, 51–91; Papashvily, *All the Happy Endings*, 153–68.

35. Anne Goodwyn Jones argues that Evans' anger stemmed not from her sense of deprivation but from her inability to transcend the narrow boundaries of southern femininity. See Jones, *Tomorrow Is Another Day*, 51–91.

36. Augusta Evans, *Beulah* (New York, 1859), 41. Hereinafter cited parenthetically by page number in the text.

37. Beulah is the only avowed atheist in domestic fiction; apparently, her quest for truth enhanced her popular appeal. See Baym, *Woman's Fiction*, 282–86. See also "Augusta J. Evans," in *Southland Writers: Biographical and Critical Sketches of the Living Female Writers of the South*, ed. Mary Tardy (Philadelphia, 1870), II, 568.

Evans wrote with authority; Beulah's realization of heroism was highly autobiographical.[38] Unlike the majority of southern domestic heroines, Beulah, like Evans herself, is a child of poverty. Orphaned in early childhood, she and her younger sister Lily spend their early years in the city orphanage. Although Beulah and Lily know no want, they are always conscious of their inferior social and economic position; like Evans, they have no definite niche in southern society and are victimized by the southern aristocracy. A wealthy society matron, impressed with Lily's exquisite beauty, decides to adopt her. Beulah, who is exceptionally ugly, is left behind. Lacking beauty, talent, and wealth, she has no value in fashionable society. From that moment onward, her heart is hardened; like Ida Ross, Beulah loses the ability to feel.

A series of implausible circumstances draws Beulah into the southern aristocracy. A wealthy physician, Guy Hartwell, becomes her guardian and offers her social position and access to numerous cultural and educational advantages. But Beulah fails to appreciate her good fortune. Using her proximity to fashionable society to issue an indictment of the southern aristocracy, Beulah decides that rather than gratefully accept Hartwell's generosity, she will merely use his assets to achieve complete self-sufficiency. Reasoning that because society has robbed her of all she holds dear, she owes it nothing, Beulah renounces her duties as an aristocratic southern female.

Retreating to the library, Beulah, like Evans, searches for community. "Books are, to me, what family, and friends, and society are to other people," she admits candidly (197). Instead of providing her with comfort and companionship, though, the literary and philosophic diatribes she studies increase her isolation. "Possessed by an active spirit of inquiry, which constantly impelled her to investigate, and as far as possible to explain the mysteries which surrounded her," Beulah delves into "systems" and "processes" best left unexplored. Her intellect causes her no end of misery. "Have your books and studies brought you to this?" an acquaintance asks. "Beulah! Beulah! Throw them into the fire" (256). Paradoxically, Beulah believes her overwhelming thirst for knowledge and con-

38. See Louise Manly, "Augusta Evans Wilson," in *The Library of Southern Literature*, ed. Edwin A. Alderman, Joel Chandler Harris, and Charles William Kent (Atlanta, 1921), XIII, 5841.

sequent ambition to be divinely inspired. "Duty," she explains to a classmate, "is a vast volcanic agency, constantly impelling me to action. What was my will given to me for, if to remain passive and suffer others to minister to my needs?" (141). Beulah's sense of duty, however, is purely selfish; she works not to benefit her fellow southerners but to satisfy her own need for legitimation. Far from cementing the bonds of community, Beulah destroys them.

Beulah capitalizes on her intellectual abilities and, shunning Hartwell's assistance, prepares to teach and to write professionally. Ironically, an early literary effort set forth the tenets of "female heroism." Contending that "female intellect was capable of the most exalted attainments," Beulah urges her audience to action: she "conjured them, in any and every emergency, to prove themselves." "Ornaments of the social circle, angel guardians of the sacred hearthstone, ministering spirits . . . women qualified to assist in a council of statesmen, if dire necessity ever required it" (171). Yet Beulah's definition of female heroism is at odds with her actions. She herself lacks the conviction to serve in the capacities outlined in her address. While she enjoins southern women to embrace their femininity and use their position within the home and family to stabilize southern society, she shuns domesticity as unworthy of her talents. Seizing control of her destiny, she steps outside the domestic circle to make her own way, motivated not by necessity like Linda Walton or Isabel Douglass but by the fierce ambition she falsely perceives as her duty.

Evans defined limits of southern female independence by contrasting Beulah Benton, her flawed heroine, with Clara Saunders, a representative of traditional femininity. Forced by limited financial resources to seek employment, Clara enters the working world with great trepidation. "Woman was intended as a pet plant, to be guarded and cherished," Clara declares. "Isolated and uncared for, she droops, languishes and dies" (141). If Clara's declaration reveals her excessive dependency, Beulah's indignant response illustrates the opposite extreme: "You are less a woman than I thought you, if you would be willing to live on the bounty of others when a little activity would enable you to support yourself" (140). The truth, Evans argued, lay somewhere in between. Women must seek and find independence within the domestic sphere. Although economic exigencies were themselves sufficient reason for female employment out-

side the home—Evans justified her own activities on those grounds—
gainful employment should not be an end in itself. That Beulah finds no
peace from either her teaching or her writing, that she gains little satisfaction from the purely intellectual life she has chosen, underscored
Evans' prescription for southern salvation. Women must cleave to home
and hearth if southern society were to remain intact: "If the wives,
and mothers, and sisters did their duty all [instability] might be rem-
edied. If they carefully and constantly strove to shield their sons and
brothers," southern civilization would remain free from northern contagion (270).

Beulah discovers a world of opportunity when she surrenders her
drive for complete independence. Marrying Hartwell and joining the
southern aristocracy, she willingly accepts the duties commensurate with
her social position. Renouncing her public career, Beulah dedicates her
life to the service of her family and her region. Her ambition redirected,
Beulah becomes the heroine she described; her difficulties in achieving
heroism only make her victory sweeter. "There is nothing a woman cannot do," Evans assured her readers, "provided she puts on the armor of
duty and unleashes the sword of a strong, unbending will" (233).[39] Beulah's
marriage to Hartwell and subsequent abandonment of her career provide
important insight into the southern domestic novelists' collective notion
of female heroism. Firmly convinced, like the majority of Victorian
Americans, that men and women were fundamentally different with
unique abilities and obligations, the southern domestic novelists saw no
contradiction in defining independent heroines in domestic terms. "We
are not cherubim,—nor yet slaves;—not your superiors," Ida Ross tells
the men of America. "Your happiness and ours would be enhanced if you
would throw sentimental nonsense overboard, and take this practical, everyday view of the case."[40] Beulah's exchange of work for marriage and
motherhood, then, is not, as some would argue, a disavowal of "selfhood"
but the actualization of female heroism. If women realize autonomy only

39. Evans continued her own professional activities after her marriage in 1868 to Lorenzo Wilson, although she subordinated her literary endeavors to her domestic responsibilities.
40. Terhune, *Alone*, 129.

in the domestic sphere, Beulah's ultimate embrace of domesticity represents her total independence.[41]

Personal and political considerations directed southern domestic fiction
and gave definition to its heroines. Conscious that political tensions between North and South threatened the stability of southern society, as
early as 1833 southern women novelists looked to their elite sisters as one
source of social regeneration. As stewards of southern culture and guardians of morality, novelists asserted that southern women of privilege had
the ability and obligation to catalyze a regional return to virtue and thus
bolster the South's immunity to northern individualism. Seeking to inspire
southern women to heroism, domestic novelists advanced an active, intelligent, and morally autonomous model of southern femininity worthy of
emulation. Dramatizing any number of implausible situations in which
southern heroines championed the honor of the South, novelists illustrated the imperative of female virtue and encouraged women to play an
active role in strengthening and stabilizing their region.

Gilman, Hentz, McIntosh, Terhune, and Evans clearly recognized the
complex interaction between the home and the world. They did not con-
ceptualize the public and private spheres as mutually exclusive; rather,
they contended that the two were indissolubly linked. In this context,
women's roles were necessarily flexible; women's ability to act without
compromising their femininity was infinitely possible. The writers themselves illustrated the enormous possibilities available to intelligent, reso-
lute southern women. They built their careers on the conviction that
through the printed page they could influence the character of their less
astute southern sisters. Defining themselves as southern heroines in fact,
they devoted their efforts toward inspiring female heroism through fiction. The personality and achievements of the southern domestic heroine
over some five decades reflected her creators' collective faith that life
could indeed imitate art.

Three-quarters of the way through her letter to Congressman Curry,
Augusta Evans abruptly changed her mind. Perhaps her sensitivity to the
problems of elite southern women convinced her that one less familiar

41. Anne Goodwyn Jones discusses problems with the resolution of *Beulah* in *Tomorrow
Is Another Day*, 91.

with the subject could never do it justice. Perhaps she simply was not certain of the point she wished to make; the numerous qualifications that punctuate her prose suggest that she struggled to frame her argument. In any case, the novelist recommended an alternative topic, one that Curry "might handle with magnificent effect, and incalculable usefulness." [42] Curry accepted the novelist's suggestion, and so his speech came to be titled "Political and Social Quicksands of the Future." The lecture on southern women and slavery was held, instead, in the pages of domestic fiction.

42. Evans to Curry, July 15, 1863, in Curry Papers, Library of Congress.

2

Prejudice Is a Tough Old Knot

*I*n the spring of 1836, Caroline and Samuel Gilman made their way to Massachusetts for the first time since their marriage almost twenty years before. Their journey north was most deliberate; stops in Washington, D.C., Baltimore, Philadelphia, and New York were calculated to put the two in Cambridge by September 8, Harvard College's bicentennial. For the Reverend Mr. Gilman, the destination was all-important. A member of the class of 1811, he had written the lyrics to a song to commemorate the occasion and was anxious to hear its first performance. For Mrs. Gilman, the trip itself took precedence. Eager to explore in detail the changes along the eastern seaboard that had occurred since her journey south as a bride in 1819, Caroline Gilman prayed that spring would last forever.

The trip began auspiciously. The Gilmans set sail from Charleston April 24 and for the most part enjoyed fair weather. "A fresh, pure breeze threw new life into my frame; friends, as agreeable as kind, beguiled the way; and the sun, bright and clear, shone above without exhausting me," Caroline wrote that day. While her husband lingered below deck putting the final touches on "Fair Harvard," she drank in the scenery. "Spring was slowly advancing, and it was pleasant to see strips of green struggling through the discoloured grass on the banks, like a smile on a harsh countenance." [1] But Gilman did more than admire her surroundings. Ever alert to opportunities to portray her adopted homeland positively, she characteristically turned her northern odyssey into a compelling discussion of life North and South, using her keen powers of observation to compare and contrast the manners and morals of the inhabitants of both regions.

1. Caroline Gilman, *The Poetry of Travelling in the United States* (1838; rpr. Upper Saddle River, N.J., 1970).

"One feels, on leaving the quiet South, . . . as if inhaling gas," Mrs. Gilman recorded in early May, 1836. "Any one of the attractions . . . would be great singly, but when one combines the imposing view of the public buildings [with the] refined and various society . . . all these things coming suddenly on a retired individual, are . . . bewildering." Still, with consummate faith in her cause and credentials, Caroline Gilman struggled to sort out the differences between North and South, to identify the distinctive characteristics of each region and to demonstrate the compatibility of the two separate cultures. "The intention was to present something . . . attractive to both the Northern and Southern reader," Gilman recalled two years later in her preface to the log she published as *The Poetry of Travelling in the United States*. If her endeavor in some small measure were able "to increase a good sympathy between different portions of the country," she would gain "sufficient satisfaction."[2]

Yet the structure and substance of *The Poetry of Travelling* belied Gilman's conciliatory aims. Instead of writing a single narrative to illustrate how a multitude of regional characteristics fused into a single national identity, Gilman detailed her adventures in two discrete volumes, *Travel in the North* and *Travel in the South*. Furthermore, the variety of short stories and poems that Gilman included to dramatize the compatibility of northerners and southerners actually underlined the attitudes and opinions that many Americans believed made inhabitants of each region essentially different. More critically, Gilman's observations grew out of existing stereotypes of North and South even as she labored to promote national harmony. In her analysis, the fast-paced, frenzied North was counterpointed by the leisurely, ordered South, the calculating merchant contrasted with the aristocratic planter. In spite of her argument to the contrary, *The Poetry of Travelling* only highlighted distinctions between North and South, giving credence to an increasingly popular notion that, by the fourth decade of the nineteenth century, America was composed of two separate and fundamentally unequal regions.

Gilman's contribution to the growing body of travel literature reveals important disjunctions in southern domestic fiction; the sectionalist consciousness she inadvertently formalized in *The Poetry of Travelling* permeated her fiction as well as that of Caroline Hentz and Maria McIntosh.

2. *Ibid.*, 2–3, preface.

Although all three novelists promoted their novels as vehicles of national conciliation, the images their fiction popularized ultimately accentuated bad feelings. Building on existing stereotypes and consistently depicting the North and South as distinct regions with manners and morals as different as their climates, Gilman, Hentz, and McIntosh unconsciously widened the chasm they had intended to bridge.

That Gilman and her colleagues could view their literary endeavors as a means of national conciliation highlights the divided loyalties of the first generation of southern domestic novelists. Residents for extended periods of time in the North, Gilman, Hentz, and McIntosh maintained close ties above the Mason-Dixon Line. Gilman and Hentz corresponded regularly with family members in Massachusetts; McIntosh moved in with her New York relatives after her mother's death. All three novelists won initial fame through the efforts of northern publishers; all three depended on substantial sales in the North to provide them with an adequate income.[3] These vital connections convinced Gilman, Hentz, and McIntosh that, with a little effort, all Americans could enjoy private and public relationships that cut across regional boundaries. Yet it was that same network that helped doom their self-proclaimed crusade to eradicate sectional prejudice. Unable to admit to their southern partisanship in light of their vested interest in national union, Gilman, Hentz, and McIntosh churned out novels that were, in fact, at odds with their intent. By depicting the United States as composed of two mutually exclusive regions while at the same time professing their commitment to alleviating sectional bias, they unwittingly helped lay the intellectual foundations for civil war.

The dualistic vision that drew Gilman and her colleagues into that elaborate web of self-contradiction was embedded in the American imagination. From the inception of the Republic onward, Americans customarily conceptualized their country in terms of North and South. Writers,

3. Biographical information does little more than note the existence of the novelists' ties to North and South; for the most part it fails to explore the role these attachments played in shaping the consciousness—and consequently the fiction—of Gilman, Hentz, and McIntosh. An outstanding exception is Howe's "A Massachusetts Yankee." See also Whichard, "Caroline Lee Hentz," and Mary Katherine Walsh, "Caroline Howard Gilman" (M.A. thesis, Duke University, 1941). Mary Kelley gives attention to the financial circumstances of these writers in *Private Woman*, 14–17, 145, 164–68.

politicians, travelers, and a host of other observers concurred that the United States was composed of two self-contained regions inhabited by men and women of markedly different temperaments.[4] Thomas Jefferson's pointed discussion of the northern and southern personality is representative: "In the North," Jefferson wrote, "they are cool, sober, laborious, persevering, . . . interested [and] chicaning." But "in the South," he continued, "they are fiery, voluptuary, indolent, unsteady, . . . generous [and] candid."[5]

For a time, the Yankee merchant, the popular symbol of the North, and the aristocratic planter, the symbol of the South, stood together in tension reflecting America's need to reconcile its republican ideals with the rapid social and economic changes of the antebellum period. By the late 1830s, however, economic depression, population shifts, and political realignment threatened to reduce the South to minority status; southerners, anxious to rationalize their fall from preeminence, sought and found an explanation and an enemy in northern society. The North, southerners argued, was driven by a competitive value system antithetical to the communitarian ethic of the South. As products of their individualistic culture, northerners were morally deficient, inferior to their southern counterparts. The merchant and the planter were—and ever would be—at odds.[6]

The first wave of southern domestic fiction played a critical role in recasting the relationship between North and South as antagonistic; the novels of Gilman, Hentz, and McIntosh illuminate the development of the antebellum South's defensive mentality and provide penetrating insight into a uniquely feminine segment of southern propaganda. Although they argued that politics fell outside their provenance—"Let us leave the great national question . . . for statesmen to settle. My head always aches, when I try to grasp anything so vast," a Hentz heroine declares—the southern domestic writers were nevertheless pivotal in shaping the politi-

---

4. In *Cavalier and Yankee*, William R. Taylor argues that this particular way of viewing the United States grew out of a postrevolutionary mandate to define a uniquely American character.

5. Thomas Jefferson to Chastellux, September 2, 1785, in Merrill D. Peterson, ed., *The Portable Thomas Jefferson* (New York, 1975), 387–88.

6. Taylor, *Cavalier and Yankee*, 15–22, 145–76. See also Watson, *The Cavalier in Virginia Fiction*, 12.

cal consciousness of America.[7] Using their fiction to focus on day-to-day experiences common to northern and southern women, they employed a vocabulary and a set of images designed to affect the heart.

While they argued publicly that they were interested only in union—"The North and the South, Thou hast created them," McIntosh proclaimed frequently—the body of antebellum southern domestic fiction reveals glaring contradictions between its writers' promulgated mission and the message their fiction ultimately conveyed.[8] For example, while McIntosh dutifully set her tales both in the North and the South and included northerners and southerners in her cast of characters, heroes and heroines typically hailed from the South. Action usually began and ended below the Mason-Dixon Line; conflict invariably arose once the action shifted north. In the notable cases when Hentz employed a northern hero or heroine, she typically paired the northern protagonist with a southerner on the premise that the northerner had imbibed sufficient southern virtue through association to render his or her predatory northern instincts innocuous. Variations in narrative and characterization notwithstanding, the consistent triumph of the South and southerners at the expense of their northern counterparts reflects each author's contradictory attitudes toward the developing national crisis.

That Gilman, Hentz, and McIntosh projected the very message they publicly condemned, that southern domestic fiction contributed to the ideological polarization of America, testifies to the insidious power of the novelists' words and pictures. In spite of their alleged objectivity, the three writers, and consequently their audience, found it impossible to separate their highly sentimentalized pictures of family life from their profoundly moralistic vision of the North and South; writers, and therefore readers, found it impossible to remain morally neutral when confronted with political issues in the context of domesticity. In a very real sense, Gilman, Hentz, and McIntosh were unwitting victims of their own propaganda.

7. Hentz, Lovell's Folly, 256.

8. McIntosh, The Lofty and the Lowly, epigraph. Mary Kelley notes contradictions in domestic fiction as a whole but explains them in terms of the anxiety women suffered upon entering the male world of belles lettres. Kelley's argument is supported by the fiction of the seven New England writers that form the majority of her sample. See Kelley, Private Woman, and Kelley, "The Unconscious Rebel: Studies in Feminine Fiction, 1820–1880" (Ph.D. dissertation, University of Iowa, 1974).

Gilman initiated the discussion of the relative merits of northern and southern society that dominated antebellum southern domestic fiction with the publication of her complementary novels *Recollections of a House-keeper* (1834), better known by its title in a later edition, *Recollections of a New England Housekeeper*, and *Recollections of a Southern Matron* (1838). Convinced that sectional dissension stemmed from lack of knowledge rather than the inherent incompatibility of northerners and southerners, Gilman designed her two major works of fiction to familiarize her audience with the dimensions of everyday life in the North and South. Both *New England Housekeeper* and *Southern Matron*, she explained in 1837, were "penned in the same spirit, and with the same object . . . to present as exact a picture as possible of local habits and manners." [9] Yet the two novels, which Gilman clearly intended to be read as a set, failed to bear out the author's commitment to union. In fact, far from affirming the essential similarity of northern and southern domesticity, Gilman's novels highlighted the differences between the North and the South, translating contemporary political debate into a uniquely feminine language. In *New England Housekeeper* and *Southern Matron*, Gilman made the predictable themes of stasis and change accessible to all literate American women by phrasing her argument in terms of northern and southern domesticity. [10]

In *Recollections of a New England Housekeeper*, Gilman chronicled the adventures of Clarissa Grey Packard, daughter of the upper middle class and quintessential New England housewife. Born in the final years of the eighteenth century, Clarissa's childhood, with the exception of her privileged economic status, mirrored Gilman's own. A somewhat perfunctory academic education—"The utmost term of my *solid education*," Clarissa recalls, "was one year of attendance at the town school"—coupled with extensive training in the domestic arts prepared both young women to assume their prescribed roles in antebellum society. "Our pecuniary

---

9. Gilman, *Southern Matron*, vi–vii.

10. In politicizing the domestic sphere, Gilman, Hentz, McIntosh, Terhune, and Evans wrote not to subvert authority but to uphold tradition through strengthening the institutions of home and family; they wrote to defend their region against attacks from the North, not to protest their oppression as southern women. But that particular interpretation of domestic fiction remains popular. See, for example, Tompkins, "Sentimental Power," 81–104; and Voloshin, "The Limits of Domesticity."

circumstances enabled us to indulge in the luxuries of life," Clarissa confides, "but none of these interfered with my education for usefulness . . . I made my own bed, swept and dusted the apartment, mended my own clothes, and when pudding or cake was to be made, rolled up my sleeves."[11]

Clarissa's mastery of her uniquely feminine curriculum (like Caroline Gilman's) was richly rewarded when, in her late teens, she met and married Edward Packard, a rising young lawyer; Gilman herself wed an ambitious clergyman at the age of twenty-three. Cornelia, most assuredly speaking for Gilman, insists that domestic expertise helped her win a sterling husband: "Though my mother was one of the most unostentatious women in the world, . . . before [Packard] left, she made him understand that I could skewer a goose, roll puff paste, complete a shirt, and make a list carpet, as well as I played on the spinet and worked a tent-stitch."[12] Within a space of several months, Clarissa finds herself mistress of a fine home in one of Boston's better neighborhoods; Gilman took up housekeeping in Charleston, South Carolina. At this point, the obvious parallels between Clarissa Packard and Caroline Gilman end. Gilman readily assumed her new identity as a southern matron and a woman of letters; Clarissa Packard's tribulations were purely the product of Gilman's rich imagination.

Although Gilman intended to portray the private sector of northern society in *New England Housekeeper* as the stronghold of the immutable social values of personal independence and community responsibility, in reality she advanced an illustration of tradition under attack. Clarissa Packard's 1834 Boston had less in common with the Boston of Gilman's youth, where "our pastor . . . resided at the head of the Square—the Mays, Reveres, and others, being his neighbors," than with the bustling center of industry and commerce that McIntosh described less than twenty years later in *The Lofty and the Lowly* (1853). By the 1830s the close-knit population bound by common heritage, the informal class structure— Gilman, daughter of a shipwright, learned to read at the governor's residence—both were in the throes of economic development. Whereas Gil-

11. Gilman, *New England Housekeeper*, 318 *Cf.* Gilman, Autobiographical Essay (MS in South Carolina Historical Society).
12. Gilman, *New England Housekeeper*, 323–24.

man could remember the generosity of her "countrypeople" when as a child she was mistakenly deposited at the wrong address yet nevertheless received a warm welcome—"I have never forgotten that long, long day with the kind and hospitable, but *wrong Phillipses*," she recalled decades later—as an adult she realized that this sort of community bond no longer existed in the North.[13]

New England Housekeeper reflected Gilman's perception that the structured society of her girlhood was rapidly fading into memory. Unlike the smoothly regulated domestic circles of an earlier day, Clarissa's household, a microcosm of the world at large, is characterized by uncertainty and change. Clarissa controls neither her time nor her money: an endless number of people and responsibilities command her every waking moment, and her household budget is tied to her husband's current position in the constantly fluctuating business community. That Clarissa perseveres in spite of these challenges, that she manages (with the assistance of her staff) to keep her house moderately neat and her husband reasonably well dressed, hints not, as modern critics argue, at the strength of the domestic sphere but at its inherent instability.[14] Increasingly isolated from the world by the polarization of society into public and private spheres, at the mercy of forces beyond her comprehension, Clarissa can order only her immediate physical environment and then only with great difficulty.

The chaos of Clarissa's household illustrates the tenuous hold the middle-class matron exerted on the domestic sphere. Typically meals are late and poorly prepared, cleaning is haphazard, mending is ignored. A string of servants, all temperamentally unsuited for domestic service, troop through Clarissa's kitchen and keep the household in an uproar. Nancy, Clarissa's first cook, lasts all of a week; Sally, Nancy's successor, stays for just two months before she surrenders her position for marriage. The Packards keep their third cook, Lucinda, for almost ten months before she takes "a notion to see a little more of the world" and moves to exotic Roxbury. Lucy, Lucinda's replacement, dies in service; Becky, Clarissa's fifth cook, runs off with the butcher. Matters are further complicated when, soon after the birth of the Packards' first child, the nursemaid,

---

13. Gilman, Autobiographical Essay (MS in South Carolina Historical Society), 5.
14. For an alternative reading, see Baym, *Woman's Fiction*, 66–70.

Mrs. Philipson, robs her employers of their silver and their maid-of-all-work, Polly.[15]

Clarissa's persistent servant problem makes her home a seat of conflict rather than a safe haven; instead of solace, the Packard household affords unrelieved tension. Servants challenge or ignore Clarissa's orders, constantly overstepping their bounds. For example, Nancy, the first cook, refuses to make the dinner pudding according to Clarissa's specifications; when Clarissa protests, Nancy quits her job and tells Clarissa to do it herself. Lucinda, cook number three, refuses to remain in the kitchen when guests call; she persistently embarrasses her employer with her familiarity. Becky, cook number five, goes through Clarissa's personal belongings and spills candle wax on a precious book of engravings. Mrs. Silter, cook number eight, drinks heavily and, during her brief tenure, breaks most of the Packards' china. Under these circumstances, it is not surprising that Edward Packard spends the majority of his time at the office.[16]

Clarissa's limited control over her household affairs, her inability to dispatch her duties alone (or, for that matter, with assistance), her husband's erratic fortunes, and her servants' recalcitrance illuminate strains within the fabric of northern domesticity. Clearly, Gilman's humorous description of the difficulties of replicating everyday life masked her gnawing fears that the northern home and family lacked the order and stability to withstand the pressures of contemporary society. Significantly, Gilman attributes the circuslike atmosphere of the Packard household not to Clarissa's shortcomings—on the contrary, Gilman repeatedly emphasizes her heroine's proficiency in the domestic arts—but to the unpredictability of modern life. A world of uncertainty and change, she contended, rendered even the best housewife and the strongest family ineffective. That Gilman failed to carry her argument to its logical conclusion, that she left the Packard household teetering on the brink of disaster rather than pushing it to certain destruction, testifies less to her optimism than to her

15. Gilman, *New England Housekeeper*, 327–47.

16. Edward Packard's complete absence from the home suggests the beginnings of the polarization of public and private spheres characteristic of the mid- to late Victorian period. Significantly, the hero of *A Southern Matron* plays a major role in the administration of the home. Clearly, Gilman perceived women's roles in the South as more flexible than in the North.

ambivalent attitude toward the land of her birth. For in spite of Gilman's fundamental distrust of the social disequilibrium she associated exclusively with the North, she could no more overtly condemn the region that provided her with a store of happy childhood memories than she could make explicit the connection between what she perceived as the tumult of northern society and the fragility of the domestic sphere. Gilman's apprehensions remained confined to the printed page and the private letter; her nagging suspicions of what she loosely defined as "progress" were buried in a novel that, on a purely superficial level, resembled a treatise on New England domesticity.

While Caroline Gilman consciously resisted the urge to publicly identify her interests with either the North or the South, her affection and loyalty to her adopted homeland and its institutions resonated throughout her second novel. *Recollections of a Southern Matron*, the companion piece to *New England Housekeeper*, portrayed a stable, ordered world that sharply contrasted with Clarissa Packard's Massachusetts.[17] Where Clarissa's life was characterized by constant movement and change, Cornelia Wilton, the southern matron, found order and harmony in both her landscape and her relationships. Punctuated by the noisy clip-clop of horses' hooves and the strident cries of street vendors, Clarissa's day was one of unpredictability; Cornelia's, on the other hand, was reassuringly monotonous. "Change! Sameness!" Cornelia wonders as she contemplates her destiny. "What a perpetual chime those words ring on the ear of memory."[18]

Although Gilman freely admitted that her beloved South had its problems—after all, Cornelia Wilton's character was conceived in part to battle the moral lethargy of the planter class—she remained firmly convinced that the plantation system nourished a communitarian ethic inherently more virtuous than the burgeoning individualism she identified in the North. Protected from the wiles of the city, sheltered from the greed and exploitation of a rapidly modernizing economy, southerners, according to Gilman, enjoyed a morally superior society by virtue of their geographical and intellectual isolation. Loyalty to the past, reverence for tra-

17. William H. Pease and Jane Pease muster convincing support for Gilman's analysis of the differences between North and South in *The Web of Progress: Private Values and Public Styles in Boston and Charleston, 1828–1843* (New York, 1985).

18. Gilman, *Southern Matron*, 6. Hereinafter cited parenthetically by page number in the text.

dition, and suspicion of new things, particularly within the planter class, fostered social stability and, Gilman believed, nurtured a sense of community obligation lost to northern civilization. In an era when many Americans questioned the viability of the republican experiment, Gilman's assurances that the ideals of the Revolution permeated the aristocratic South and galvanized the southern community provided readers with comfort and security.

In the opening pages of *Southern Matron*, Gilman evoked images of stability and permanence: "I write in my paternal mansion," Cornelia Wilton declares. "The Ashley, with a graceful sweep, glitters like a lake before me. . . . Occasionally . . . a boat, with its urging sail, passes along, and the woods echo to the song or the horn of the negro" (5). Unlike Clarissa Packard, who revels in the new and the fashionable—Clarissa's residence, furnished with "new carpet, new chairs and new mahogany," is located in "one of the most genteel quarters in . . . Boston"—Cornelia cherishes the past: "The avenue of noble oaks, under which I sported in childhood, still spread their strong arms and rustle in the passing breeze. My children are frolicking on the lawn where my first footsteps were watched by tender parents, and one of those parents rests beneath yonder circling cedars" (5).

The prominence of the Wiltons' family burial ground, to which Cornelia repeatedly refers during her narrative, illustrates the high value southern culture placed on tradition. In that enclosure, "sacred to the domestic dead," undisturbed by "the tumult of the city," lay the physical remains of the men and women who fought for southern greatness. Their "whitened bones" served to remind the living of the cost of freedom and the sanctity of the Republic; their words and deeds, memorialized by "princely" monuments, inspire their progeny to uphold the ideals of the Revolution. It is while contemplating the deeds of "the fair, the good, and the brave" that Cornelia finds courage to crusade for feminine virtue, just as it is by familiarizing her children with the achievements of their ancestors that she prepares them to take their place in the southern aristocracy. They "love to lead me to the spot where they may spell the inscription . . . to their grandfather, and hear the tale I have to tell," she explains (6).

A host of time-honored rituals united planter, artisan or small-holder, and slave, perpetuating the values of personal independence and community obligation that formed the bedrock of southern society. Births,

deaths, Christmas celebrations, and summer square dances nurtured relationships that cut across the boundaries of caste and class. "We are as
one," Cornelia proudly asserts. "Misfortune is not required to develop
kind neighborhood at the South. A system of attentions is going on in
prosperity so tranquilly, that, when adverse circumstances befall one, no
surprise is excited at a great benefit" (105). For instance, when Roselands,
the Wiltons' plantation, catches fire, friends, family, and total strangers
rush to offer their assistance, risking their lives to rescue slaves and salvage
family heirlooms from the blaze. Once the flames are extinguished, every
member of the Wilton clan, including the slaves, is taken in by neighbors,
who insist that the refugees regard their temporary quarters as "another
home" (105).

Cornelia characterized the ethos of the southern community with elegant simplicity. "Remembrance," she asserted, "was our . . . watchword."
Every day provided southerners, regardless of economic class, with countless opportunities to demonstrate interest and concern for their fellows.
"The question was not asked, Have they this preserve, or that flower?
would they like to read this book, or copy that pattern?" Cornelia explained. "But the preserve or the flower, the book or the pattern, were
sent as testimonials of good-will" (105). Thus, when the Wiltons hear that
Mrs. Alwyn, "a neighbor, a widow has lost her only child, a daughter,"
Cornelia immediately sets out for parts beyond to offer her sympathies
and assistance (216).

Differences in class notwithstanding—Mrs. Alwyn manages a small
farm and often takes to the fields herself—Cornelia and the bereaved
mother share their grief as equals. It is Cornelia, daughter of the aristocracy, who comforts the grieving widow and prepares the body for burial,
and it is Cornelia who hears Mrs. Alwyn's confession that she had hoped
her daughter one day might have married into the planter class. "I have
toiled night and day, I've worked like a nigger, and more than any nigger,
I've been up early and abed late, to get that girl a genteel education, and
what has it all come to?" Mrs. Alwyn asks Cornelia indignantly. "She sat
so lady-like at the table, as if she had been born and bred genteel," Mrs.
Alwyn mourns. "It tan't no mercy. I wouldn't treat a dog so." Cornelia,
disturbed by the revelation, later recorded the incident as "a startling representation of an irreligious, uncultivated mind" (218).

Cornelia's encounter with Mrs. Alwyn simultaneously points up the flexibility and the rigidity of the southern social hierarchy, lending insight into Caroline Gilman's explanation for the stability of southern society. For while it was accepted that the extreme interdependence of the three orders of southern society necessitated a high degree of informality in day-to-day contact between classes, as Bertram Wyatt-Brown and others have noted, that informality was, in itself, part of a larger pattern of deferential behavior that reinforced distinctions between class and caste.[19] Most often it was the planter elite who initiated and set the boundaries for community interaction. Thus, while it was right and proper for Cornelia to heed the distress of Mrs. Alwyn, her social inferior, and in the shadow of death to listen with compassion to Mrs. Alwyn's dreams of upward mobility, it was just as correct for the planter's daughter when removed from the immediate situation to discount the yeoman's wife's yearnings for gentility as the fancies of "an irreligious, uncultivated mind." If Cornelia was bound by the aristocratic principle of noblesse oblige to attend to the physical and spiritual needs of her inferiors, members of the southern middle and lower classes were equally expected to observe the limits of their authority (221).

While Gilman took great pains to emphasize that the stability of southern society depended on the exchange between all three orders, she nevertheless placed the greatest emphasis on the interaction between master and slave. It was this peculiar bond, Gilman argued, that stabilized the South, that perpetuated the values of community and preserved the ideals of the Revolution intact. Slavery strengthened the moral currency of the South by consistently demanding sacrifice on the part of the planter class; it ensured the persistence of the Christian ethic—Gilman contended that there were "passages in the teachings of the New Testament" that had relevance only in context of southern slavery—and, more important to the domestic novelists, it reinforced the authority of the institutions of home and family (234). "None but those who live under our peculiar institutions can imagine the strong bond existing between faithful servants and the families with whom they are connected," Gilman argued through her heroine. "They watch our cradles; they are the companions of our

19. Wyatt-Brown discusses the psychological foundations of planter culture in *Southern Honor*. See also Stowe, *Intimacy and Power*.

sports; it is they who aid our bridal decorations, and they wrap us in our shrouds" (107).

Her professions of political neutrality aside, Gilman's celebration of the peculiar institution brought her southern partisanship into sharp relief. Her discussion of the role slavery played in stabilizing southern society was anything but impartial; in fact, on this particular issue, Gilman's tone was almost aggressive. In examining the master-slave relationship, Gilman went so far as to imply that southerners were harder workers, more responsible citizens, and generally the moral superiors of their northern counterparts (234–35). Slavery subjected planter women to any number of demands unfamiliar to their upper- and middle-class sisters in the North. "Instead of a limited household," Gilman explained, the plantation mistress's "dependents are increased to a number which would constitute a village." She was responsible for hearing "cases of grievance," nursing the sick, and distributing the "half-yearly clothing," Gilman pointed out. "The mere giving out of thread and needles is something of a charge on so large a scale." She admitted, "A planter's lady may seem indolent, because there are so many under her who perform trivial services, but the very circumstance of keeping so many menials in order is an arduous one" (50–51).

If slavery exacted a toll from the planter's wife "of which a Northern housekeeper knows nothing," it placed an equally heavy burden on the planter (50). Cornelia's husband, Marion, spends his lifetime "preparing . . . for usefulness." He attends "medical and surgical lectures that he might supply with advice the accidental wants of his people; and interests himself in mechanics as a means of saving labor on his plantation." Cornelia observes, "He felt the responsibility of his situation, and looked with a steady and inquiring eye on his duties, removing evil where it was practicable. . . . It was not gain only that he sought; he was aware that he controlled the happiness of a large family of his fellow-creatures" (234).

By exercising a "strict superintending hand," Cornelia and Marion, representatives of the planter class, maintain that discipline without which the social hearth cannot be preserved free from strife (78). Through the sublimation of personal interests to community good, the two, like planter families throughout the South, establish order and ensure the prosperity of their region. By guarding their virtue and considering the needs of

others first, they set a sterling example for their social and economic inferiors; by perpetuating the values of community, they achieve a coherent,
integrated society that is the mirror image the North. "No manufactories,
with their overtasked inmates to whom all but Sabbath sunshine is a
stranger, arose on our plantation," Cornelia enthuses. "Long before the
manufacturer's task in other regions is closed, our laborers were lolling on
sunny banks, or trimming their gardens" (122). Slavery, in sum, drew out
and reinforced the nobler instincts of men and women, thereby endowing
southern society with a superior culture and morality.

Gilman's decision to explore the precarious relationship between
North and South was undoubtedly influenced by the Nullification controversy that rocked South Carolina during the late 1820s and early 1830s.
The challenge, issued by planters intent on refuting the authority of the
United States government to levy a protective tariff, divided South Caro-
linians and forced all southerners to consider, at least on an ideological
level, union or secession.[20] When Caroline Gilman depicted the North as
a land of relentless progress and the South as a bastion of timeless values,
she drew upon contemporary political rhetoric; her implicit argument that
(northern) development imperiled domestic institutions and thereby
threatened the stability of society as a whole echoed the oratory reverber-
ating through the halls of the state capitol.

That this particular debate informed Gilman's literary vision is hardly
surprising. Historians long have regarded the Nullification controversy as
a prelude to national tragedy, a chilling rehearsal of the drama of civil war.
They argue that the focus of the South Carolina planter class was misdirected; planters were, in fact, formulating the philosophical defense of
state's rights that would figure prominently in the proslavery agitation of
the next three decades. At issue, then, was not that the national government had no power to impose a protective tariff that planters argued dis-
criminated against producers, but that state government had the right,
indeed the obligation, to choose which, if any, national mandate to obey.[21]

20. See William W. Freehling, *Prelude to Civil War: The Nullification Controversy in
South Carolina, 1816–1846* (New York, 1966).
21. See Freehling, *Prelude to Civil War,* 134–76; John McCardell, *The Idea of a Southern
Nation: Southern Nationalists and Southern Nationalism, 1830–1860* (New York, 1979), 1–48.
McCardell dates the beginnings of southern nationalism from the onset of the Nullification
controversy.

Caroline Gilman's personal correspondence reflected her avid interest in the developing crisis. "To think . . . that we should live to see a Civil War!" she wrote her sister-in-law Louisa Loring in 1833 upon learning that South Carolina governor Robert Hayne and his district commanders were mobilizing an army of nullifiers.[22] "Our Nullifiers are just as determined & the mass are as conscientious as the Whigs of '76 . . . the passions of men of both sides run so high, that we should not be surprised to see them anticipate the last sad crisis." Several weeks later she reported to her sister Anna: "It is utterly impossible to calculate on the result. Our greatest apprehension is, that in the excited state of feeling which prevails, some inflammatory, though perhaps unintentional aggression, may cause the flame to burst out on either side."[23]

"Families are sadly divided," Gilman lamented in her letter to Anna. One friend was a "Union man, an officer in the State Bank," while his son was "a nullifier & officer in a new corps of Artillery, got up for the express purpose of defending the State." The father told Gilman "mournfully" that he could only hope that "if they drive me from South Carolina they will give the fruits of my labor to my son."[24] Another acquaintance, Gilman wrote Anna in horror, "told me a short time since, that she would not own her son (a lad of 16) if he did not turn out against the Government forces."[25] Gilman's anxious comments about the ability of political dissension to dissolve familial bonds were revealing. The novelist was well aware of the potential for dissension within her extended family; many relatives were active in abolitionist circles. Samuel Gilman's sister Louisa, for example, was married to Ellis Gray Loring, the lawyer-activist; Caroline's niece Maria was the wife of James Russell Lowell. Although Caroline eventually came to realize that "all love does not stand trials," over the years she diligently worked to maintain family ties; even in the throes of civil war, she regularly sent her "best wishes to the Lorings" and to "Mr. Lowell."[26] For the most part, the conciliatory tones Gilman adopted in her private missives north echoed the message of moderation she sought

22. Caroline Gilman to Louisa Loring, December 17, 1833, in Caroline Howard Gilman Papers.
23. Caroline Gilman to Anna Maria White, January 15, 1834, *ibid.*
24. *Ibid.*
25. *Ibid.*
26. Caroline Gilman to "My dear Annie," February 17, 1865, *ibid.*

to promulgate through her fiction; however, just as Gilman's southern partisanship permeated her fiction, so did it spill over into her letters. "The South is all to me now," she told Louisa Loring.[27]

Caroline Gilman's imperfectly concealed southern loyalties revealed her growing suspicions that the future of America lay in the South, where a static, hierarchical community ensured the primacy of domestic values. Try as she might, she could not convince herself that the North exhibited the stability and homogeneity requisite for a virtuous society. Her optimistic contention that proper education could alleviate sectional tensions, that she, as a resident of both regions, could foster better communication between northerners and southerners through her literary endeavors, indicates her inability to confront and resolve her deep-rooted fear that the North was beyond redemption. If, indeed, southern society was the nation's stronghold of virtue and northern society was its mirror image, no amount of education could restore the North to virtue. Caroline Gilman, daughter of the North and the South, found this conclusion unconscionable.

Caroline Hentz shared Gilman's inner turmoil. Committed to the removal of sectional biases through education, Hentz was equally determined to mute her obvious preference for the people and the culture of her adopted homeland. Like Gilman, Hentz grew up in Massachusetts and moved south after her marriage to accommodate her husband's career.[28] Like Gilman, Hentz maintained a lively correspondence with her northern relatives, traveling north for visits whenever her budget permitted, and like Gilman, she sought to remain actively engaged in the lives of her distant friends and family. But whereas Gilman quickly acclimated herself to her new environment and became a leader of Charleston society, Hentz remained forever an outsider. Whereas Gilman immersed herself in cultural affairs, Hentz found intellectual stimulation primarily through her rich imagination.

The wife of Nicholas Hentz, a mentally unstable itinerant school-

27. Gilman to Loring, December 17, 1833, *ibid.*

28. Nicholas Hentz's interests were many and varied. In addition to teaching, he attended medical school in Paris, painted miniatures, studied and painted insects, and wrote poetry and novels. His posthumously published *Spiders of the United States: A Collection of the Arachnological Writings of N. M. Hentz, M.D.* (New York, 1875) remained the definitive work in the field for years after its publication.

teacher, Caroline Hentz had little opportunity to establish roots in her community.[29] Just as soon as she settled her family and adjusted to her new home, her husband, who suffered from an undiagnosed emotional disorder his wife referred to as "unsheathed nerves," invariably decided to move on; the Hentzes lived in six states over a twenty-year period.[30] Inevitably, the strain of constant dislocation took its toll. "I sometimes fall into hypochondria fits & feel as if there were no one in the world to love me," Hentz confessed to her diary, "as if I were removed from all that were once interested in my happiness!"[31] Near the end of her life, Hentz observed that only her memories of her youth, "that joyous period" in Massachusetts when she was surrounded by familiar objects and faces, had sustained her during years of constant tribulation. "If a 'thing of beauty is a joy forever,'" she reflected, "surely a scene of happiness has a life as long. What is once taken into the heart blooms perennial there."[32]

Nicholas Hentz's erratic behavior accentuated his wife's isolation. An exceptionally jealous man, Hentz opposed any moves the gregarious Caroline made toward establishing a degree of independence; he relentlessly scrutinized her friends and activities. After one of Nicholas' uncontrollable fits of temper forced the Hentzes to leave town in order to avert a scandal, Mrs. Hentz wisely decided to limit her contacts with the outside world.[33] Under these circumstances, a letter or a visit from friends was

29. See Rhoda Ellison, "Caroline Lee Hentz's Alabama Diary, 1836," *Alabama Review*, IV (1951), 254–70; and Ellison, "Mrs. Hentz and the Green-eyed Monster," *American Quarterly*, XXII (1950), 345–50.

30. Caroline Hentz to Mrs. Stafford, March 5, 1851, in Hentz Family Papers, Southern Historical Collection, University of North Carolina. See also Dr. Charles A. Hentz, Unpublished Autobiography (MS in Hentz Family Papers, Southern Historical Collection).

31. Caroline Hentz Diary, April 27, 1836. Kelley discusses Hentz's intense loneliness in *Private Woman*, 222–32. See also Ellison, "Alabama Diary."

32. Caroline Hentz to Mr. and Mrs. Willard, August 21, 1851, in Clifton Waller Barrett Author Collection (#9040), Clifton Waller Barrett Library, Manuscripts Division, Special Collections Department, University of Virginia Library.

33. Ellison discusses Mr. Hentz's history of irrational behavior and the incident that provoked the family's departure from Cincinnati in "Green-eyed Monster." Both Helen Papashvily and Mary Kelley believe that Mr. Hentz's mental illness influenced Caroline Hentz's fiction and led her repeatedly to emasculate her male characters in an effort to work through the pain. See Papashvily, *All the Happy Endings*, 75–94; and Kelley, *Private Woman*, 222–32.

cause for rejoicing; an infrequent trip to the North was a source of endless pleasure. "I remember your annual journey to the White Mountains," she wrote her friends, the Willards, on the one-year anniversary of her stay at their Massachusetts home. "You are probably even now wending your way among the snow-clad hills and sun-clothed valleys." By the time the Willards returned from the mountains, Hentz observed, her "little token of friendship" would have "knocked vainly at your door" for weeks on end; she comforted herself, however, with the thought that "I can wait in the [post] office for your return & be one of the first friends who has the happiness to greet you to your own home." [34]

In the end, Caroline Hentz's extreme loneliness and intense hunger for community drew her to the South and made her one of its most ardent defenders. Embracing the South and southern culture as the ideal of social stability and cohesion, Hentz erected a compelling monument to the South and its people. Enlarging upon the themes of stasis and change that dominated Caroline Gilman's discussion, Hentz celebrated the strength and coherence of plantation culture as manifestations of a superior society.

The complexity of Hentz's fictional investigation of the potential for national harmony, however, came at high personal cost. While Gilman avoided taking sides by restricting her discussion to the parameters of the domestic sphere, Hentz boldly explored the interaction between the public and private sectors of society. While Gilman attempted to bury her partisanship beneath a welter of domestic details, allowing the reader to draw her own conclusions about the meaning in the text, Hentz forced herself to argue both sides of the question. And while Gilman would privately admit her loyalty for the South on the rare occasion when she could not sidestep the issue, Hentz did not allow herself that freedom. In spite of her apparent affinity for the southern life-style, she remained committed to the ideal of political neutrality that she propounded in her fiction, struggling to reconcile her uneasy recognition of what was with what ought to be between the covers of a single volume.

Caroline Hentz's letters and diary echo the tension that permeated her fiction. "We see here a strong contrast to the North," she wrote her

---

34. See Caroline Hentz to Mr. and Mrs. Willard, August 21, 1851, Caroline Hentz to "My Dear Friends," October 22, 1850, and Caroline Hentz to [?], August 28, 1850, all in Barrett Author Collection.

family in 1826. "I look in vain for Northern neatness and comfort," she complained. "You see such a swarm of greasy negroes filling the houses & streets, it is enough to put one out of conceit with everything."[35] Her 1836 diary underlined her ambivalence. "Oh! that we were far removed from the red men of the wilderness, as well as the children of Africa," she declared on May 20. Another entry roundly condemned a local planter for marrying a woman who was "not handsome, not even pretty, nor witty." "Her father has some 4 or 500 negroes," Hentz noted wryly, "and that makes her lovely, in this southern land." The same year, however, that Hentz recorded her anger at the "credulous and prejudiced parents and guardians" of her students in Alabama, she proclaimed, "Ye snows of New England—ye merry sounding bells—ye have lost your charms for me." The same year that she lamented the "angry and ungentlemanlike" behavior of the planter class, she implored heaven to "give me a more genial clime, where the gales of the south, melt the flakes in the upper regions of air." Hentz's attraction to the South, coupled with her commitment to the unbiased discussion of northern and southern relations, could not be reconciled easily.[36]

In spite of, perhaps because of, her dissatisfaction with certain aspects of southern society, Caroline Hentz became one of the South's most effective proponents. The delicate balance through which she privately maintained the fiction of her political neutrality sustained the plots of a series of novels concerned with the domestic ramifications of sectional dissension. Hentz's relentless demands for a thorough and honest investigation of each side of the question gave her fiction an urgency and credibility that eluded more straightforward propaganda novels; her (reasonably) plausible, easy-to-understand synopsis of the fundamental issues that threatened to dissolve the Union brought politics within the purview of the literate female population. Yet Hentz's insistence that she herself had nothing at stake and that she was no more than a disinterested party disseminating vital information rang hollow. For all her efforts otherwise, every novel Hentz wrote ostensibly to further better relations between North and South in reality illustrated her fervent belief in the superiority of southern civilization.

35. Caroline Hentz to "My Dear Sisters," November 5, 1826, in Hentz Family Papers.
36. Caroline Hentz Diary, February 18, May 20, May 24, 1836.

In her first novel, *Lovell's Folly* (1833), Hentz outlined the argument she revised and refined over her twenty-year career as a woman of letters. Written at the same time Caroline Gilman was wrestling with the Nullification question in Charleston, *Lovell's Folly* reveals Hentz's similar awareness of and concern with the growing distance between North and South. Yet, while Gilman merely hinted at a solution to the problem, Hentz used her fiction to illustrate the potential of sectional conciliation through the establishment of a meaningful dialogue between northerners and southerners, especially between women. Asserting that if women would actively seek out points of agreement rather than accepting arguments that the North and the South were inherently incompatible, sectionalist sentiment could be quelled, Hentz urged her readers to keep an open mind, to question conventional wisdom. But Hentz's own commitment to union, as evidenced by the message in her text, was hardly overwhelming.

Unlike Hentz's subsequent fiction, *Lovell's Folly* opens in the North, in Cloverdale, a village situated in a "beautiful valley in New England." Like Clarissa Packard's Boston, however, Cloverdale is in transition. Long celebrated for the "superior intelligence and refinement of its inhabitants," the little town has been infiltrated by the residents of a nearby city, and through their negative influences, "like a rustic beauty, inflated by the consciousness of her charms," it has begun "to assume the refinements and graces of the metropolitan belle." While an influx of the rich and the famous labor to transform the pristine countryside into a center of fashion and culture, Cloverdale's "venerable oracles," stunned by the invasion, fold their hands and "sigh . . . for the rustic simplicity of olden times." [37]

The physical organization of Cloverdale brings social tensions into sharp relief. The rich occupy the center of town; the good reside on its perimeter. Looming over the whole is Lovell's Folly, a "fantastic white elephant of a house" that serves simultaneously as the seat of fashionable society and the symbol of corruption (9). A Cloverdale landmark, Lovell's Folly has been renovated and renamed "La Grange" by a Mr. Merriwood, a fabulously wealthy businessman. Intent upon bringing the sophistication of the city to the country, Merriwood, assisted by his "ugly but extremely

---

37. Hentz, *Lovell's Folly*, 7–8. Hereinafter cited parenthetically by page number in the text.

rich" daughter, Penitence, undermines the integrity of Cloverdale in much the same way that he destroys the character of his new home (10).

Into this morally and economically polarized landscape, a microcosm of the North as a whole, Hentz introduces another source of conflict in the form of two members of the southern aristocracy. Mrs. Sutherland and her beautiful daughter, Loralley, accompanied by servants Blackey, Aunt Venus, and November, are en route to a northern resort favored by well-to-do planters when a carriage accident forces them to take shelter in Cloverdale. Ignoring Venus' dire predictions of "no good in Yankee country," the Sutherlands retire to a local hotel (23). At once, fashionable Cloverdale rushes to greet the newcomers. Eager to confirm rumors of southern depravity through firsthand observation, a petty and small-minded delegation, led by Penitence Merriwood, hastens to the Sutherlands' room in the Hotel Washington.

Penitence's airs of superiority and impertinent questions immediately alienate Loralley Sutherland. Puzzled by Venus' address of Mrs. Sutherland as "Miss Fanny," Penitence observes to Loralley: "*Surely* your mother is married" (48). When Penitence wonders at Loralley's reference to her slave attendant as "aunt"—were the two related?—the southerner loses her temper. Accusing her visitor of calling for the explicit purpose of adding "insult to misfortune," Miss Sutherland proclaims that her "spirit of a true Virginian, which never stoops a second time to degradation," forbids her to continue the conversation (48). Demanding that Penitence leave immediately, Loralley announces, "I detest them all—the whole race of cold, selfish, calculating Yankees" (55).

While Mrs. Sutherland initially protests her daughter's vehemence on the grounds that "it is unjust, it is unfeminine, to cherish such bitter prejudices," she is hard-pressed to defend the close-mindedness that the two repeatedly encounter at northern hands (55). United by their extreme ignorance, fashionable Cloverdale residents exploit every opportunity to make the Sutherlands feel not only unwelcome but also morally degenerate. A tea party to honor the southerners provides a forum for one social maven to air her views on slavery. "Slavery is an evil, a crime," Mrs. Elmwood states emphatically. "Man has no right to hold his fellow-man in bondage, nor to barter human blood for gold" (253). A picnic affords an opportunity for others to familiarize the Sutherlands' slaves with abolitionist sentiments, with disastrous consequences. "I'm no more a slave than you be—and I ain't going to be ordered around about anymore like a nigger when I can be a free gentleman," November concludes after an abolitionist informs him of his rights. "I tell [Mrs. Sutherland] that she better stay at home, if she want nigger slave to dog after her" (249).

Still, the northerners are not the only ones at fault; Hentz argues that the southerners' willingness to take offense and refusal to countenance honest curiosity are equally deplorable. Rather than explaining the unfamiliar customs that have Cloverdale in an uproar, the Sutherlands, particularly Loralley, fly into a rage and prohibit further discussion. This typically southern response to typically northern overtures, Hentz commented, merely perpetuated regional dissension: "the empire of prejudice will never be shaken, but continue to extend, encroaching more and more on the limits of good feeling and good sense," unless women in both regions endeavored to gain a more complete knowledge of life above and below the Mason-Dixon Line (253).

Hentz contended that sectional misunderstandings could be reconciled easily if northerners and southerners would put aside their preconceived notions. For instance, when Mrs. Sutherland represses her anger and responds to Mrs. Elmwood's accusations of southern inhumanity rationally, she is able to make some headway in correcting false impressions of the plantation South. Acknowledging that although the image of "southern soil moistened by the blood of the negro drawn from his back by the lash of his tyrant master is an image familiar to all" in the North, Mrs. Sutherland claims nevertheless that this picture is wholly inaccurate. "I will not venture to contend with you in argument," the southerner declares calmly, while at the same time assuring Mrs. Elmwood that she herself has never seen any evidence of the brutality northerners associate with slavery (255). Thus mollified, Mrs. Elmwood hastens to assure Mrs. Sutherland that the abolitionists who sought to incite the rebellion of the Sutherland slaves were but a small portion of society, and she urges the southerner not to judge the North "by its dregs" (253–54). The two women part amicably. "We ought to be willing to let your opinions balance ours, and I know all your best feelings are in favor of us, as human beings," Mrs. Sutherland concludes (255–56).

Loralley Sutherland is similarly persuaded that northerners and southerners are not fundamentally incompatible. Rescued from danger by

Russel Rovington, a noble young man who lives with his mother and his sister Catherine on the outskirts of town, Loralley learns, much to her chagrin, that not all northerners are as meanspirited as Penitence Merriwood and her cohorts; in fact, conversations with Russel and his family reveal that the Rovingtons cherish a sense of independence and community obligation congruent with Loralley's own. Loralley apologizes for her ignorance at once: "I have been a child of prejudice," she confesses, "and never before had an opportunity of knowing how utterly groundless were some of my illiberal prepossessions—and how greatly exaggerated were others" (188). In return, the Rovingtons acknowledge that they, too, have harbored misconceptions. Loralley realizes that "all frankness, cordiality, and hospitality were not monopolized by favored children of her genial clime." The Rovingtons become aware that "all the kindliest charities of the heart might flourish in a soil moistened by the sweat of the negro's brow" (70–71). That settled, Loralley is free to become fast friends with Catherine Rovington and eventually to accept Russel's proposal of marriage.

The union of Russel and Loralley, the moral northerner and the almost perfect southerner, was dictated less by literary convention than by Caroline Hentz's profound optimism that sectional differences could be resolved if only men and women would take the trouble to learn about their northern and southern counterparts. If political arguments could be set aside and the issues dividing North from South considered in the context of domesticity, that is, in terms of relationships within the family and the larger community, Hentz believed that northerners and southerners would find that they were more alike than different. For instance, once Russel and Loralley reject their preconceived ideas concerning northern and southern morality, they realize that neither North nor South holds a monopoly on virtue, that in fact virtue has more to do with the character of the individual than with that of his or her region.

Yet the substance of Hentz's story undercuts her moral. Willing to grant at least theoretically the possibility that northerners and southerners had an equal capacity for good, Hentz nevertheless weighted her story toward the South. Significantly, Russel Rovington moves to Virginia after his marriage, exchanging immoral Cloverdale, where he is forced to live on the periphery of town, for a smoothly ordered, inherently virtuous plantation where he will serve as the moral arbiter of his community. Penitence Merriwood and other persecutors of the southerners are punished; the few enlightened souls who showed the Sutherlands comfort in their need are rewarded. While Hentz does criticize Mrs. Sutherland's lassitude and Loralley's impetuosity, she fully redeems the two and by the novel's end presents them as exemplary women. In spite of her conscious attempts to balance her narrative, Caroline Hentz unconsciously depicted the South as the persecuted, the North as the persecutor.

But if Hentz managed to assure herself that *Lovell's Folly* presented northern and southern grievances in a straightforward unbiased manner, she failed to convince her readership at large. Almost immediately after publication, *Lovell's Folly* was withdrawn from circulation on the grounds that its unfavorable portrayal of northerners was potentially libelous. Although no evidence of Hentz's reaction exists, the twenty-year period that separated *Lovell's Folly* from her second novel, *Linda* (1850), coupled with the dramatically different approach to the subject of national division exemplified in her later fiction, suggests that challenge to her nonpartisanship considerably shook Hentz's confidence.[38]

In *Eoline* (1852), Hentz went beyond the polemics of *Lovell's Folly* and the sentimentality of *Linda* to explore the causes of regional dissension. Reiterating her fundamental conviction that morality was not the exclusive province of either region, she focused on the particular personality traits that gave rise to damaging northern and southern stereotypes and argued that it was imperative that women, particularly southern women, take immediate action to correct inappropriate behavior of community members that fostered negative beliefs. Women, stewards of morality, must take responsibility for setting the moral tone of society. By providing a sterling example and demanding similar behavior from their friends and family, they could take important steps toward defusing the controversy that racked America.

At first glance, *Eoline* closely resembles Hentz's earlier efforts. Like Loralley Sutherland, Eoline lacks self-discipline; her high spirits, quick temper, and keen sense of injustice—typically southern traits—cause her consistently to fall short of the domestic ideal of southern femininity. She possesses the same energy and independence as Linda Walton; in fact,

---

38. Although *Lovell's Folly* was withdrawn from circulation almost immediately, it remains the clearest expression of Hentz's contradictory vision of North and South.

Eoline, like Linda, leaves home when her father proposes that she marry a man she does not love, justifying her actions on moral grounds. "My choice is made, then," Eoline tells her father angrily. "Be it poverty and banishment—it cannot be disgrace."[39] But *Eoline* is more than the reworking of an old romance; it demonstrates Hentz's growing sophistication as a propagandist as well as her heightened confusion as to where her true loyalties lay. For Hentz defended the South best as she criticized its institutions and its people; she convinced her audience of the superior morality of southern civilization by enumerating its shortcomings. In *Eoline*, Hentz came into full command of her powers as a southern propagandist, all the while persuaded that the novel she wrote conveyed another message altogether.

Set exclusively in the warm and pleasant South, *Eoline* advances an image of plantation society designed to soften the hardest heart. Hentz's novel, laden with domestic imagery, illustrated the numerous physical and emotional intersections between master and slave. Magnolia-scented breezes whisper around the "massy rows of columns" of the big house, carrying melodious slave songs to the planter's parlor. In the house, master and slave enjoy a close relationship (13).[40] Eoline's maid, Gatty, sleeps in Eoline's room and wears her mistress's clothes. The two consult on personal matters, the slave often providing a unique and welcome perspective on puzzling questions. For example, when Eoline expresses reservations about a certain Horace Cleveland, Gatty volunteers that her sources tell her that Cleveland is a "mighty good young master. . . . He mighty smart, too—know a heap, folks say" (27). This high degree of interaction between masters and their chattel, Hentz argued, ensured the benevolence of the planter regime; furthermore, it fostered a cohesion and a strength within the southern community that made it inherently more virtuous than its chaotic northern counterpart.

But the plantation South, Hentz repeatedly noted, was far from perfect. In the long run, its capacity for virtue depended directly on the

39. Caroline Hentz, *Eoline; or, Magnolia Vale* (Philadelphia, 1852), 11. Hereinafter cited parenthetically by page number in the text.

40. Eugene Genovese describes the reciprocal relationship between master and slave that piqued Hentz's imagination in "Life in the Big House," in *A Heritage of Her Own: Toward a New Social History of American Women*, ed. Nancy Cott and Elizabeth Pleck (New York, 1979), 290–97. See also Clinton, *The Plantation Mistress*, 16–35.

conduct of its people, and unless its people remained ever vigilant, its moral strength would wane. The southern temperament that Hentz, like others before her, described as potentially volatile, demanded a high degree of self-awareness and self-discipline to keep it in check. Without self-government, contemporary southerners could easily destroy the commonwealth of virtue that had been established over the centuries. By focusing on the internal as opposed to the external challenges facing the antebellum South, Hentz attempted to protect her work from the charges of partiality leveled at *Lovell's Folly* and to gain a broader audience than would have been attracted by an explicitly political tract. Using the language of domesticity to investigate the problems and possibilities of southern society, Hentz won the South and its people a hearing before a sympathetic female audience.

Eoline Glenmore, Hentz observed, was no different from the majority of young southern aristocratic women. Beautiful, wealthy, and intelligent, she grows to maturity without event, cosseted by her loving widowed father and his houseful of slaves. Indulged and rarely contradicted, Eoline has little opportunity to learn self-denial; she comes to believe that her will should reign supreme. Thus, when her father apprises her in her late teens that he has chosen her husband, indeed, arranged her marriage years before, she immediately rebels. Even though the would-be bridegroom, none other than Horace Cleveland, is eminently suitable, Eoline rejects him. Arguing that she will not marry a man of Horace's cool, intellectual temperament, Eoline flies into a passion and decides that she would rather work as a music teacher than marry the "cold, distant, reserved, and haughty" Cleveland (8).

In taking such extreme action, Eoline seems to mimic another heroine, Linda Walton; however, similarities between the actions of the two are purely superficial. Eoline's flight into the world is motivated not by her father's immorality but by her uncontrollable emotions. Her anger blinds her to the wisdom of her father's actions in recommending the level-headed Cleveland as her mate. Whereas Linda Walton's rebellion is legitimated by her father's greed and her would-be husband's reprehensible character, Eoline Glenmore leaves home because she will not tolerate opposition to her will. The first case illustrates the circumstances under which women are morally bound to subvert authority; the second exemplifies the destructive potential of the southern character, for Eoline's lack of discipline leads her to reject an ideal husband and jeopardize the future of southern civilization. If, in *Linda*, Hentz challenges the women of the South to catalyze a regional return to virtue, in *Eoline*, she acknowledges the circumstances that make that challenge both necessary and difficult.

Repudiating her life of luxury, Eoline takes a position as a music teacher at Magnolia Vale, an exclusive girls' school doubtlessly modeled after the Hentzes' establishments. Trading her extravagant suite for a tiny, poorly furnished dormitory room, Eoline is initially dismayed by her surroundings and responsibilities. No longer is she queen of all she surveys; rather, she is a working woman, subject to the commands of not only her employer but also her students. Although her teaching load is not arduous, Eoline finds her subordinate position vexing. She receives no special treatment; if anything, she is forced to work harder to prove her commitment to teaching in light of her privileged background. And although she suffers no great humiliation—on the contrary, she is recognized and treated as the lady she is—Eoline nevertheless endures what would have been privation and humiliation in the context of her former life.

Yet it is in the sequestered environment of Magnolia Vale that Eoline realizes the domestic ideal of femininity. Finding time and reason to confront her debilitating temper and to consider her obligations to her region and her class, she gives thought to the virtues of abnegation and sacrifice that she has previously discounted. Bereft of power and money, Eoline gains fuller appreciation of the things of the spirit and, in so doing, prepares herself to serve as a beacon of morality within her community. It is as a teacher that Eoline learns the lessons requisite to the successful discharge of her duties as an aristocratic southern female; it is as a member of the working class that she earns the moral credentials necessary to rule.

Ironically, Eoline's metamorphosis from undisciplined girl to disciplined woman is facilitated through the efforts of two northerners: Miss Manly, the principal of the school, and Louisa More, the head teacher. From Miss Manly, affectionately nicknamed "the colonel" because of her rigid bearing, Eoline learns the importance of system and order. Miss Manly, who has dedicated her life to teaching, routinely molds the fragile flowers of the South into exemplary young women through the force of her intellect and her personality. "Miss Manly had a remarkable power of awakening the ambition of her pupils," Hentz observed. "She had so constantly placed before them heroic and striking examples, that almost all

looked forward to the time, when the epithet *Great* would be attached to
their name and immortality their portion" (150). Eoline, no less than her
students, accepts Miss Manly's challenge to excel and applies herself diligently to her "lessons." She commences her "new duties with feelings of
awkwardness and repugnance," but inspired by "the all-exacting Miss
Manly," she learns to love her work (55).

Manly forms the characters of her pupils through rigorous instruction
and strict discipline. "She never threatened, never scolded. She laid down
her rules, fixed, *immutable* rules, and their violation was immediately followed by the known penalty. She might have represented justice, with her
scales" (150). Eoline is not spared the principal's relentless attentions. She
is forced to respect the stipulations of her contract and the authority of
her superiors even when she feels less than agreeable. For instance, when
an acquaintance stops in at Magnolia Vale unexpectedly, Eoline leaves her
classes to enjoy a long conversation. When Miss Manly objects to Eoline's
behavior on the grounds that her pupils have been left unattended and
that there is no time to make up the lessons, Eoline complains, "I did not
expect to be considered such a slave to hours . . . as not to have the privilege of greeting an old friend" (64). Manly responds that she herself never
leaves school during recitation hours, and she expects her teachers to follow her example. Eoline, realizing her error, apologizes.

If Miss Manly teaches Eoline intellectual discipline, Louisa More,
daughter of a New England minister, teaches her emotional control.
Greatly beloved by her students, Louisa complements Miss Manly's education of the mind with instruction in the ways of the heart. A sterling
example of Christian love, Louisa teaches those around her to think of
others first, to swallow a harsh reproach, and to look for the good in all
people. With Louisa's encouragement, Eoline begins to curb her temper,
to cultivate the self-discipline she sorely lacks. "I feel, since I have known
you," Eoline tells Louisa, "as if my life had been one tissue of selfishness.
Yet I dared to glorify myself as a martyr" (56). Louisa's message of charity
has an immediate impact on Eoline's turbulent emotions. For example,
when Miss Manly imposes upon Eoline's good nature and asks her to share
her room with a girl as "wild and uncultivated as an animal," as wild "as
ever was caught in the deep pine woods of the South," Eoline thinks of
Louisa's injunctions and gracefully submits to her superior's wishes. "It *is*

wrong to laugh at the personal defects of any human being; wrong to look upon them with scorn and derision," Eoline admits (126). With the assistance of "dear, angel Louisa," Eoline realizes a greater maturity.

Through the unremitting efforts of the two northerners, Eoline gains the wisdom and self-control she needs to take her place in the southern aristocracy. "I came here a very proud, inexperienced young girl, born to affluence and indulgence—a perfect novice in the school of discipline and action," Eoline observes toward the end of her tenure at Magnolia Vale. "I should have found my service hard, and I have no doubt pride has magnified my trials and darkened my judgment" (153). That her judgment has been clarified, that her appreciation of her extensive duties to her region has been enhanced through her months of gainful employment, is confirmed when Eoline reverses her decision not to marry Horace Cleveland. She accepts his suit and leaves her job to become mistress of his plantation.

"You were formed for a different sphere," Miss Manly observes to the young southerner early in her stay, "one to which I doubt not you will shortly return" (153). Through careful instruction, Miss Manly and Louisa More have prepared Eoline to uphold the institutions of home and family central to the stability of southern society. By providing Eoline with the discipline she needs to realize virtue, the two northern women increase the South's store of virtue and ensure the benevolent character of the plantation regime. Both Eoline and her region, Hentz suggests, are enriched greatly through her extensive interaction with northerners.

Still, in spite of Hentz's positive tone, the substance of the novel contradicted her claim that she wrote to promote national harmony. *Eoline*, just like *Lovell's Folly*, betrayed the author's loyalty to her adopted homeland; minor criticisms of the plantation South and its people did little to hide Hentz's belief in the moral superiority of southern civilization. While Hentz asserted on the one hand that virtue was not restricted to either North or South, her characterization of northerners and southerners argued just the opposite. For example, for all her admirable qualities, Miss Manly exhibits the northern traits Hentz openly condemned in *Lovell's Folly*: she is petty, jealous, cold, humorless, and often unforgiving. Louisa More fares somewhat better, yet she, too, pales alongside her southern colleague. While Eoline is warm, generous, and glowing with health,

Louisa is sickly and frequently inadequate to her teaching responsibilities. Eoline's vibrancy and effortless charm immediately endear her to her southern students. Where Miss Manly and, to a lesser extent, Miss More govern by respect and dignity, Eoline controls her classroom with affection.

Hentz offers little hope that the northern women will succeed in fulfilling their highest destiny of wife and mother. Miss Manly, her name chosen to reflect her masculine qualities, never marries. Her unrequited love for a Creole ne'er-do-well serves as the novel's comic relief while, at the same time, illustrating the northerner's inability to make responsible choices. Whereas Eoline can recognize her shortsightedness and correct her mistakes, Miss Manly's self-righteousness, another damning northern characteristic, forbids her to admit her stupidity. Louisa More eventually marries, but the heightened color of her cheeks and a persistent cough suggest that her days are numbered. Only Eoline, the southern aristocrat, marries an appropriate husband and mothers a new generation. Her southern impetuosity tempered with northern discipline, Eoline now is capable of fulfilling her duties to her community.

Eoline illustrates the ideological inconsistencies characteristic of the first wave of southern domestic fiction. Conceived to further national understanding, in reality the novel exacerbated sectional tensions through its unflattering portrayal of northerners. Like antebellum southern domestic fiction as a whole, *Eoline* argued, on one level, that men and women from the North and the South could profit from interaction while, on another level, the novel illuminated its author's implicit belief that southerners, with few exceptions, had more to teach and less to learn. By employing regional stereotypes, by consistently portraying northerners as fundamentally flawed and southerners as capable of infinite virtue, Caroline Hentz and Caroline Gilman—and also Maria McIntosh—merely reinforced the sentiment they professed to condemn: northerners and southerners were neither cultural nor moral equivalents.

"The South! the sunny South! The land where the snow-spirit never comes, where the forest-trees are never stripped of their green corona," Maria McIntosh rhapsodized in *Woman in America*. "Let us stand beneath her soft skies, inhale the perfume of her myrtle-bowers and orange groves, press her violet-covered turf, and weave fragrant wreaths of the jessamine."[41] McIntosh's invitation to her readers, issued in 1850, was tinged with nostalgia. A resident of New York City for some fifteen years, McIntosh had not seen her native Georgia since the sale of her plantation in 1835. In the beginning, financial disaster and personal misfortune conspired to keep her in exile from the home of her heart; later, a flourishing literary career tied her to the North.[42] Memories offset McIntosh's geographical distance: "When bruised and worn with the conflicts of life," she wrote, "we shrink from great emotions and long only for repose, the memory of [the South's] peaceful loveliness comes back on our spirits, with an influence soothing as that of the mother's smile which lulled our infancy to rest" (111).

Still, in spite of McIntosh's celebration of the South as the bastion of national virtue, she found much to like about the North. During her lengthy tenure above the Mason-Dixon Line, she had regained the fortune she had lost in the panic of 1837 and, in the process, established her name as a household word. A string of successful juvenile books and domestic novels had won her a loyal following and enabled her to command considerable respect in the antebellum publishing community. A minor celebrity, she enjoyed the company of leading literary figures; after the war, her home became an incubator for creative talent.[43] If McIntosh once had been ostracized by the northern elite as a result of her financial reverses, by 1850 she had gained access to the best homes in the country: women and children, regardless of regional affiliation, looked to Maria McIntosh for counsel.

Not surprisingly, McIntosh's personality reflected northern and southern influences. A model of southern gentility, she openly condemned the activities of the "manly" women who swelled the ranks of organized feminism and abolitionism. Women should exercise their power, she ar-

41. McIntosh, *Woman in America*, 110. Hereinafter cited parenthetically by page number in the text.
42. Baym, *Woman's Fiction*, 86–109; Kelley, *Private Woman*. See also Freeman, *Women of the South*, 163–70.
43. See Freeman, *Women of the South*; and Colles, *Authors and Writers*, 174–76. See also Marian Hornberger, "Maria Jane McIntosh," in *Notable American Women, 1607–1950: A Biographical Dictionary*, ed. Edward James, Janet Wilson James, and Paul S. Boyer (Cambridge, Mass., 1971), II, 468–69.

gued on one occasion, "not by public associations, debates, and petitions, but in the manifestations of all feminine grace, and all womanly delicacy" (118–19). Yet if McIntosh exemplified female decorum in her personal life, in her public career she was anything but retiring. Indeed, her rapid rise from poverty to affluence mirrored the determination and energy she typically assigned to northerners. McIntosh's commentary on the virtues of northern society, while directed to the men of America, accurately described her own achievements: "There are few, comparatively here," she wrote in 1850 from New York City, "who may not hope by industry, sobriety, and economy, to obtain an income sufficient to lift them above sordid poverty" (140).

McIntosh's ability to appreciate certain aspects of northern society, however, left her no less convinced of the superiority of southern civilization; although she made a sincere effort to portray life above and below the Mason-Dixon Line realistically and without bias, her overwhelming loyalty to the South consistently compromised her objectivity. Her use of northern and southern settings and characters merely underlined her psychic division. Crises always occurred in the North and were resolved in the South; northern villains were punished whereas southern villains were redeemed. If northern heroes and heroines occasionally triumphed, they did so only after they had exchanged the aggressive traits of their region for the communitarian ethos of the southern aristocracy. In spite of her prominence in northern literary circles, McIntosh, no less than Gilman or Hentz, was driven to assert the moral superiority of the South by a force she neither recognized nor controlled.

McIntosh articulated her dualistic vision of the North and the South in *Woman in America*. In the South, "we find some vestiges of the old feudalism," the novelist observed. "Changes of property are less frequent and violent . . . families remain longer in their relative positions . . . a higher value [is given] to blood,—to family distinction" (120). Celebrating a land of clear skies, open spaces, and unparalleled hospitality "where you will often find the highest intelligence in the land," McIntosh argued that the "inartificial life of the country" nurtured a population that "unites in a rare degree, refinement and simplicity." Impervious to change, the region offered the whole of its white population a "simple, unostentatious" life of virtuous independence (120).

Although McIntosh acknowledged her hesitancy in discussing in detail the "domestic institution" from which the South derived "many of those traits which have given her a distinctive character, and assigned to her a distinctive part in the great drama acting in this land," in fear of alienating a portion of her audience, she credited slavery with establishing the high moral tone of southern society (112). Southerners, regardless of economic class, were to zealously guard their virtue, constantly bearing in mind their accountability for the "temporal and eternal" interests of slaves. Women in particular were enjoined to moral vigilance: "She should be there to interpose the shield of her charity between the weak and the strong, to watch beside the sick," McIntosh wrote, "to soothe the sorrowing, to teach the ignorant, to soften by her influence the haughty master, and to elevate the debased slave" (118).

Lacking the organizing principle of slavery, the North, according to McIntosh, exhibited a greater propensity for widespread immorality; its diverse population, its concentration of "wealth, talent, and energy" in cities, and its emphasis on commerce fostered a high degree of social instability and personal dependence (117). "A great kaleidoscope of ever-shifting forms and colors, without plan or definite arrangement," the North was composed of "bustling crowds . . . moving hither and thither . . . jostling and even trampling each other" (127). In such an environment, McIntosh warned, the home and the family, core institutions of society, came increasingly under threat. "The rapid variations of fortune resulting from commercial enterprise, have a tendency to engender feverish dreams and wild speculations," the southerner commented. "Life, under such circumstances, becomes a great game of chance" (128).

While the burgeoning industrial centers of the North presented citizens with a greater potential for advancement than the South, McIntosh averred that it also held greater temptation for evil. Lured by hopes of monetary gain, northerners repeatedly betrayed their families, sacrificing all that was good and true at the altar of mammon. "It is by . . . the anxious, self-absorbed spirit of the gamester—that the movements of most [northern] men are impelled," McIntosh argued, lamenting her inability to exempt "the lawyer, the physician, and even the divine" from censure (128). "*Most men,*" the novelist concluded, often had "the product of years of labor placed . . . in some popular stock, or surprisingly lucrative business, where, at some acknowledged hazard, it promises to double, or treble, or quadruple itself in an incredibly short time" (128).

"We are nearing the abyss of strife—we feel its hot fires burning on our brow and kindling a flame in our heart," McIntosh proclaimed from her vantage point in New York City; unlike Gilman and Hentz, who relied primarily on newspapers and letters from relatives for information about the state of affairs in the North, McIntosh had a firsthand view (113). What she saw alternately moved her to disgust or despair. "We gladly turn from the acts of men, inconsistent [and] vacillating," she remarked on one occasion, "to those of the all perfect one, 'with whom is no variableness nor shadow of turning'" (113). Writing in the wake of the controversial Compromise of 1850, McIntosh inevitably suspected that the formal statement of northern and southern grievances had pushed the nation one step closer to tragedy. No legislation, however comprehensive, could effectively combat the deep-seated prejudices of northerners and southerners, McIntosh argued; national harmony must be pursued through less divisive channels.

McIntosh explored the causes and consequences of prejudice in *The Lofty and the Lowly* (1853). Subtitled *Good in All and None All-Good*, the two-volume novel argued that the differences between North and South were purely superficial. Tracing the origins of sectionalism to inadequate information and unfamiliarity with regional customs, McIntosh emphasized that the negative behavior and attitudes that perpetuated dissension could be effectively transformed through proper education. Prejudice was the inevitable result of ignorance, McIntosh stressed. If northerners and southerners would take the trouble to form their own opinions rather than accepting those of others, sectional tensions would rapidly abate. In a convoluted narrative that ran over seven hundred pages, Maria McIntosh reiterated a central tenet of antebellum southern domestic fiction: that northerners and southerners were essentially the same.

The Lofty and the Lowly chronicles the struggle of two sets of brothers and sisters to overcome their deep-seated prejudices against the North. Children of a northern mother and southern father, Alice and Charles Montrose are forced from their Boston home when the untimely death of their profligate father leaves them penniless. Receiving no sympathy from their mother's wealthy brother, Thomas Browne, who offers instead to put the family to work, the children turn in desperation to their paternal uncle, Colonel John Montrose. In true southern fashion, Montrose takes his brother's children into his home and rears them with the same affection he accords his own son and daughter, Donald and Isabelle. "Your children are henceforth mine," he writes his sister-in-law, "and you must relinquish to me all care for their future maintenance and settlement in life."[44]

Colonel Montrose is infuriated by Browne's proposals to prepare his niece and nephew for "a life of toil." He gives the children everything they want in order not to awaken the materialism and greed he associates with Browne and the North. To squelch their ambition, he takes steps to secure their future financially. Any show of independence is promptly discouraged on the grounds that it is improper behavior for a southern aristocrat. For example, when Charles Montrose seeks his help in establishing himself in a profession, his uncle responds indignantly to what he calls "northern" ideas. "Do you think that I would ever permit you or . . . Alice or your mother to want anything—that I shall not provide for you?" the colonel demands (I, 46).[45] Through careful education, he erases any evidence of his niece and nephew's northern heritage.

Time passes quickly. With Colonel Montrose's permission, the Montrose cousins develop some of the worst traits of the southern aristocracy. Donald Montrose, the heir apparent, is impetuous, indolent, and thoughtless; his quick temper and extravagance keep him in trouble. Charles Montrose fares somewhat better; impulsive and careless, he nonetheless has a keen sense of responsibility, the legacy of his northern mother, that keeps him from indulging in destructive behavior. Donald's sister, Isabelle Montrose, and his first cousin, Alice, exemplify the darker side of southern femininity; beautiful, intelligent daughters of the ruling class, they represent the merely ornamental type of femininity that southern domestic fiction condemned. Although McIntosh implied that these traits were not damning in themselves—they can be and are overcome through hard work—she argued nevertheless that they diminished the strength of the aristocracy and thereby threatened the stability of the South. Ironically, when Colonel Montrose seeks to protect his region by purging his family

44. McIntosh, *The Lofty and the Lowly*, I, 18. Hereinafter cited parenthetically by volume and page number in the text.

45. Chapter 1 of *The Lofty and the Lowly* compares the different reactions of the northerners and the southerners to the death of Charles Montrose, Sr. Predictably, the Brownes are reluctant to put aside their worldly interests for an appropriate period of mourning while the Montroses are catapulted into the depths of despair.

of northern characteristics, he is placing the southern community in jeopardy.

Far more important to McIntosh's story, however, is the cousins' virulent antinorthernism, the direct result of Colonel Montrose's personal prejudices. Taught to view the South and the North in terms of good and evil, noble planter and ignoble merchant, Donald, Isabelle, Charles, and Alice come to believe that "a manufacturer and a mechanic could hardly exhibit the dignity and courtesy and . . . heroism of a chevalier" (I, 153–54). On the contrary, Colonel Montrose tells them, northern society is dominated by "very shrewd men of business, ready to take advantage at every turn of [the] easy good-nature and thoughtless generosity" of southerners (I, 156). Holding up Thomas Browne as the personification of the greed and insensitivity he attributed to the northern population in general, Montrose proclaimed that the word *Yankee* marked "not a geographical, or national, but a moral distinction" (I, 152).

The cousins have no reason to question the authenticity of Colonel Montrose's statements. Certainly Thomas Browne, the only northerner they know, conforms to the colonel's portrait of northern depravity. A wealthy merchant, Browne takes every opportunity to vent his hostility toward the South in general and the Montroses in particular. "I am a plain man, and know nothing of *Southern Chivalry*," he declares on more than one occasion. Proud of his rapid rise from poverty, Browne scorns the aristocratic ethic of noblesse oblige as financially unsound; he openly condemns Colonel Montrose's gentlemanly demeanor as evidence of southern dissipation. Montrose is "quite too high to condescend to have any . . . association with a Yankee shopkeeper, as he calls all Northern merchants," Browne remarks, happily including himself in the slighted class (I, 26). A signal representative of "the enterprising North," Browne will go to any length to distinguish himself from "the chivalrous South" (I, 29).

On a tour of the North, the Montrose cousins find much to reinforce their existing prejudices. In fashionable Newport and later in Boston, they encounter a variety of people whose behavior confirms their uncle's dicta. Particularly offended by the many representatives of the new rich who displayed their wealth "with a bustling ostentation too little softened by . . . the refinements which [they] had not had time to study," they conclude that the South is the last bastion of national virtue (I, 93). Over a period of weeks, northerners ridicule Isabelle, Alice, and Mrs. Montrose for their provincial dress and genteel demeanor, insult Charles and Donald for their courtly manner, and generally make the southerners feel ill at ease. The visit culminates when Donald is victimized by a pair of northern "sharpers" who play on his prejudices to swindle him out of his inheritance. Only the timely intervention of a northern industrialist named Robert Grahame saves the Montrose family from complete financial ruin.

Owners of a large Massachusetts textile mill, Robert and his sister, Mary, symbolize the North at its best. Intelligent, sensitive, and ambitious without being exploitative, Robert and Mary have nothing in common with the northerners the Montroses have previously encountered. Unlike the Thomas Brownes of the North, whose characters have been warped by inordinate greed, Robert and Mary use their substantial assets to benefit their community. Their mill is a model of benevolent capitalism: working conditions are excellent, pay is better than average, workers are treated with respect. Mary, an example of the active feminine ideal that southern domestic fiction promoted, teaches the predominantly female labor force in a special schoolhouse after the evening bell signals work's end.

Robert and Mary Grahame play a critical role in recasting the antinorthern ideology of the Montrose family. Not content with merely rescuing Montrose Hall from the auction block, Robert takes it upon himself to convince the cousins of the North's fundamental morality. Inviting the Montroses into his home, Robert provides them with numerous opportunities to observe the power of northern industry to transform lives for the better. Slowly but surely, the cousins reevaluate their attitudes toward the North and its people. "A GENTLEMAN is the same everywhere in fundamental qualities," Charles concludes in a burst of insight, "though he may differ in the cut of his clothes, in the language he speaks, or in any of those things which are the result of social prescription, rather than the spontaneous expression of the man. North or South . . . the gentleman is still unchanged" (I, 248). When Donald Montrose, the most resistant to the idea that not all northerners are criminals, admits that "ignoble labor" is not necessarily incompatible with "education and refinement," the victory is complete.

Their prejudices set aside, the Montroses discover that they can learn much from their northern hosts. For example, Robert teaches Donald that a gentleman can, and indeed should, manage his own finances, and after helping Donald settle his debts, Robert teaches him economic principles

that will help him run his plantation more efficiently. Mary Grahame inspires Isabelle and Alice to shake off their torpor and start a slave school.
"I tried at first to excuse myself, under the plea of different circumstances," Alice explains, "and to persuade myself that I had none whom I
could teach and influence, . . . but then I remembered the negroes, and
how much I could teach them" (I, 205). The eventual success of Alice's
venture, McIntosh argues, proves that the "different circumstances" Alice
cited as an impediment to activity were really not so different after all.

A double wedding legalizes the relationship between the Montroses
and the Grahames and ensures the maintenance of cross-cultural ties.
Robert departs for Massachusetts with Alice as his bride; Donald installs
Mary as the mistress of Montrose Hall. Regular visits to the North and to
the South, McIntosh explains, will militate against the redevelopment of
sectionalist sentiments and enable the next generation to grow up free
from prejudice. Robert leaves Montrose Hall promising to convince his
northern colleagues that southern planters were hardly "the monsters of
selfishness and cruelty which partisan writers had represented" (II, 317–18).

McIntosh's disparaging remarks about northern propagandists indicate her lack of self-awareness; critical of those who used their literary
skills to foment sectionalism, she failed to recognize that this was precisely
what she herself was doing. For all McIntosh's professions of objectivity,
The Lofty and the Lowly is peppered with examples of northern inhumanity. For instance, the Thomas Brownes, symbols of the northern merchant class, complain loudly that they must cancel numerous social en-
gagements to observe the death of Alice and Charles Montrose's father.
They spend their perfunctory mourning period criticizing the deceased
for his lack of assets. A doctor called to tend to Donald Montrose when
he is taken ill in Boston uses his visit to discourse on the shortcomings of
southern planters: "Idle, dissipated . . . that's the history of these chaps,"
he observes with disdain (I, 139). Another northern doctor refuses to give
Alice Montrose credit in order that she may obtain the medicine he prescribed for her desperately ill mother; that same day, a hardhearted Boston
landlord threatens to evict the southerners. McIntosh's warnings about the
dangers of sectional prejudice aside, she herself found it impossible to
avoid.

Paradoxically, McIntosh's most conscious affirmation of her nonpartisanship was, at the same time, her boldest assertion of southern moral

superiority. Her use of a northern hero and heroine whose characters exhibited none of the traits she had painstakingly attributed to the North brought her southern sympathies into bold relief. Robert and Mary Grahame are truly exceptional northerners. Generous, hospitable, and always aware of their duty to their inferiors, the Grahames are better southerners than the Montroses; in fact, it is under their conscientious tutelage that Donald, Isabelle, Charles, and Alice realize their potential as southern aristocrats. Robert's responsibilities parallel those of the noble planter: Robert is "a ruler and guide to many," Mary explains, "availing himself of this position only for good. Around him are some who came to him untutored clods . . . into whom he has infused intelligent souls, and whose aspirations he has directed heavenward" (I, 154).

The Grahames, like the Montroses, have nothing in common with the North as portrayed by Maria McIntosh; Robert and Mary, like the southern cousins, exhibit none of the greed and pettiness McIntosh attributed to the northern population at large. For instance, Robert is trained not for factory work but, like Donald and Charles Montrose, for scholarly pursuits; he takes over the mill not to make money per se but to keep a deathbed promise to his father to clear his outstanding debts. Reluctant to "lead a life in which all intellect and refinement must be lost," Robert continues his studies in his spare time and uses his education to transform his business into a humane endeavor (I, 38–39). That Robert's factory resembles Donald's plantation is hardly coincidental; for all practical purposes, they are the same. Under these circumstances, Robert's comment that "no man who felt that life's highest object was to labor for the advance of man and the glory of God, need mourn that he was born a Southern slave-holder" becomes less a declaration of tolerance than a reaffirmation of his commitment to his own people (II, 320). Morally and intellectually, Robert is of the South.

In spite of McIntosh's attempts to balance her narrative by dividing action equally between the North and the South, by overtly criticizing the behavior of the planter class, and, most important, by using a northern hero and heroine, she could not mute her southern partisanship. For all her efforts to emphasize diversity within the North, she ultimately portrayed the North as a place where evil ran rampant, permitted, if not encouraged, by an economy of exploitation; in contrast, she depicted the South as a land where, if perfection did not exist currently, it had the potential to be realized in the near future. Certainly McIntosh, a dispossessed southerner in northern society, appreciated the fluidity of the class structure in the North that had facilitated her rapid rise to social prominence, but at the same time, she could not forget the instability that initially had propelled her into poverty. While McIntosh could revel in the rewards northern society accorded her energy and creativity, she would never forget the indignities she had suffered at northern hands. McIntosh's contradictory attitudes toward her adopted home doomed her self-styled mission of conciliation to failure.

Perhaps McIntosh sensed the inconsistencies in her narrative; certainly she felt compelled to restate her objectivity. In the preface to *The Lofty and the Lowly*, she explained that the work, like all her fiction, had originated "in the desire to remove some of the prejudices separating the Northern and the Southern United States." She had not entered "armed for combat," McIntosh explained, but to stand between "the contending parties, bearing the olive-branch, and desiring only to pour balm into the wounds given by more powerful hands." She intended to offend no one and wrote only the truth: "Every instance of sacrifice to a sense of duty . . . had its foundation in fact known to the author, not by report, but by actual observation." But even with these qualifications, McIntosh felt the need to claim "the privileges accorded to her sex by the chivalry of every age" as she ventured "unwillingly within precincts which others have made an arena of controversy." Seeking to further the cause of "peace and goodwill to man," she inadvertently illustrated the fundamental incompatibility of North and South.

Beginning in the decade that started the descent into civil war, Caroline Gilman, Caroline Hentz, and Maria McIntosh, the first generation of southern domestic novelists, launched an ambitious campaign to eradicate sectionalism. Convinced that regional bias stemmed primarily from ignorance, the three writers devoted their energies toward educating their audience. Drawing authority from their extensive residences above and below the Mason-Dixon Line, they argued that if Americans would put aside their preconceived notions about the North and the South, they would discover that northerners and southerners had much in common. Yet antebellum southern domestic fiction failed to bear out its authors' commitment to union; rather, it pointed up the distinctiveness of North and

South and suggested that rapprochement was less a real possibility than a praiseworthy ideal. By consistently portraying North and South as opposites, by refusing to rehabilitate northern villains while at the same time restoring southern ne'er-do-wells to prominence, and, most important, by transposing the southern planter-ideal into the context of the industrial North, Gilman, Hentz, and McIntosh unwittingly fanned the flames of sectionalism.

The contradiction between the authors' conciliatory intent and the divisive message their fiction actually conveyed embodied the divided loyalties of the first generation of southern domestic novelists. Gilman, Hentz, and McIntosh were linked by ties of blood and affinity to both the North and the South. Over the years, they continued to correspond with friends and family, frequently denying or at least muting their political beliefs in the interest of maintaining relationships in both regions. The need to remain on good terms with northern publishers played an additional part in the novelists' struggle to remain objective; all three were heavily dependent on northern sales for their livelihood and could not risk endangering their contracts by publicly announcing their southern sympathies.

Still, the disjunctions that characterize antebellum southern domestic fiction were not the result of a conscious decision to deny prosouthern sentiment. Gilman, Hentz, and McIntosh believed fervently in the principle of union. Their ongoing struggles to reconcile their feelings through whatever strategy were motivated not by self-interest but by the belief that northerners and southerners should be as one. Political actors themselves, they labored to familiarize their predominantly female audience with the dimensions of contemporary political debate with the objective of establishing national equilibrium. Using the language and images of domesticity to illustrate the complicated relationship between the public and the private sphere, they sought to convince their audience that the merchant and the planter could coexist. "We write not for men, who make and may therefore unmake the laws," McIntosh wrote, "but for women, whose benevolence and charity should be a law unto themselves, softening the pressure of the fetters which they cannot break and lightening the darkness which they may not wholly dispel." [46] Demanding no less than total com-

---

46. McIntosh, *Woman in America*, 117.

mitment from their audience, Gilman, Hentz, and McIntosh demanded the same from themselves. Their all-encompassing belief in what ought to be ultimately compromised their objectivity and transformed them from agents of conciliation to inadvertent southern sectionalists.

As early as 1836, Caroline Gilman, the most pragmatic of the southern domestic novelists, had a premonition of what was to come. On the same trip north that prompted her dualistic disquisition entitled *The Poetry of Travelling in the United States*, Gilman had the opportunity to attend a Senate session. As she watched from the gallery, enthralled by the drama unfolding on the floor, she experienced some puzzling feelings. "I see other great men beside C[alhoun] and P[reston] in the senate," she observed, "but how is it that when they rise I feel as if the reputation of a father or brother was at stake? . . . I am carried away by the stream, and a word against Carolina is a personal offence to me." At the end of the day she reflected: "If anything can remove prejudices, it is coming here and seeing this variety. But prejudice is a tough old knot, and will not be removed half the time without killing the root and branch too." As the Civil War grew closer, Gilman's words would come back to haunt her.[47]

47. Gilman, *The Poetry of Travelling*, 10–11, 5.

3

Two Sides to Every Picture

*I*n 1863, Maria McIntosh broke her silence of nearly a decade to castigate a prominent member of the northern literary community. For years, the southern domestic novelist had devoted her career to the eradication of sectionalism, muting her southern loyalties; for years, she had minimized her personal commitment to the plantation South in order to discuss objectively the issues dividing the nation. Dismissing northern charges of depravity as the product of a fundamental ignorance about the plantation regime, struggling through personal example to prove her region neither morally nor intellectually deficient, McIntosh had battled regional prejudice resolutely with her pen.

Two years into the Civil War, however, even the redoubtable Miss McIntosh had to concede defeat; clearly, no amount of travel above and below the Mason-Dixon Line or marriage between northerners and southerners—favorite literary remedies to soothe regional tensions— could ensure a happy ending for the real-life drama currently playing on the American stage.[1] Unable to offer a viable solution for the contemporary crisis, fighting the gnawing suspicion that she could have done more to avert national tragedy, McIntosh in desperation turned her attention to the past. Seeking to justify her literary efforts toward national harmony, as well as those of fellow writers Caroline Gilman, Caroline Hentz, Mary

---

1. Caroline Hentz's *Lovell's Folly* (1833) contains perhaps the earliest example in domestic fiction of the settlement of sectional grievances through the marriage of northerner to southerner. McIntosh herself regularly employed that formula. See, for example, McIntosh's *Two Lives; or, To Seem and To Be* (New York, 1846) and her *Charms and Counter Charms* (New York, 1848). And of course one of the most ambitious attempts to resolve sectional tensions in that manner occurs in McIntosh's epic *The Lofty and the Lowly* (1853), in which two pairs of northern and southern heroes and heroines wed and pledge their lives toward the eradication of sectionalism.

Virginia Terhune, and Augusta Evans, McIntosh searched her memory to determine what had gone wrong: what had thwarted antebellum southern domestic fiction's promotion of national harmony?

In the closing pages of her ninth and final novel, *Two Pictures; or, What We Think of Ourselves and What the World Thinks of Us* (1863), McIntosh offered a partial explanation for the failure of the self-defined mission of conciliation. The scene is one of domestic tranquillity. Georgia aristocrat Augusta Moray and her northern husband, Hugh, are seated in their spacious library, engrossed in their mail. All of a sudden Augusta flinches. Holding up a northern newspaper, she points to a review of *Uncle Tom's Cabin*. "Oh Hugh! how unjust," she cries in horror. "That they should think thus of you!" Harriet Beecher Stowe's "unflattering portraiture of southern planters" could not help but further turn northern readers against the South, Augusta worries. While southerners would dismiss the "picture of the vulgar and beastly tyrant" as the product of a morbid imagination, northerners would surely accept it as fact. And although Augusta tries to comfort herself with the thought that southerners were "not obliged to see [them]selves or each other as the false world" saw them, both she and Hugh realize that it is impossible to discount the impact of Stowe's work in galvanizing antislavery sentiment. There might well be, as Hugh argued, "two sides to every picture," yet propaganda along the lines of *Uncle Tom's Cabin* made it highly unlikely that the majority of Americans would seek out the truth.[2] Hugh and Augusta Moray realize what Maria McIntosh recognized only in retrospect: *Uncle Tom's Cabin; or, Life Among the Lowly*, published in 1852, must have hastened the coming of the Civil War.

While McIntosh's charge clearly reflected her professional biases—a didactic writer herself, McIntosh was inclined to exaggerate the role of fiction in shaping public opinion—her accusations were not wholly without merit. If Stowe's seminal work was neither necessary nor sufficient cause of the debacle that rocked mid-nineteenth-century America, certainly it contributed to the ideological polarization of the nation by providing northerners and southerners with a list of grievances around which to coalesce and, in so doing, eroded support for the Compromise of 1850.

2. See McIntosh, *Two Pictures; or, What We Think of Ourselves and What the World Thinks of Us* (New York, 1863), 474–75.

If it did not swell the ranks of organized abolitionism as McIntosh implied, it ensured a hearing for less strident activists and made the antislavery impulse more acceptable to the northern mainstream.[3]

More important for the purposes of McIntosh's argument, if *Uncle Tom's Cabin* was not solely responsible for the failure of the crusade against sectionalism conducted in southern domestic fiction throughout the 1830s and the 1840s, it undeniably made the literary peace initiative harder to sustain. By graphically illustrating the horrors of slavery, by posing the "Negro question" in absolute terms of good and evil and condemning the many who professed a desire to remain uncommitted, Stowe challenged the notion of peaceful coexistence and forced McIntosh and her colleagues to defend the peculiar institution in detail. After 1852, northern critics could no longer be placated by vague assurances of southern benevolence; with the publication of *Uncle Tom's Cabin*, Stowe placed the burden of proof upon the South and irrevocably altered the course of antebellum southern domestic fiction.[4]

The phenomenal success of *Uncle Tom's Cabin* stemmed primarily from Stowe's ability to tap into the persistent anxieties of a nation exhausted by years of sectional infighting. Appearing first as a serial in the anti-slavery organ the *National Era* over the months of 1851, *Uncle Tom's Cabin* roused America from the political torpor of the immediate aftermath of the Compromise of 1850 and reminded a generation anxious for peace on any terms that moral rectitude must take precedence over political expediency. Divine law interdicted slavery in any form, Stowe argued; therefore, the Compromise of 1850, which sanctioned slavery by promising legal assistance to masters eager to reclaim runaways under the terms of the Fugitive Slave Law, ran contrary to God's will. That Stowe managed to reopen political debate in an era of relative prosperity—cotton

3. Although historians now question the authenticity of Abraham Lincoln's supposed designation of Stowe as "the little lady who started the big war," they continue to emphasize the phenomenal impact of her book in shaping northern opinion. See, for example, Gossett, *"Uncle Tom's Cabin" and American Culture*, 164–84; Clement Eaton, *A History of the Old South* (New York, 1966), 197, 466–91; Holman Hamilton, *Prologue to Conflict: The Crisis and Compromise of 1850* (Louisville, 1964), 171; and David M. Potter, *The Impending Crisis, 1848–1861* (New York, 1976), 140.

4. See Ryan, *The Empire of the Mother*, 130; and Taylor, *Cavalier and Yankee*, 300–13.

sold for thirteen cents a pound and northern industry expanded steadily—
and that she convinced many Americans to reject compromise measures
and almost single-handedly made the Fugitive Slave Law unenforceable
testifies to the verisimilitude of Stowe's narrative.[5] *Uncle Tom's Cabin*
voiced the unspoken concerns of millions in a language all could understand, reminding northerners and southerners alike of their ultimate
accountability.

Ironically, the author of the volume that William R. Taylor observes
did more to alter America's perception of the South "than any book ever
published" failed to recognize the inflammatory content of her work: "I
have tried, during this whole investigation to balance my mind by keeping
before it the most agreeable patterns of Southern life and character,"
Stowe declared in 1852. "Many who have attacked the system [of slavery]
have not understood the Southern character, nor appreciated what is really good in it," she wrote. "I think *I* have."[6] In fact, there is some suggestion that when Stowe would concede the possibility that *Uncle Tom's
Cabin* might offend, she was concerned primarily with the North. Years
later, Stowe continued to protest her innocence. In the preface to the 1879
edition of her then long-established novel, Stowe stated that in spite of
arguments to the contrary, she had indeed "painted slave-holders as amiable, generous and just," showing examples of their "noblest and most
beautiful traits of character." A northern friend of hers who had "many
relatives in the South" had assured her that her book was going to be "the
great pacificator," Stowe wrote. It would "unite both north and south."
She recalled that she was astonished when "the entire South . . . rose up
against [*Uncle Tom's Cabin*]."[7]

Whether or not Harriet Beecher Stowe's astonishment was sincere or
merely an attempt to disassociate her novel from the chain of events that
propelled America toward civil war remains open to question; nevertheless, it is clear that Stowe was unprepared for the violent reaction her
novel provoked.[8] No less than fourteen formal "replies" to *Uncle Tom's
Cabin*, along with countless shorter rebuttals, appeared within three years

5. Eaton, *A History of the Old South*, 478–79.
6. Stowe quoted in Taylor, *Cavalier and Yankee*, 307–308.
7. Gossett, *"Uncle Tom's Cabin" and American Culture*, 164–84, 116.
8. *Ibid.*, 116.

after the novel's publication, and responses from indignant southerners continued to pour forth for the rest of the decade.[9] But while the South was championed in a variety of forums by a broad cross-section of its sons and daughters, the most consistent and convincing effort came from the handful of southern domestic novelists.[10] United by their commitment to the South and their conviction in the moral superiority of its people, Gilman, Hentz, McIntosh, Terhune, and Evans sprang to the defense of their native or adopted region, using their considerable skill with the written word to counter Stowe's accusations.

Given the nature of Stowe's assault on slavery, it is hardly surprising that she met her most formidable opposition in the field of southern domestic fiction. After all, *Uncle Tom's Cabin* borrowed heavily from the southern domestic novelists; its plantation setting and black and white characters were, at least superficially, standard fare for northern and southern readers.[11] Yet for all its similarity, *Uncle Tom's Cabin* differed strikingly in structure and substance from novels written by Gilman,

9. In "Pro-Slavery Propaganda," Jeanette Tandy identifies at least fourteen fictional "answers" to *Uncle Tom's Cabin* published over the three-year period after its 1851 serialization; Gossett finds no fewer than twenty-seven published responses between 1851 and 1861. Some of the more intriguing titles include Mary Eastman's *Aunt Phillis's Cabin; or, Southern Life as It Is* (1852) and John W. Page's *Uncle Robin in His Cabin in Virginia and Tom Without One in Boston* (1853).

10. Tandy, "Pro-Slavery Propaganda." See also Gossett, *"Uncle Tom's Cabin" and American Culture*, 212–38; and Brown, *The Sentimental Novel*, 241–80. Hilldrup surveys the response of southern women writers to *Uncle Tom's Cabin* but fails to place their efforts in the context of domestic fiction in "Cold War Against the Yankees," 370–84.

11. For all its similarity in theme and characterization to plantation fiction, the domestic tradition remained distinct. Written by and for women, domestic fiction told a specific story of female development and necessarily accorded women the larger role in the drama. In contrast, plantation fiction, which was, for the most part, written by and about men, typically assigned women to peripheral and traditional roles. For discussion of the origins of the plantation tradition see Taylor, *Cavalier and Yankee*, 178–92. Gaines's *The Southern Plantation* remains the definitive work on plantation fiction. More recently, Mary Ann Wimsatt has surveyed the leading practitioners of the genre in "Antebellum Fiction," 92–107. John C. Ruoff notes the marginal role of women in plantation fiction but fails to distinguish between novels written by men and women in "Frivolity to Consumption." For definition and discussion of the terms of domestic fiction in general, see Baym, *Woman's Fiction*, 11–50. Kathryn Lee Seidel discusses the relationship between the plantation and the domestic genres in *The Southern Belle in the American Novel*, 3–17, 171n.

Hentz, and McIntosh during the 1830s and 1840s. Unlike these southern writers, Stowe did not struggle to keep an open mind when it came to political controversy; neither did she attempt to moderate her partisanship.[12] Focusing specifically on the institution of slavery rather than the benign images of plantation life favored by the southern novelists, Stowe explored the marginal living conditions, unremitting toil, and brutal punishment that she held characterized the slave regime. Rejecting the conventional romance between chivalrous planter and beautiful belle, Stowe thrust the plight of the slave into the center of her narrative and permitted the black characters previously used by southern writers exclusively for comic relief to testify to their own humanity.[13] Repeatedly and relentlessly, Stowe challenged a set of images and assumptions designed by southern writers to assuage sectional anxieties. Bringing the "Negro question" to the fore, turning the southern domestic literary tradition upon itself, she forced its authors, however reluctantly, to confront the problems of slavery.

Caroline Hentz opened the dialogue with Harriet Beecher Stowe. The oldest writer of domestic fiction in the South to refute *Uncle Tom's Cabin* actively—Caroline Gilman contented herself with reissuing *Recollections of a New England Housekeeper* and *Recollections of a Southern Matron* and securing their stereotypes from her northern publisher—Hentz was also the best qualified to frame the southern response. As biographer Rhoda Ellison observes, Hentz and Stowe had much in common. Both came from distinguished Massachusetts families, married improvident intellectuals, moved repeatedly, and earned a substantial portion of the household income from the sale of their fiction. More significant, the two had known each other during the Hentzes' ill-fated residence in Cincinnati, Ohio, in the early 1830s, when both were members of the Semi-Colon Club, an exclusive local literary society. Although no record of

12. In fact, Stowe would have considered the self-consciously nonpartisan position adopted by the first generation of southern domestic novelists as nothing short of sinful. She viewed the struggle to eradicate slavery as a holy cause and pursued her crusade with messianic fervor. Gossett discusses the evolution of Stowe's attitude toward slavery in *"Uncle Tom's Cabin" and American Culture*, 64–86.

13. Mary Ann Wimsatt and Robert C. Phillips, "Antebellum Humor," in *The History of Southern Literature*, edited by Louis D. Rubin, Jr., et al. (Baton Rouge, 1985), 136–56.

more than a passing acquaintance exists, it is likely that the celebrated
Hentz, who by 1833 had published her first novel and seen two of her
plays produced in Philadelphia and Cincinnati, provided inspiration and
moral support to the aspiring author eleven years her junior whom she
knew as Hattie Beecher.[14]

Certainly Hentz's extreme and extended reaction to *Uncle Tom's
Cabin* suggests that to a certain extent she took Stowe's antislavery diatribe as a personal affront. Taking time out from her extensive nursing
duties—Nicholas, her husband, had become an invalid in the late 1840s
and required constant attention—Hentz assured her publisher, Abraham
Hart, that "slavery as [Stowe] describes it is an entirely new institution to
us." It was inconceivable that "a woman could write such a work," Hentz
told Hart, although she was forced to acknowledge the New Englander's
considerable skill. If there was "no danger of a surfeit" of responses
(Hentz made it clear that she thought that was not the case), she proposed
to write a comprehensive refutation. Which "particular phase of the subject" should she discuss? "There shall be no *Cabin* in it most assuredly,"
Hentz declared as her project unfolded. "The public have had enough for
one century."[15]

"Not for the sovereignty of worlds" would she "attempt to remove
[northern] prejudices by the sacrifice of *truth*," Hentz stated on another
occasion; calling Stowe's veracity into question, Hentz asserted that truth
"inspires and sustains me in all I utter."[16] But how, then, Hentz wondered,
could she explain the outright lies of another sentimental writer, one
whom McIntosh had called "a daughter of the skies"?[17] How could she
counteract the negative impression of the South set forth in *Uncle Tom's
Cabin*? "I could go on and speak volumes on the subject," Hentz pro-

14. See Hentz, *The Planter's Northern Bride*, vii–xxii. See also Papashvily, *All the Happy
Endings*, 63–94. Papashvily goes so far as to suggest that a villainous abolitionist couple,
Mr. and Mrs. Softly, who appear in *The Planter's Northern Bride*, were modeled after Calvin
and Harriet Beecher Stowe.

15. Caroline Hentz to Abraham Hart, December 14, 1852, in Caroline Hentz Papers,
Huntington Library, San Marino.

16. Caroline Hentz, *Marcus Warland; or, The Long Moss Spring* (Philadelphia, 1852),
149. Hentz's skepticism at the specifics of Stowe's indictment is understandable. Apparently
Stowe made her only visit to a slave state in 1834 when she visited a teaching colleague in
Washington, Kentucky.

17. McIntosh, *Letter in Relation to Slavery*, 13.

claimed through Marcus Warland, hero of a prosouthern novel she published the same year as Stowe's diatribe. But while Hentz could and did work prodigiously to reduce the impact of *Uncle Tom's Cabin*, she never could figure out what led Stowe to make such wild accusations in the first place.[18] Had Stowe succumbed to greed, Hentz puzzled, or could it be that Stowe, who had lived much of her life in the shadow of her celebrated brothers and sisters, hungered for fame?[19]

Perhaps Hentz's endless musings on the motivation behind *Uncle Tom's Cabin* prompted her concern that her own noble intentions might be mistaken; clearly, she was anxious to establish that her rebuttal of Stowe's novel was written to further "the interests of those whom a dispensation of Providence has made me the lonely guardian" rather than for financial gain. Negotiating the terms of her latest novel, Hentz defended her decision to seek remuneration. "I have written in sorrow and struggled with the darkest misgivings," Hentz wrote mournfully to Abraham Hart at the end of 1851. First, the Hentzes had been "defrauded" of their property by an unscrupulous creditor. Then Mr. Hentz had fallen victim to a nervous complaint, and as if that were not enough, Caroline's favorite brother, "to whom [she] might have looked for aid if absolutely required," had suddenly died. "The pillar of strength on which I felt I could lean for support has fallen as if struck by lightning from heaven & it seemed as if I were shivered by the stroke," Hentz confessed. "Till this era, I have written for self-gratification, animated by the hope of public favor."[20] Now, at the worst possible time, when she as a champion of the South was most vulnerable to charges of self-interest, Hentz was forced to "turn her brains to gold," to put a price on her literary defense of southern culture.[21] Only sheer desperation, Hentz stressed, could have moved her to such action.

But although Caroline Hentz pleaded with Hart to deal generously with her in view of her wretched existence—"You are a husband & a father

18. Hentz, *Marcus Warland*, 149. Southern writers and reviewers devoted countless pages to speculation on Stowe's motives. See, for example, George Frederick Holmes's review in the *Southern Literary Messenger*, XVIII (1852), 721–31. More recent criticism accepts Stowe's declarations of innocence at face value. See Taylor, *Cavalier and Yankee*, 307–308.

19. Caroline Hentz to Abraham Hart, November 18, 1852, in Overbury Collection, Special Collections Library, Barnard College.

20. Hentz to Hart, November 30, 1851, *ibid.*

21. Hentz to Hart, November 18, 1852, *ibid.*

[and] I have heard a kind & feeling one[.] Can you not feel for a woman in circumstances like mine?"—she steadfastly refused to permit personal crisis to overshadow her perceived responsibility to her adopted home.[22] Keeping a lonely vigil by her husband's bedside, Hentz hurried to the defense of the South, interrupting her labors only to implore her two grown sons to replenish their father's dwindling supply of tobacco and laudanum.[23] Rushing out her response to Stowe, Hentz fought with her publisher to release *The Planter's Northern Bride* earlier than Hart originally had planned, in order to stave off growing antisouthern sentiment.[24] When Hart resisted, Hentz persevered, arguing that her travels and her contacts in the North told her that, in view of the current political situation, there was no time to waste. "Everyone says that the excitement produced by the Nebraska bill will be favorable to [the novel's] reception," Hentz reported after a trip to Massachusetts in 1853. "There is a great deal of interest expressed here about it as well as in the South." Still, Hentz saw ominous signs that the public was becoming less willing to consider the possibility that *Uncle Tom's Cabin* was an inaccurate portrayal of slavery. "Antislavery lectures & meetings are the order of the day in Boston," Hentz noted glumly; the number "who have not defiled their garments" shrank daily.[25]

"Would that we had the power to encircle with flowery bonds the North and the South, and draw them together in sweeter, closer union," Hentz enthused in an uncharacteristic flight of fancy.[26] Lacking a wreath of suitable proportions, however, she was forced to content herself with more conventional tools of sectional conciliation: "an unprejudiced mind, a truthful spirit, and an earnest and honest purpose." With a nod in Stowe's direction, the novelist stated: "No one will accuse us of having set down *aught in malice*, so we can assert we have in *nothing extenuated*."[27]

22. Hentz to Hart, November 30, 1851, *ibid.*

23. In one of the last letters written before her death, Hentz continued to remind her two sons, both doctors, of their unusual filial obligations. See Caroline Hentz to Dr. Thaddeus Hentz, [no month or date given], 1855, in Hentz Family Papers.

24. Hentz to Hart, November 30, 1851, in Overbury Collection.

25. Hentz to Hart, February 13, 1854, *ibid.*

26. Hentz, Introduction to "Magnolia Leaves," in Hentz, *The Banished Son*. Hentz's opening remarks are dated May, 1853.

27. Hentz, *Marcus Warland*, 7.

By the fall of 1852, the writer who twenty years before had expressed unbounded optimism that "great national questions" could be resolved through education and understanding found herself embroiled in a war of words that severely tested her faith.[28] Bewildered by the success of *Uncle Tom's Cabin* and puzzled by the circumstances that prompted a fellow novelist and former associate to launch a campaign against her beloved South, Caroline Hentz struggled to reassert the moral superiority of her region while refraining from passing judgment.

In *The Planter's Northern Bride* (1854), Hentz couched her unmistakably proslavery argument in numerous protestations of her sincere disinterest, criticizing other writers, unnamed, who ventured into the literary forum with less exalted motives. Yet while Hentz proclaimed her "sacred regard" and "undying attachment" to the scenes of her youth, the substance of her "answer" to *Uncle Tom's Cabin* left no doubt of her loyalty to the South.[29] Clinging to her stated principles of noninterference while at the same time acknowledging the necessity of a more aggressive response to Harriet Beecher Stowe, Hentz attempted the impossible: to discredit her nemesis while remaining above the political fray.

The preface to *The Planter's Northern Bride* reflected Hentz's dilemma. Simultaneously revealing her inability to dismiss the slurs spewed southward and her unwillingness to sever her ties to New England, Hentz's address to her readers alternated between paeans to the "noble, liberal minds" and "warm, generous, candid hearts" of the majority of northerners and warnings against "the unhappy consequences of that intolerant and fanatical spirit, whose fatal influence we so deeply deplore." Tracing the spread of sectionalist sentiment to the efforts of a misguided few, in her prefatory remarks Hentz stressed the potential of enlightened discourse to alleviate regional tensions. Yet the novel itself ran contrary to its opening statement. Whereas in previous novels Hentz had portrayed northerners with some degree of consistency, emphasizing the common humanity of residents above and below the Mason-Dixon Line, in *The Planter's Northern Bride* she depicted Yankees as largely reprehensible. Whereas earlier Hentz had depicted even the most depraved

28. Hentz, *Lovell's Folly*, 256.
29. Hentz, *The Planter's Northern Bride*. Hereinafter cited parenthetically by page number in the text.

northerner as holding the possibility of redemption, *The Planter's Northern Bride* painted northerners and northern society as inherently flawed,
blighted by an overweening love of money, an exaggerated sense of self-
importance, and an overwhelming desire to impose their false values upon
the South.[30]

The novel's disjointed quality reflects Caroline Hentz's struggle to
contain her rising partisanship. Although at one time Hentz was able to
set aside her preference for the South in the interest of national harmony
with relative ease, by 1854 her ability to deny her prosouthern leanings
had considerably declined. In 1853, for example, Hentz extolled the singular spirit of New Englanders in a poem written to commemorate the
centennial of Lancaster, Massachusetts. "I consider it an exalted privilege"
to participate in "so interesting an occasion," Hentz wrote. "I earnestly
hope, that what I have written may prove an acceptable offering."[31] Less
than a year after praising the "high and glowing" spirits, "eagle hearts,"
and "home-born virtues" of her native New England, however, she wrote
Abraham Hart denouncing the prevailing aura of self-righteousness that
prompted northerners to flock to abolitionist meetings.[32] That Hentz was
to some degree aware of her fluctuating opinions is suggested by her pro-
fuse apologies to the centennial committee for what she sensed might be
viewed as an inappropriate display of emotion. "Perhaps I have allowed
private feeling to have too great a way in the tribute I send," she admitted.
"If so I pray to be forgiven."[33] Still, in spite of her fears that the exaggerated tone of her ode to the North might ring false, Hentz remained characteristically indifferent as to the origin of her excessive sentiment. That
her rhetorical flourishes might be read by some as an index to her growing
alienation from the North never crossed her mind.

In *The Planter's Northern Bride*, Hentz combined romance and prop-

---

30. Rhoda Ellison observes that before *The Planter's Northern Bride*, Hentz's "New
England characters are usually deluded but amiable creatures who, faced with the reality of
southern plantation life, are quickly converted to a more enlightened attitude." See Ellison,
Early Alabama Publications: A Study in Literary Interests (Tuscaloosa, 1947), 175–76.

31. Caroline Hentz to J. M. Washburn, May 27, 1853, in Evelyn Hardy, "Mrs. Caroline Lee Hentz, A Woman of Her Times" (M.A. thesis, Auburn University, 1935),
Appendix 12.

32. Hentz to Hart, February 13, 1854, in Overbury Collection.

33. Hentz to Washburn, May 27, 1853, in Hardy, "Mrs. Caroline Lee Hentz."

aganda to refute Stowe's negative depiction of the South once and for all. Liberally borrowing plot twists and characters from *Uncle Tom's Cabin*, Hentz essentially rewrote the tale of life among the lowly from the opposite perspective. In Hentz's version of the story, a plantation owner articulates the true principles of the early Republic, an abolitionist's daughter champions slavery, northern laborers envy southern slaves, and, in perhaps the most obvious inversion of Stowe's plot, a mulatto slave crosses the Ohio in desperate flight from freedom. Although Hentz's narrative lacked fluidity—like *Uncle Tom's Cabin*, *The Planter's Northern Bride* is rife with editorial intrusions—her excellent mimicry of Stowe's style and skillful manipulation of the northern novelist's message lent Hentz's interpretation a freshness and vigor that distinguished it from the spate of replies issued by less talented southern writers.[34]

From the moment he crosses the Mason-Dixon Line accompanied by his devoted servant Albert, Russell Moreland meets with hostility. Residents alternately ignore and insult him, encourage his slave to rebel, and in more extreme cases try to convert him to abolitionism. Moreland's polite responses fail to rebuff the meddlesome northerners; they simply cannot resist an opportunity to interfere. For example, when Moreland declines an innkeeper's offer to serve Albert at the same table as the other guests, the innkeeper will have none of it. "When folks come among us we don't see why they can't conform to our ways of thinking," the innkeeper asserts. "I'm an enemy to all distinctions myself, and I'd like to bring everybody round to my opinion" (24). Moreland's calm in the face of disaster does credit to his region and his class. While he cannot dismiss the innkeeper's invitation as the product of ignorance—"He knows our customs at home, and that nothing could be done in more positive violation of them than his unwarrantable proposition," Moreland reflects—the southerner refuses to spar "with a man so infinitely my inferior" (22).

Moreland meets a more formidable opponent in his future father-in-law, Mr. Hastings. A rabid abolitionist, Hastings epitomizes the intoler-

---

34. In her introduction to *The Planter's Northern Bride*, vii–xxii, Ellison speculates that part of the novel's strength comes from Hentz's perception of herself as a peacemaker. *The Planter's Northern Bride*, while clearly more defensive than Hentz's previous works, lacks the "narrow focus and fanatical tone" of contemporary plantation fiction.

ance and hypocrisy Hentz held out as quintessentially northern. Having squandered his own inheritance on a variety of "fruitless speculations and visionary schemes," Hastings is in a poor position to judge the moral and financial failings of others; nevertheless, the self-described "sturdy, independent Yankee" has no inhibitions whatsoever in denouncing southerners as a "selfish, aristocratic, lazy, self-indulging, cruel set of people" (40, 103, 107). Drawing Moreland into his home under false pretenses, Hastings defies the southerner to defend his region and his class. "I should like to have you explain the tales of cruelty and suffering, the cries of anguish that have rent the very heavens," Hastings demands, while at the same time openly acknowledging his determination not to give Moreland a hearing. "We might talk in this way for six thousand years, without changing my immutable conviction," the abolitionist emphasizes, "that, as long as you allow the existence of slavery, you are living in sin and iniquity . . . you are violating the laws of God and man, incurring the vengeance of heaven, and the retributions of eternity" (85). Moreland can only shake his head in dismay.

Mr. Hastings intensifies his interference upon Moreland's engagement to his daughter. Although Eulalia Hastings for some inexplicable reason is not prejudiced against the South, sincerely loves the planter, and would like nothing better than to accept his suit, her father categorically refuses. "Were I to consent to this union, I should destroy by a single act, the labor and devotion of years," Hastings says (104). "You have read from my own pen a sentence I know you must have remembered," Hastings rages to Moreland, "'that I would rather see a daughter of mine laid in the deepest grave of New England than wedded to a Southern planter'" (104).[35] When Moreland quite naturally protests, Mr. Hastings agrees to the union on one condition: "Liberate your slaves; remove the curse from your household and your land; come to me with a pure, unburdened conscience, and I will oppose no barrier to your love" (109). And although Moreland tries to explain the impossibility of meeting with Hastings' request—"I cannot, even to secure Paradise itself, cast upon the Northern

---

35. In heralding the restorative properties of the southern climate, Ellison notes, Hentz cleverly challenged the conventional portrayal of the region as one conducive to illness, particularly the dreaded consumption. *Ibid.*, note to p. xv.

world the large family dependent upon me for comfort and support," he tells his accuser—Hastings remains unyielding (104).[36] Only when Eulalia falls desperately ill does her father stop his manipulations and then only after great deliberation.

Ultimately, Moreland's good humor and liberality are pushed to the limit; he steps in to shield himself, his servant, and, more significantly, his region from the endless stream of northern criticism. Confessing his fury that a handful of northern incendiaries would deliberately misrepresent the circumstances of slavery and use their written and oratorical talents to sway opinion against the South, Moreland admits that he, a Christian and a gentleman, nevertheless cannot hold the whole of the North responsible for the evil deeds of a few. "If I believed one-fourth part of what I see stated here," Moreland comments after reading one of Mr. Hastings' abolitionist tracts, "I would forsake my native region . . . [and make] my whole life an expiatory sacrifice for the involuntary sins of my bygone years" (78).

Part of the misunderstanding, Moreland acknowledges, arose from northerners' fundamental ignorance of the character of the Negro. "God never intended that you and I should live on *equal* terms with the African," Moreland tells Eulalia; for that reason, "He created a barrier between his race and ours." To deny that boundary, the planter continued, was to contradict divine law and, more important, to deny the responsibility to minister to "this subservient and benighted race" with which God had charged men and women of a lighter hue. "I look upon every master and mistress in our Southern land, as missionaries appointed to civilize and christianize the sons and daughters of Africa with a kindling countenance," Moreland announces. "To them Ethiopia is stretching out its sable hands, and through them they are lifted to God" (108–109).

Russell Moreland enunciated Caroline Hentz's views on Stowe and her adherents with clarity and passion. "At a distance [northerners] stretch out their arms, and call [the slave] brother and exclaim, 'Are we not children of the same Father?'" Moreland notes bitterly, but the "ties of consanguinity" were quickly forgotten once the slave drew near (202). Those same "philanthropists" who with honeyed words urged the slave to flee

36. Hastings tells Moreland that if he were a poor farmer from New England, he would pose no objection to the union.

the South themselves disdained "social communion with [those] on whom God has affixed the seal of a darker dispensation," the planter fumes. Once they had accomplished their "noble purpose" of bringing the slave north, they cast him aside, "an isolated, degraded being, without caste or respectability,—a single black line running through a web of whiteness" (204). Condemning those who "rave" of the slave's injuries, yet "hold out no hand to redress them," Moreland stands firm against his northern critics. "We [planters] have the *power* to do many things which reason and right forbid," he tells the antislavery advocates who question the motivation of southern slaveholders. "We have the power to cast thousands of helpless, ignorant, reckless beings on their own resources . . . but we believe it our duty to take care of them" (82–83). While it was indeed true that planters reaped the benefit of the slave's labor and the fruit of his toil in his day of vigor, those years of service were richly rewarded. Nursed in sickness, provided for in old age, and protected "from the horrors and miseries of want," the slave was given ample opportunity to realize his highest potential (83).

If Russell Moreland's declamation at first glance seemed to reassert Caroline Hentz's frequently articulated idea that the preponderance of northerners took issue with the South only because they were ignorant of southern ways—"There are a host of [northerners] that will bear us out in our views of Southern character, and feel with us that our national honour is tarnished, when a portion of our country is held up to public disgrace," Hentz wrote in the preface to *The Planter's Northern Bride*— his critical attitude toward much of northern society betrays the novelist's growing determination to take a more aggressive stance against the North (4). Although Moreland generously acknowledges the difficulties novice readers of abolitionist propaganda might have in sorting fact from fiction, he has little patience for those who accept the rhetoric without question. It was ridiculous to believe "that the North was one wide garden of the Lord where nothing but the peaceable fruits of righteousness grow—and the South a howling wilderness of sin and crime and pollution," Moreland rails. What about the large number of criminals in the North? What about mob rule? He himself has witnessed a lynching in Boston and has heard of even worse things. What is he to make of this? Should he follow northern example and blame these atrocities on the institutions of the region in which they occurred (196–97)?

And, Moreland reflects, what should he make of the stories of "the thousand toiling operatives of the Northern manufactories . . . the poor, starving seamstresses" (28)? How should he view the desperate circumstances of the domestics he had observed at work in the very same home his detractors portrayed as the bastion of American freedom? In the Hastings household, for example, one Betsy Jones labors harder than "three of Moreland's stoutest slaves" (65). Working dawn until dusk for a tiny stipend, Betsy spends her free time caring for her invalid brother. Nancy Brown's situation is even more depressing. Employed by the innkeeper who was first to impute Moreland's morality, Nancy has ruined her health working to support herself and her elderly mother. Succumbing to tuberculosis, Nancy loses her job and her income. With no savings and no hope of assistance from her community, Nancy's future is bleak. No wonder that Betsy and Nancy envy Moreland's slave Albert (65). No wonder that Russell Moreland, a representative of the much-maligned planter class, bitterly resents northern accusations that the South is its moral inferior.

Caroline Hentz's wide-ranging discussion of slavery exhibits the strengths and weaknesses typical of the proslavery ideology advanced through southern domestic fiction. Less consistent than the doctrinaire defenses of the peculiar institution offered by contemporary male propagandists—Hentz alternately portrayed slavery as a positive institution that uplifted both master and slave and an onerous burden entailed upon the white man by God above—Hentz's vision of the plantation regime made up in feeling what it lacked in theory.[37] Speaking directly to the concerns of her female audience, Hentz drew heavily upon slave testimony, biblical

37. According to Drew Gilpin Faust and others, as early as 1832 male propagandists rejected the idea that slavery was a necessary evil; by the middle 1840s, leading polemicists had come to believe that the peculiar institution served a positive good. While male propagandists argued that point from a variety of positions—some found scientific justification for race slavery, and others focused on biblical injunction—their formal declarations evidenced a high degree of uniformity. Hentz's willingness to consider both the older argument—that slavery was but a temporary state that would, over time, wither away as more and more slaves became suited to assume the responsibilities of Christian citizens—and its newer version—that slavery played a pivotal role in maintaining southern civilization—distinguishes her propaganda from the mainstream and suggests that perhaps male and female proponents of slavery viewed the so-called Negro question quite differently. That Hentz's ideological flexibility was echoed by her fellow southern domestic novelists would further support this speculation.

injunction, and personal observation of life in the North and in the South to offer a compelling defense of the plantation regime that asserted the primacy of the southern community.[38] Rejecting the scientific and sociological arguments favored by men as too restrictive, Hentz used the language and symbols of domesticity to counter northern arguments, particularly those advanced in *Uncle Tom's Cabin*, that slavery threatened the fabric of America by undermining the home and the family. Slavery stabilized and harmonized the South, Hentz asserted; it called upon the higher nature of whites and facilitated the optimum development of the Negro's spiritual and intellectual character. Providing an organizing principle for society, slavery cemented the South into a single whole and prevented the dread disease of individualism from infecting those who lived below the Mason-Dixon Line. Addressing not so much the mind but the heart, playing upon the fears of social and economic dislocation that pervaded antebellum America, Caroline Hentz offered *The Planter's Northern Bride* as both a vindication of southern morality and a convincing rebuttal of the arguments circulated by the nefarious Mrs. Stowe.[39]

But while Caroline Hentz conscientiously sketched what she believed to be an accurate portrait of the plantation South and its inhabitants, she doubted that her endeavor could sway public opinion in favor of her adopted home and its institutions. Cognizant of the growing power and superior organization of her northern adversaries—for all their bombastic declarations, southern propagandists could hardly be described as presenting a united front—Hentz recognized that the task facing the southern domestic novelists was becoming more difficult with each passing day.[40] And although the sales of *The Planter's Northern Bride* reconfirmed her standing as one of America's most popular writers, Hentz could

38. After 1832, "scientific" evidence increasingly came to replace the more subjective arguments favored by earlier propagandists. See Faust, *The Ideology of Slavery*, 10–12.

39. Rhoda Ellison notes that the novel contains six different arguments supporting slavery that together form a "strange mixture of the fatalistic, the pragmatic and the humanitarian." See Ellison, *Early Alabama Publications*, 174–75.

40. At least one historian has argued that there was far from universal support of slavery within the immediate environs of the South; propagandists worked to convince their fellow southerners of the rightness of slavery as much as they labored to convert northern readers. Perhaps Hentz's calculated appeal to the South reflected her awareness of a certain indecision below the Mason-Dixon Line.

not shake her fear that her efforts to establish the moral superiority of the South through the medium of fiction were all for naught and that regional conflict was the inevitable result of northern agitation.[41]

The conclusion of *The Planter's Northern Bride* reflected the novelist's concerns about the continued viability of the Union and illuminated her growing willingness to indict the North for the perpetuation of sectional tensions. An abolitionist disguised as a minister travels south, where he places himself under the protection of Russell Moreland (495). Once established within the community, the abolitionist, Brainard, uses his oratorical skill to foment rebellion amongst Moreland's slaves (450–53, 500–503). Although Moreland manages to squelch the incipient insurrection by appealing to the loyalties of his people, he is unable to prevent Brainard from escaping to the North. "I have a glorious career before me," the abolitionist exults as he gallops to safety across the Mason-Dixon Line. "I will go back to the North, deliver such lectures on the South as will curdle the blood with horror. No matter what I say—I'll find fools to believe it all." He vows: "I'll rave of blood-marked chains, of flesh torn from the body with red-hot pincers, of children roasted alive, of women burned at the stake. The more horrors I manufacture, the more ecstasy they will feel!" In an obvious reference to Harriet Beecher Stowe and her extraordinary ability to mobilize antislavery sentiment through the power of her prose, the dastardly Brainard declares, "Thank Heaven for the gift of eloquence!" (526).

Why did abolitionists "light the brand of discord, and throw it blazing into the already burning heart of a community"? Hentz wondered. Why, "with frantic zeal," did they pursue their diabolical plans "when the stars of the Union may be quenched in the smoking, and the American eagle flaps its wings in blood?" (237–38). But while Hentz persisted in her efforts to understand her northern persecutors—she enjoined readers who felt even the slightest twinge of sympathy for Stowe's position "to pause and think of the consequences of all this"—she could not ignore indications that the South was losing ground rapidly (237). She had seen the

---

41. George Frederick Holmes anticipated Hentz's concerns that fiction, at least the fiction that had appeared in the immediate wake of Stowe's indictment, was not an adequate deterrent to northern aggression. See Holmes, "Review of *Uncle Tom's Cabin*."

turnout for abolitionist lectures during her 1853 trip to New England; with the enormous popularity of *Uncle Tom's Cabin*, she had no reason to believe that attendance at similar gatherings would not continue to rise.[42] Hentz's parting words pointed up her fear that her best efforts were not enough to avert national tragedy: "Should the burning lava of anarchy and servile war roll over the plains of the South, and bury, under its fiery waves, its social and domestic institutions, it will not suffer alone," the southern novelist wrote somberly. "The North and the South are branches of the same parent tree and the lightning bolt that shivers the one, must scorch and wither the other" (579). While her ailing husband slept in the cool that came after nightfall, Caroline Hentz sat alone in the darkness and shivered at her apocalyptic vision of America.

Antebellum popular culture seemed to confirm Hentz's apprehensions that the rising tide of sectionalism threatened to engulf the nation. When *Uncle Tom's Cabin* was initially issued in book form in the spring of 1852, it sold over 10,000 copies within the first week. By the end of that year, the novel had broken all existing sales records: 300,000 copies were purchased in the United States alone. Cheaper editions brought the novel within reach of many households. Lending libraries, which were obliged by overwhelming demand to keep as many as six copies in circulation at any given time, gave Harriet Beecher Stowe an even larger audience. And the novel's influence extended well beyond the literary marketplace. Candles, toys, and figurines modeled after the protagonists of *Uncle Tom's Cabin* bedecked northern parlors; games in which players competed to reunite slave families occupied leisure hours. In a single year, three hundred infant girls in Boston alone were christened "Eva" after the pious heroine, and some enterprising northern churchgoers went so far as to introduce a movement to adopt the novel as part of the Sunday school curriculum.[43] Finally, after 1852, any number of independent theatrical troupes adapted the novel for stage and brought Stowe's story to auditoriums across America.[44] In one form or another, the antislavery appeal

42. Hentz to Hart, February 13, 1854, in Whichard, "Caroline Lee Hentz," 28–29.

43. Gossett, *"Uncle Tom's Cabin" and American Culture*, 164–84.

44. *Uncle Tom's Cabin* ranks among the most successful theater productions of all time. See *ibid.*, 260.

articulated in *Uncle Tom's Cabin* touched the lives of most northerners and, directly or indirectly, exerted a tremendous impact on the minds of the South.

None of the southern domestic novelists was more attuned to the disruptive potential of *Uncle Tom's Cabin* than Maria McIntosh. Whereas Caroline Gilman and Caroline Hentz and, for that matter, their successors, Mary Virginia Terhune and Augusta Evans, typically relied on second- or even thirdhand information to apprise them of the North's growing antipathy toward the South, McIntosh had but to step outside her New York City residence to test the waters of public opinion.[45] A transplanted Georgian, McIntosh had weathered numerous sectional crises since her move north in 1835; her first inclination was to ignore the latest disturbance. Yet as time passed and popular enthusiasm for Stowe's diatribe against the South continued to escalate, McIntosh began to panic. Infuriated by Stowe's narrow-minded portrayal of the peculiar institution, appalled at the intensity of the antisouthern rhetoric that Stowe's novel engendered, McIntosh, the daughter of one of the South's founding families and a former slave owner, temporarily set aside her professional scruples to cast her fortune with her native home formally.

McIntosh took up the southern banner at great personal risk. Having experienced both wealth and poverty, the popular novelist was reluctant to alienate the national following that, after years of effort, had restored her to relative affluence.[46] Neither was McIntosh eager to risk her near-celebrity status in northern literary circles by espousing ideas at odds with those of her colleagues. Shunned by fashionable society upon the loss of her fortune in 1837, McIntosh had not forgotten how quickly northerners could withdraw their friendship when it was no longer socially advantageous. But while McIntosh's public professions of neutrality on sectional

45. The difficulties in obtaining accurate information about the North were complicated by overt and, frequently, covert censorship of northern literary materials below the Mason-Dixon Line. For example, it was almost impossible for some southerners to obtain even a used copy of *Uncle Tom's Cabin*. See *ibid.*, 185–211.

46. For biographical information on McIntosh see Kelley, *Private Woman*, 33–35, 145–48, 257–58; and Baym, *Woman's Fiction*, 86–109. Contemporary accounts portray McIntosh as a romantic heroine. See, for example, Hart, *The Female Prose Writers*, 63–69.

issues initially made it possible for her to enjoy a sort of dual citizen-
ship—"Gladly would we claim [Miss McIntosh] by birth as well as adoption," a northern biographer enthused, "but 'honor to whom honor is
due' "—after 1852 she found it increasingly difficult to ignore the claims
of her southern heritage.[47] Unwilling to relinquish the rarefied existence
she enjoyed as one of America's leading writers, McIntosh nevertheless
knowingly jeopardized her personal happiness and professional standing
to formulate a coherent response to Stowe.

Yet McIntosh did not enter into dialogue with the author of *Uncle
Tom's Cabin* precipitously. Just as she decided to champion her homeland
explicitly only after considering the public and private implications of that
activity, she waited to open her one-sided conversation with Stowe until
the ideal occasion. When word arrived that the enormous popularity of
Uncle Tom's Cabin in Great Britain had prompted some 500,000 women
under the auspices of the Duchess of Sutherland to deliver to Stowe a
massive petition to abolish slavery, McIntosh could no longer contain her
indignation.[48] Gaining access to the editorial page of the New York *Ob-
server*, she unleashed her fury at the northern woman whom the British
had recognized as the symbolic head of antislavery activity in America,
portraying Harriet Beecher Stowe as a traitor to both her country and her
gender.

What later was published (with the addition of a biographical sketch
of the author) as *A Letter on the Address of the Women of England to
Their Sisters of America in Relation to Slavery* depicted the peculiar institution and its supporters as gravely misunderstood victims of a northern
campaign to ruin the South. Adopting the injured tone of the unfairly accused, Maria McIntosh pardoned the "injudicious" action of "the women
of England" from the outset. "It was a mistake which we can readily forgive," McIntosh conceded, "when we recollect the influence under which
it was made." Nevertheless, she expressed her incredulity that Christian

47. Freeman, *Women of the South*, 163.
48. While Stowe's *Uncle Tom's Cabin* sold approximately 350,000 copies in the United
States during its first year after publication, about one million copies were purchased in
Great Britain during that same period (Gossett, *"Uncle Tom's Cabin" and American Culture*,
239–40). William Gladstone, for instance, used the volume in his drive to eradicate
prostitution.

women could believe the grossly exaggerated account of life on the southern plantation that had precipitated the missive.[49] Slavery bore little or no resemblance to the exploitative economic relationship detailed in *Uncle Tom's Cabin*, McIntosh asserted. "Slaves are not regarded as mere articles of merchandise, valued only at the number of dollars and cents they may bring," the southern novelist explained. On the contrary, they commanded the unlimited "kindness" and "sympathy" of their masters to the extent that slaveholders would typically "resist any temptation and submit to much privation" before permitting their chattel to pass into other hands (27).

Harriet Beecher Stowe's wild allegations obscured the efforts of enlightened southerners to improve the condition of the slave, McIntosh contended; furthermore, they distorted the real gains the Negro had made under slavery. "Brought hither not, as romance would teach, from the enjoyment of the dear ties of home, from a life of freedom and of simple pleasures," McIntosh wrote, "but from a condition the lowest to which humanity could sink," the slave population had been systematically civilized through the unremitting efforts of the southern aristocracy. "Now wearing in their features more of the aspect of humanity, exhibiting in their habits more of the decencies of life," "this people," as McIntosh called the African race, provided living testimony of the kindness and compassion of the South's ruling order (15–16). "We claim not that we or our fathers have done for them all that we ought," the southerner admitted. "We acknowledge that more, far more might and should have been done" (16). Nevertheless, she wrote with a nod toward her northern nemesis: "Against the examples of . . . debasement and cruelty, so industriously sought out by our enemies I might set examples of such self-devotion as would compel the admiration of the world" (22–23).

If Maria McIntosh was taken aback by the petitioners' implications

---

49. Maria McIntosh, *Letter in Relation to Slavery*, 13. Hereinafter cited parenthetically by page number in the text. McIntosh's ready forgiveness may have been more strategic than genuine. Many southerners and some sympathetic northerners were convinced that Great Britain's support of Stowe's antislavery crusade was merely a means through which the British could publicly claim moral superiority over the United States. Great Britain abolished slavery in 1834. See Gossett, *"Uncle Tom's Cabin" and American Culture*, 257–59; and Edmund Wilson, *Patriotic Gore: Studies in the Literature of the American Civil War* (1962; rpr. Boston, 1984), 62.

that masters regularly sacrificed the physical and spiritual well-being of their slaves for personal gain, she was horrified by their assertions that slaveholders as a group failed to respect the integrity of the slave family. However, in keeping with the "spirit of . . . charity" in which she commenced her reply, the southern novelist directed her hostility at the one she held ultimately responsible for the missive from abroad: the dastardly Mrs. Stowe (12). Citing the paragraph of the British petition that described slavery as an "awful system" that separated, "at the will of the master, the wife from the husband, and the children from the parents" as a prime example of Stowe's use of sensationalism to discredit the South, McIntosh confessed her surprise that, in light of such prejudicial information, her British sisters "could still believe us not wholly dead to human sympathies" (14). "Represented to the world as tearing without remorse the wife from the husband, the mother from the child . . . by names so fair and generally reliable," she wrote angrily, "we can scarcely hope to be believed when we affirm such cruelty would be met with as fierce an indignation" in the South as anywhere else in the world. "You accuse us—woe to us if you accuse us justly" (25). Ironically, McIntosh avoided criticizing the notorious duchess whose alleged displacement of her Scottish tenants had made her a favorite target of southern derision. Although the current duchess was not guilty—the crime in question had been perpetrated by a predecessor—many outraged southerners, among them former First Lady Julia Gardiner Tyler, failed to make that distinction and branded the well-meaning duchess a hypocrite.

Midway through her ringing denouncement of Stowe, however, McIntosh recalled herself. Perhaps, she considered, her efforts were all for naught; perhaps the damage occasioned by *Uncle Tom's Cabin* was, in the final analysis, irreparable. "I am opposed, in the statements I have here made . . . by the power of genius and the sensibilities it has aroused," McIntosh wrote, acknowledging the superior literary talents of the unnamed northern authoress. "A volume" that had made "its way across the Atlantic" offered "confirmation strong as proof of Holy Writ" of the depravity of the central institution of the South; conceived and executed by "a daughter of the skies," the sheer force of its argument put McIntosh, a mere mortal, at a hopeless disadvantage (28).[50] While "the impressions

50. Not only *Uncle Tom's Cabin* was crossing the Atlantic. In March, 1853, Harriet and

thus created" were clearly injurious to the South, McIntosh could do little to combat the damaging message other than to assert that she had "spoken truth, and that truth will abide, let falsehood oppose it as she may" (28–29). "As I think of the unheeding ears and the unbelieving hearts I am addressing, I am ready to throw aside my pen," McIntosh wrote wearily. "But . . . difficult as it is, I will with God's help speak the truth, and speak it in love, even though conscious that I speak it to those who are not likely to credit my assertions" (26).

"Every unjust accusation, every bitter and insulting word uttered against the South, in England, or in the Northern United States," McIntosh warned, hardened hearts and added to prejudices, ultimately erecting an "insuperable barrier" to the attainment of more favorable conditions for the slave (22). More important, the novelist contended, allegations of southern inhumanity along the lines of those made in *Uncle Tom's Cabin* thrust southerners on the defensive and in so doing endangered an already fragile Union. McIntosh argued that by accepting the message of antislavery propagandists without question and refusing to consider an alternative view of the slave regime, men and, more particularly, women tacitly endorsed the sectional division such rhetoric engendered; conversely, by insisting that the portrait of slavery submitted by Stowe and others like her be judged against those submitted by expert witnesses like McIntosh herself, readers could take steps to halt the momentum of the antislavery movement and help pave the way for sectional rapprochement.[51]

McIntosh's message to the women of England featured many of the

---

Calvin Stowe took their message directly to the people of Great Britain. Undoubtedly, McIntosh read about the trip in the New York papers. See Gossett, *"Uncle Tom's Cabin" and American Culture*, 255–56; and Wilson, *Patriotic Gore*, 61–62. On the Duchess of Sutherland and Harriet Beecher Stowe see Ian Grimble, *The Trial of Peter Sellar: The Tragedy of Highland Evictions* (London, 1962), 98–108, 149; and Evelyn L. Pugh, "Women and Slavery: Julia Gardiner Tyler and the Duchess of Sutherland," *Virginia Magazine of History and Biography*, LXXXVIII (1980), 186–202.

51. At least one reader was thoroughly convinced by McIntosh's credentials. The editor of the New York paper that originally published her reply to the women of England endorsed her enthusiastically: "Miss M'Intosh is the fit representative of that numerous band of self-appointed missionaries under whose labors so many of their poor negroes have become joyful disciples of Jesus Christ." See introduction to McIntosh, *Letter in Relation to Slavery*, 9.

distinctive properties of the uniquely feminine proslavery ideology articulated in antebellum southern domestic fiction. Although she rehearsed the basic tenets of mainstream propaganda—that slavery was economically beneficial to North and South, that it stabilized society and provided a congenial environment for the potentially dangerous African population—unlike the majority of male writers, McIntosh considered the slave system in the context of domesticity.[52] Devoting the balance of her attention to the emotional component of slavery, McIntosh justified the peculiar institution in terms of the intense relationships and the sense of community it fostered. Slavery was much more than a sort of legalized exploitation, the southerner asserted; in its purest form, it was an ideal system of social organization. Predicated on mutual need, sustained by a keen awareness of moral obligation, slavery enriched the national store of virtue by demanding that men and women, regardless of color, respect their responsibilities to their fellows. In reducing a complex system of relations to a simple economic equation, McIntosh contended that Stowe and her supporters robbed slavery of its most outstanding characteristic: its fundamental humanity.[53]

But if McIntosh's initial foray into explicitly political commentary afforded her the opportunity to answer Stowe and other agitators, it brought her perilously close to violating her belief that women had no place in the political arena.[54] Man, not woman, was in charge of making and therefore unmaking the laws, McIntosh had argued in 1850; though her concern for the safety of her native home had prompted her to speak out against opponents of the South in 1853, she had not changed her opinion about women's proper role in legislating political change. "Proclaimed at the first . . . lord of this lower world," McIntosh told her female audience, man was entrusted "by Heaven" with "the fashioning of the external forms of

---

52. It was, of course, Stowe's use of the domestic genre to articulate clearly the case against slavery that galvanized the antislavery movement of the 1850s. See Ryan, *The Empire of the Mother*, 130–40.

53. Stowe, on the other hand, argued that she was well aware of that aspect of slavery. She admitted, in fact, that visitors to Kentucky might be convinced that slavery exerted a positive good. See Harriet Beecher Stowe, *Uncle Tom's Cabin; or, Life Among the Lowly* (1852; rpr. New York, 1981), 51. George Frederick Holmes, for one, believed that Stowe's admission made her novel all the more nefarious. See Holmes, "Review of *Uncle Tom's Cabin*."

54. Cf. McIntosh, *Woman in America*, 22–27.

social and political life." Woman, on the other hand, who was gifted by God "with capacities of sympathy," was to assume the "unobtrusive but not less important task [of] imbu[ing] those forms with the Spirit of peace and love" (31). By using her "gracious influence," McIntosh postulated, woman "may inspire the colder reason and move the stronger arm of man" (30). In urging her "sisters of England" to respect this division of responsibility between the sexes, McIntosh revealed herself as a woman of convention; however, by pushing this distinction to the edge, as she did in her *Letter in Relation to Slavery*, she indicated that her overwhelming commitment to the South took precedence over propriety—at least temporarily.

Although McIntosh enjoined her "sisters" to retreat from the political forum and channel their professed concern for the slave into a broader agenda of general domestic reform—"Let us each, in our own land and our own sphere, labor to teach the ignorant, to comfort the sorrowing, to reclaim the vicious in whatever condition we find them," she proposed—she then declined to follow her own advice (31). Unwilling to resign the fate of southern civilization to the hands of contemporary politicians, the majority of whom she believed incompetent, and unable to shake her sense that the ramifications of the ongoing debate over the theory and practice of slavery had long ago spilled over the boundaries of organized politics, McIntosh remained vitally engaged in current affairs. Still, for all her early enthusiasm for overt propaganda, after the publication of her letter to the women of England, McIntosh returned to the more familiar—and more acceptable—medium of domestic fiction, in which she used her proximity to the domestic sphere to indulge in the sort of sweeping moral judgments she believed her gender interdicted in the generally recognized public arena of political debate.[55]

With McIntosh's withdrawal to the genre of domesticity came a noticeable moderation of her tone; her subsequent fiction, like that which had preceded the *Letter in Relation to Slavery*, demonstrated the temperance and restraint toward sectional issues that had come to be the signature of the antebellum southern domestic novelists in general. Although after the spring of 1853 McIntosh would again shroud her defense of the South in the dense prose and multilayered plots characteristic of senti-

55. *Ibid.*, 21–30.

mental fiction, her ideas and opinions remained consonant with the avow-
edly partisan *Letter*. Relying on a tried-and-true cast of characters and
store of plot devices, comparing and contrasting life above and below the
Mason-Dixon Line, McIntosh continued to criticize the North in general
and Stowe in particular, though in a more creative and less obvious vein.
Perhaps McIntosh, who fancied herself at home both in the North and in
the South, had surprised herself with the intensity of her feelings. Perhaps
she realized that her style of argument was best suited to the realm of
fiction. Perhaps she simply found the space limitation that a political tract
imposed too restrictive. For whatever reason, after the publication of the
Letter in Relation to Slavery, McIntosh consciously muted her partisanship to answer Stowe on her own terms, reappropriating the conventions
of the antebellum southern domestic novel and reasserting that vehicle as
an effective tool for political action.

The Lofty and the Lowly, the novel that succeeded the explosive *Letter*, illustrated McIntosh's ability to translate an overtly political message
into the language and images of the home and hearth. Ostensibly written
to further the cause of union, the two-volume investigation of the moral
foundations of northern and southern society superficially bore little resemblance to the incendiary political tract McIntosh had issued only
months before. Yet though McIntosh repeatedly disavowed her partisanship—the novel abounds with disclaimers of sectional preference—closer
examination of the message reveals that her motives were hardly disinterested. While McIntosh's skill enabled her to camouflage her commitment
to the South, her consistent use of northern villains and southern heroes,
coupled with her characteristic use of her own negative experiences to
inform her narrative, inevitably betrayed her true feelings. Just as Stowe's
self-conscious efforts to distribute the blame for the scourge of slavery
across both regions could not obscure the fact that Stowe held the South
responsible for perpetuating the perfidious system, McIntosh's literary ac-
robatics did little to conceal the ferocity of the novelist's loyalty to her
homeland.

The latter half of *The Lofty and the Lowly*, the mammoth saga of
the northern and southern branches of the Montrose family, demonstrated
the continuity of McIntosh's defense of slavery. Chronicling the efforts of
Donald and Isabel Montrose and their half-northern first cousins, Charles
and Alice, to regain the fortune Donald lost through a combination of

naïveté and northern greed, *The Lofty and the Lowly* merely rephrased the arguments concerning the salutary effects slavery exerted upon the domestic institutions of the South that McIntosh had employed more aggressively in her *Letter in Relation to Slavery*. Arguing that free labor, not slavery, threatened the fabric of American society, McIntosh painstakingly detailed the humiliation of the Montrose family upon the sudden death of the noble Colonel John Montrose, the forced sale of the Montrose slaves, and the threatened foreclosure on Montrose Hall, events that can be traced back to northern inhumanity.[56] Yet it was the heartrending tale of young Alice Montrose's tribulations above the Mason-Dixon Line that best dramatized the positive aspects of slavery that McIntosh had identified earlier. Lacking the theoretical framework so much in evidence in the *Letter in Relation to Slavery* and embellished with every sort of anxiety known to the domestic genre, this particular story line poignantly illustrated how the destructive values of individualism eroded the home and family while the communitarian ethic of slavery strengthened and stabilized them.[57]

As Volume II opens, Alice and her widowed mother, Mrs. Charles Montrose, who have depended previously on the goodwill of Mrs. Montrose's brother-in-law, the late Colonel John Montrose, for their subsistence, are in the process of removing themselves to the North, Mrs. Montrose's birthplace. Although their income is negligible—Donald Montrose lost the inheritance his father, the colonel, had intended for Alice and her mother at the end of Volume I—Mrs. Montrose is confident that her brother, the wealthy Bostonian Mr. Browne, will take care of their modest needs. Bidding adieu to Montrose Hall, the only home Alice has ever known, the two women plan to take up residence in a tiny cottage in Cambridge in the belief that their proximity to their northern relative will encourage him to meet the familial responsibilities he has until this point ignored. In view of the extreme uncertainty of her future, Alice finds it especially difficult to leave the familiar scenes of Montrose Hall; she struggles to maintain her composure. "Think what I am losing—home and friends and all," Alice cries in despair. "Of all that have loved and

56. See McIntosh, *The Lofty and the Lowly*, I.

57. Mary Ryan identifies three types of anxiety characteristic of domestic fiction: "filial, parental, and conjugal." See Ryan, *The Empire of the Mother*, 132.

cherished me so tenderly, none left but my mother."[58] That she should so leave "her old home, so long the home of love and peace, was an event Alice had never contemplated," McIntosh observed, but that she should be forced to exchange that "dear old nest" for the "cold strange world" of the North was almost unfathomable. "Can you think of that and not pity me?" Alice asks Donald (19).

Certainly, Alice deserves pity; the move north fulfills many of her greatest fears. Unaccustomed to relying upon her own efforts, acquainted only with the privileged life-style of the planter elite, the gentle Alice finds herself living in only a marginally genteel neighborhood with the prospect of moving to even less suitable quarters unless the Montroses' economic situation changes radically. Her mother, whose health has never been strong, quickly sickens under the strain; Alice must beg for money to secure adequate medical care. To make matters worse, Alice is deprived of the comfort of her devoted servant Daddy Cato. A free man under the terms of Colonel Montrose's will, Cato nevertheless considers himself bound to Alice and her mother; his heart is broken when Alice informs him that a lack of funds makes it impossible for him to join her northern household (39). Although Mrs. Montrose continues to hold out hope that when confronted with her impending poverty her brother will set aside his long-standing prejudices and contribute to her upkeep—Mr. Browne had virtually renounced his sister when she married a southerner against his advice some two decades earlier—Alice knows differently. Her uncle, to whom she secretly appeals, will do nothing to help her; in fact, he discontinues paying the small stipend he has, against his judgment, provided Mrs. Montrose. Browne tells Alice gleefully that poverty is the fitting reward for Mrs. Montrose's decision many years ago to take sanctuary in the southern home of her brother-in-law (176).

The Browne family supports Mr. Browne's inhumane policy toward their newly transplanted kin. Mrs. Browne, a social climber, has long resented her unsophisticated sister-in-law; from the beginning, she has discouraged Mr. Browne from assuming the slightest obligation toward his widowed sister and niece. Concerned primarily with impressing fashionable society, Mrs. Browne devotes most of her attention to plotting her

58. McIntosh, *The Lofty and the Lowly*, II, 19. Hereinafter cited parenthetically by page number in the text. All references in the text in this chapter are to Volume II.

daughters' prospective debuts; she goes out of her way to prevent any association that might detract from their marriageability. The two Browne girls, Anne and Eliza, share their mother's ambitions. Even though they are about the same age as their cousin Alice, they refuse to do so much as pay a call on her (71).[59] Browne's son, George, the one largely responsible for the Montroses' misfortunes—he tricked Donald Montrose into signing away his inheritance and later tries to murder an accomplice—simply pretends his aunt and cousin do not exist. Having turned over his ill-gotten gains to his father for collection, George no longer takes any interest in the family his perfidy has nearly destroyed (25–29).

Yet for the Brownes' refusal to assist Mrs. Montrose and Alice, for all their willful disregard for the precarious circumstances of their nearest relatives' existence, they cannot shatter the Montroses. When Mr. Browne flatly denies Alice's supplications, Alice assumes full responsibility for the support of herself and her mother, pleading with the doctor and the landlord to extend her credit and putting up a cherished piece of jewelry for security (80–93). Selling the produce from her small garden, taking in sewing for members of the Brownes' social class, Alice manages to stave off poverty and eventually reunites her "family" by bringing Cato north. "Your southern education has left you utterly ignorant of business," Mr. Browne smirks when he learns of Alice's plan to spend one-fifth of her annual income to send for Cato, but as McIntosh illustrates, it is precisely Alice's lack of business experience that enables her to maintain the integrity of her home (75). Alice's keen appreciation of the human bond, a direct product of slavery, enables her to maintain the integrity of her domestic circle in the face of almost insurmountable odds; in contrast, McIntosh argues, the Brownes' insistence on the primacy of money, a hallmark of the individualistic North, ensures that their home and family will be subject to any and every stress and strain.

Maria McIntosh's comparison of the two domestic circles dramatized the central theme of the domestic defense of slavery: that slavery cemented society by strengthening its key elements of home and family. Harriet Beecher Stowe had asserted in *Uncle Tom's Cabin* that a social system which sanctioned the buying and selling of human flesh necessarily

59. In Volume I, the Thomas Brownes debate the necessity of donning mourning upon the death of Charles Montrose.

precluded the existence of a stable society: because southerners willingly
tore apart slave families, Stowe reasoned, they obviously placed little value
on the domestic institutions that gave society its fundamental structure.[60]
McIntosh argued just the opposite. Northerners, not southerners, threatened America's equilibrium, the transplanted Georgian stated sagely. By
giving the individual precedence over the community, by predicating all
social intercourse on the dollar, northerners undermined the sanctity of
the domestic sphere and thereby endangered the longevity of civilization.
Although Stowe might publicly deplore the circumstances of the slave, her
unfounded concern for the well-being of the "sable race" merely served
to divert attention from the real problem, the systematic destruction of
the northern home and family generated by a social ethic fueled by greed.

The Browne family, which McIntosh intended to represent the northern merchant class in general, illustrated the falling away from the cherished principles of the early Republic that McIntosh believed contributed
to the demise of the domestic sphere in the North. The senior Browne
and his erstwhile mate teach their children by example that their first responsibility is to themselves; it is hardly surprising that Anne and Eliza
Browne devote their lives to fashion while young George Browne becomes
a criminal (224–28). In contrast, the Cambridge Montroses demonstrate
the sort of interdependence that McIntosh and her fellow domestic writers
held made the home and family a bastion of strength in a troubled world.
For instance, Alice and her mother gladly do without new clothing to
claim Cato; Cato, in turn, happily hires himself out to help his "family"
make ends meet (101–102). The fact that the southerners maintain the
stability of their household outside the salutary environment of the South
and in the worst of financial situations merely emphasized McIntosh's argument for the protective properties of slavery. It was slavery, McIntosh
contended, that ultimately ensured the perpetuation of the values in which
a true sense of community could flourish; it was slavery that held out the
last best hope for civilization.

60. Stowe argued that "so long as the law considers all these human beings with hearts
and living affections, only as so many things belonging to a master,—so long as the failure,
or misfortune, or imprudence, or death of the kindest owner may cause them any day to
exchange a life of kind protection and indulgence for one of hopeless misery and toil,—so
long is it impossible to make anything beautiful or desirable in the best regulated administration of slavery." Stowe, *Uncle Tom's Cabin*, 51.

Still, while McIntosh refrained from openly criticizing Stowe in *The Lofty and the Lowly*, she could not resist portraying the abolitionist faction with which she, like many southerners, associated Stowe. Significantly, after the Montrose family overcomes most of the hardship inflicted by the Brownes, they are menaced by an equally destructive portion of the northern population: fanatical abolitionists. Ironically, the Montroses' troubles arise after their "family" is whole, completed by Cato, who insists on acting like a slave even though he has papers that argue otherwise. At first, Cato is merely subjected to curious stares; later, he is mercilessly interrogated by one Mr. Sampson, an abolitionist lecturer who poses as a clergyman to gain Cato's trust. Completely without morals, Sampson resorts to all kinds of chicanery to get Cato to discuss his treatment at the hands of southern slaveholders, twisting the simple Negro's professions of loyalty to suit his evil ends (95–100). By appealing to Cato's extreme religiosity, the abolitionist gets an answer he can exploit. "And so, my poor fellow, you have been in bondage all your life;—in bondage to a hard master?" the clergyman asks. The former slave, who is familiar with the term *bondage* only in its spiritual sense, responds immediately: "Bondage for true, maussa, we all in bondage to bery hard maussa, work we day and night neber stop tell we fall down and dead; he feed we wid husk and make we back sore wid he heaby burden" (98–99). Sampson is overjoyed. "Hitherto, in his appeals to the popular mind," McIntosh notes, the abolitionist had been " 'indebted to his imagination for his facts,' but here was a genuine fact, and told in a manner so unusually interesting—such native eloquence—the more powerful for its simplicity" (99). Never mind that Cato divulges that the name of his oppressive master is "sin"; never mind that the newly freed man willingly testifies to the benevolence of the slave regime. Like Stowe in reality, Sampson has, through the total distortion of fact, found the example he has sought, and despite Cato's arguments otherwise, he determines to turn the slave's humble testament to the redeeming love of Christ into a scathing indictment of the slave regime.

The abolitionist's zeal sparks an attack on the Montrose home designed to liberate Cato from his alleged persecutors. Sampson, accompanied by a loyal band of fanatics, surrounds the Cambridge cottage and announces his intentions to storm its gates if Cato is not immediately released into his custody. "Tell us where to find this oppressed and downtrodden fellow-man," the multitude cries. Determined to "proclaim freedom to the captive—to loose his bonds and let the oppressed go free," the mob will hear no reason; Alice's protests that Cato is, in fact, already free fall on deaf ears. Cato's pleas are similarly ignored; the abolitionists will not believe that "he came here of his own free will, and has been detained by no bonds but those of his own affectionate, generous heart." In spite of Alice's efforts to protect her loyal servant—"Dem come for me, but don't gib me up; please my dear Misses," Cato begs, "no to gib me up"—she is largely powerless against the onslaught. While Cato cowers in the parlor, a wild-eyed woman pushes Alice aside and directs her abolitionist "myrmidons" to break down the door. "Those who place themselves obstinately in the way of the triumphal car of Liberty must be crushed beneath its wheel," the female abolitionist raves. "If woman's spiritual weapons fail, then man's strong hands must break open the prison-doors and let the oppressed go free" (167–71).

Although the timely intervention of Robert Grahame, McIntosh's idealized vision of a northern industrialist, saves the Montrose family from their attackers, she suggests that the next time they (or, more to the point, others like them) may not be so lucky (172–75). Organized abolitionism held a special appeal for the growing number of northerners who, like the Thomas Brownes, regularly indulged in psychological and, in the case of George Browne, physical violence. McIntosh argued that the insidious movement flourished in a society that denied the existence of a higher law, that same standard which Stowe found lacking in the South. Thus, while the Cambridge Montroses stand firm against the variety of external threats they encounter during their northern sojourn—circumstances eventually permit them to return to the South—the inordinate difficulties they face in maintaining their domestic circle indicate McIntosh's real fears for the stability of southern society in view of the continued threats from the North. Certainly, McIntosh's depiction of abolitionism revealed her incomplete comprehension of the antislavery movement—the fact that McIntosh, like her fellow southern domestic novelists, repeatedly labeled Harriet Beecher Stowe an abolitionist is evidence of her limited understanding.[61] Nevertheless, McIntosh's explicit link between the inhu-

61. Like McIntosh, Stowe, in fact, favored colonization, a point that led some abolitionists to take issue with *Uncle Tom's Cabin*. See Gossett, *"Uncle Tom's Cabin" and American Culture*, 164–84.

manity of the Brownes and the hypocrisy and exploitativeness of Mr. Sampson and his cohorts toward the southerners indicates her keen appreciation of the intersection between the private and the public spheres of society, a realization that held profound implications for the whole of America.

Yet for all of Maria McIntosh's insight into the problems that plagued northern society, she was no more successful than Caroline Gilman and Caroline Hentz in establishing the benevolence of the slave regime, much less in halting the spread of Stowe's perceived antisouthern message. To an author who had enjoyed a considerable measure of success for over a decade—McIntosh began her noteworthy career in 1841—the palpable failure of her self-styled peace initiative was doubtlessly most disturbing. After all, McIntosh, unlike Gilman and Hentz, was thoroughly familiar with both sides of the story. Although both Gilman and Hentz were born in New England and diligently worked to maintain their connection with their native region, only McIntosh could boast intimate acquaintance with "the varied forms of social life" both above and below the Mason-Dixon Line.[62] And whereas, if pressed, Gilman and Hentz could offer a variety of excuses for the limited success of their endeavors—Gilman, that age and infirmity did not permit her to issue a specific response to *Uncle Tom's Cabin*, and Hentz, that her husband's severe illness impeded her efforts—McIntosh could claim no such distraction. At the height of her powers and popularity, in the final analysis McIntosh had only herself to blame for the inherent improbability of her effort to block Stowe's progress.

In this context, McIntosh's observations on the failings of American women contain more than a grain of self-recrimination. If, indeed, women were responsible for controlling the "vital principle" of society, with forming the "enduring impressions" of mankind and serving as "the clear light, which should beam ever on the path of honor and truth, and shine . . . with undimmed and cheering ray, when all around [is] blackest night," then McIntosh herself had fallen short of the self-same feminine ideal she and her colleagues had labored to define.[63] In her unsuccessful

62. McIntosh, *Woman in America*, 11–12.
63. *Ibid.*, 25; McIntosh, *The Lofty and the Lowly*, II, 165.

attempts to eradicate sectional tensions through her fiction, in her inability to transform political infighting into constructive dialogue, she had
compromised the exacting standard to which she enjoined her admittedly
less talented sisters and, in so doing, had inadvertently betrayed the trust
of her beloved South. Or so she feared. McIntosh's subsequent activities
testify to the extent of her psychic discomfort: almost immediately after
the publication of *The Lofty and the Lowly*, she embarked upon a lengthy
sabbatical during which she pondered the near failure of the domestic
defense of southern culture. The single volume she issued over these
years, *Violet; or, The Cross and the Crown* (1856), chronicled the fantastic adventures of a band of pirates in New Jersey.[64] The South and all its
problems received no further mention until the middle of 1863.

The first generation of southern domestic novelists had entered the 1850s
optimistically. Having weathered a period of sectional turbulence, Gilman, Hentz, and McIntosh anticipated a decade of political stability, confident that their efforts to defuse tensions through the literary presenta-
tion of both sides of the argument had alleviated some of the strain.
Certainly, there was reason for hope. The Compromise of 1850, for one
thing, held the promise of a new era of good feelings, as it addressed many
long-standing sectional grievances and affirmed the vitality of the national
political process. And the seeming resolution of regional tensions affected
the southern domestic novelists on a personal level; with the "great national questions" apparently settled, there was no pressing need for additional weaponry in the domestic arsenal. Gilman and Hentz made arrangements to travel north, and McIntosh decided to go abroad. Yet the
projected "cease-fire" in the fifteen-year war of words failed to transpire.
The publication of *Uncle Tom's Cabin* in 1852 removed any possibility of
rapprochement within the confines of domestic fiction, forcing the three
novelists to reassess their contribution to national equilibrium and to plan
the most effective counterattack.

   Gilman was content to reassert her historical position; the reissue
of *Recollections of a New England Housekeeper* and *Recollections of a*

---

64. Maria McIntosh, *Violet; or, The Cross and the Crown* (New York, 1856). See Baym,
Woman's Fiction, 101–104, for a synopsis of the plot.

Southern Matron signified her continued belief that northerners and southerners could overcome their prejudices with proper instruction.[65] Caroline Hentz felt compelled to do more. Familiar with Stowe personally and professionally, Hentz could not let the antislavery polemic go uncontested; after two years of searching for the proper vehicle, she wrote *The Planter's Northern Bride*. McIntosh took action as well. Mustering her courage, she dealt Stowe a blistering blow with her open letter to the women of England, anticipating the objections of many northerners to slavery in her statement of southern principles. Shortly after the document was printed in pamphlet form, McIntosh published her most comprehensive discussion of the peculiar institution to date: *The Lofty and the Lowly* synthesized the ideas and arguments McIntosh and her fellow domestic novelists had worked with for almost twenty years in formulating their fictional defense of southern culture. But though the concentrated effort of the first-generation writers brought forth several of the most provocative southern domestic novels, they were unable to impede the progress of Stowe's message. Indeed, the theme and characters of *Uncle Tom's Cabin*, specifically the emphasis on slavery and its moral ramifications, significantly influenced the southern domestic novel, redirecting its focus from the planter elite to their chattel and forcing its practitioners to confront a variety of issues they had, until 1852, successfully avoided. Although Maria McIntosh's 1863 identification of Harriet Beecher Stowe as the instigator of civil war clearly was unwarranted, her awareness of the significance of *Uncle Tom's Cabin* was to the point: Stowe's tale of life among the lowly changed the course of southern domestic fiction and with it the personal and professional lives of its practitioners.

65. Gilman, Autobiographical Essay (MS in South Carolina Historical Society).

4

We Need No Prophet's Eye

*B*y the middle 1850s, a second generation of southern domestic novelists had laid claim to the audience established by Caroline Gilman, Caroline Hentz, and Maria McIntosh. Although first-generation writers continued to publish sporadically— Gilman, for example, sent random verses to several periodicals, and Hentz managed to issue one more major novel, a fantasy, that made no reference to the South whatsoever—the marginal quality and quantity of material, coupled with the complete avoidance of the divisive issues that previously had preoccupied their work, suggested their willingness to surrender the burden to other, more capable hands.[1] "Were I to detail the personal mistakes and deficiencies of this long era," Caroline Gilman confessed in 1852, "I might lose the sympathy which may have followed me thus far." Reviewing her long career, the eldest domestic novelist decided that her achievements were rather few. "My only pride," she wrote somberly, "is in my books for children."[2]

With the transfer of responsibility from the first generation to the second came a noticeable shift in the style and tone of southern domestic fiction. Whereas Gilman, Hentz, and McIntosh, self-identified southerners who retained positive feelings for the North, refused to acknowledge their southern partisanship publicly in the interest of national harmony, Mary Virginia Terhune and Augusta Evans felt no such compunctions. Coming of age in an era distinguished by conflict rather than the Revolutionary consensus familiar to their predecessors, Terhune and Evans

---

1. See Caroline Hentz, *Ernest Linwood* (Boston, 1856). Some critics believe Hentz's final novel is autobiographical. Certainly, this would explain its noticeable lack of prosouthern propaganda. See, for example, Ellison, "Green-eyed Monster," 345–50; and Papashvily, *All the Happy Endings*, 75–94. Kelley has reasserted this argument recently in *Private Woman*, 222–32.

2. Gilman, Autobiographical Essay (MS in South Carolina Historical Society).

found it difficult if not impossible to envision the sort of national unity their literary forebears so fondly recalled. Forced by time and circumstance to acknowledge sectional cleavages as well as to modify their personal and professional ambitions in response to ever-increasing tensions, the two younger writers considered the possibility of the dissolution of the Union to a degree and in a manner the domestic pioneers would have found inconceivable. Yet for all their political sophistication, the two younger writers failed to recognize the immediacy of "the coming crisis," much less to acknowledge the role their fiction and that of their predecessors played in setting the stage for national tragedy. Up until the very eve of the Civil War, Terhune and Evans continued to believe that the escalation of sectional tensions would stop short of armed conflict.

"I am often asked if we were not uneasy for the safety of the Union, while in the thick of sectional wordy strife," Terhune wrote in 1910. "The truth is that I had been used to political wrangling from my youth up."[3] Remembering the months immediately preceding the outbreak of war, the venerable novelist chided herself for her naïveté: "The fact that South Carolina and six other states had seceded . . . that, in every county and 'Cross-Roads' hamlet . . . bands of volunteers were drilling daily and nightly and that cargoes of arms were arriving . . . and in distribution . . . weighed marvelously little against the settled conviction, well-nigh sublime in its fatuousness" that there would be no war. "To my apprehension, so much that we heard was sheer gasconade, amusing for a time from its very unreasonable and illogical conclusions . . . that I failed to attach to it the importance[,] the magnitude the mischief deserved to have" (365–66).

Although Terhune, who wrote under the pseudonym "Marion Harland," publicly berated herself some fifty years after the fact for her inability to predict the coming of the war, circumstances suggest that her lack of prescience was unavoidable, the inevitable consequence of her highly politicized youth. Unlike Caroline Gilman's 1852 reminiscences, which emphasized the persistence of the Revolution's legacy (Gilman went so far as to credit what she called her "mind-birth" to the "associations" she formed while playing amidst the tombstones of the war dead), *Marion Harland's Autobiography* (1910), which purported to describe "what the

---

3. Terhune, *Marion Harland's Autobiography*, 365. Hereinafter cited parenthetically by page number in the text.

Old South was in deed and truth," chronicled the challenges offered by a
younger generation (ix–x). Dedicated to her father, Samuel Hawes, a local
leader of the Whig party, Terhune's lengthy recollections pointed up the
numerous national and regional cleavages of the antebellum era, celebrating both the vitality and the complexity of the southern electoral process.[4]

Barbecues, stump speeches, fairs, musters, and partisan and bipartisan
rallies were the stuff of Terhune's girlhood. One of her earliest memories
was of being reprimanded for chanting an off-color political verse: "My
mother . . . said it was vulgar, untrue and unkind. It was not her fault that
each of us had the private belief that there was a spice of truth in it" (122).
As her father's favorite, young Mary Virginia frequently accompanied him
on his extensive travels through Powhatan County and its environs to mobilize support for his "ancient and honorable" party (118). Election day
met with keen anticipation: "From the time when I was tall enough to
peep over the . . . fence—until I was reckoned too big to stand and stare
in so public a place, and was allowed to join the seniors . . . it was my
delight to inspect and pronounce upon the groups that filled the highway
all day long" (121).

Although Samuel Hawes did not hold elected office until the late
1840s—he repeatedly declined nomination to the state legislature, declar-
ing that "helping to put the right man into the right place" was the whole
of his political ambition—he played a critical role in determining his party's future (119). Charged with delivering a rural, predominantly Democratic county, Hawes evened the odds somewhat by recruiting voters from
the Whig stronghold of Richmond to vote in nearby Powhatan County;
under one of the more controversial provisions of Virginia law, voters
were permitted to cast a ballot in as many counties as they held land.
While Hawes, according to his daughter, held strong doubts as to the
inherent morality of that legislation, he was determined to use it to the
Whig advantage (120). Sixty-six years later, Terhune remembered her
father's anxiety as he waited for reinforcements. "As early as three o'clock
I was used to seeing my father come out of the door of his counting-room
over the way, watch in hand, and look down the Richmond road," she

4. Gilman, Autobiographical Essay (MS in South Carolina Historical Society). For
discussion of the vigorous party system in the South and the pivotal role the Whigs played
in energizing southern politics, see Eaton, *A History of the Old South*, 281–300.

wrote. As time passed, inevitably "sympathizers . . . began to speculate as to the possibility of accident to man, beast, or carriage. . . . What would happen if the Richmond voters did not come, after all?" When they came, and they always did, a "hurrah" went up for Hawes. As he doffed his hat "in courteous acknowledgment of the hands and hats waved to him from carriage and saddle-bow," Hawes reminded his daughter of Alexander, Napoleon, and Washington. "That child has been defrauded who has not had a hero in his own home," Terhune concluded, leaving no doubt that she and her brothers and sisters had been well served (123).

Terhune's political education intensified upon her family's 1844 move to Richmond. Returning to their plantation only for summers, holidays, and election days, the Haweses plunged immediately into the round of intellectual events to which Samuel Hawes's prominence within the Whig party and the local business community afforded them access. Not long after her relocation to a "quietly, but eminently aristocratic" neighborhood, Terhune dined several times with Edgar Allan Poe, an outspoken advocate of literary nationalism, and attended a private reception honoring future governor Henry A. Wise (196).[5] In early 1846, when Thomas Ritchie, Jr., and John Pleasants, the respective editors of Richmond's Democratic and Whig newspapers, dueled over Pleasants' alleged abolitionist sympathies, Terhune took a personal interest in the proceedings. Her father had long revered Pleasants, who was mortally wounded in the incident, as the conscience of liberal Virginia; Terhune herself was a schoolmate and close friend of Pleasants' daughter and niece.[6]

The outbreak of the Mexican War later that same year provided further occasion for political instruction. Hawes, who had campaigned vigorously for Henry Clay in 1844, had argued that the election of James K. Polk heralded the demise of the Republic; with the onset of war, his gloomy predictions seemed accurate. Terhune shared her father's dissatisfaction with the Polk administration. "Were you not astonished and horrified by the election?" she wrote a friend. "I never dreamt of such a thing

5. Mary Hudson Wright reports on Terhune's meeting with Poe in "Mary Virginia Terhune ('Marion Harland'): Her Life and Works" (Ph.D. dissertation, George Peabody College for Teachers, 1934), 49–50.

6. Clement Eaton discusses the tragedy in *The Freedom-of-Thought Struggle in the Old South* (New York, 1964), 179–80.

much less thought of it in my waking hours so it came upon me like a thunderclap." But she failed to adopt her father's conservative attitude toward the leading question of the day, the expansion of slavery into the western territories.[7] Long after the Virginia legislature had declared the positive good of slavery, Hawes continued to assert that the peculiar institution was morally wrong. In fact, on one occasion, he went so far as to make arrangements to free the "family servants" and send them to Liberia, only to be dissuaded by the slaves' "wild weeping" and bitter protests against their proposed "exile." That overwhelming display of emotion convinced Hawes "to wait for further indications of the Divine will" before he acted; still, he remained deeply troubled (194–95).[8]

Perhaps it was the constant threat of slave unrest that prompted Terhune to repudiate a portion of her father's political ideology and conclude that slavery was the only answer to the so-called Negro question. "I cannot recollect when the whisper of the possibility of 'Insurrection' (we need not specify of what kind) did not send a sick chill to my heart," Terhune recalled. "To the present hour I am conscious of a peculiar stricture of the heart that stops my breath for a second, at the sudden blast of a hunter's horn" (191). That the rumors were, more often than not, of no consequence failed to quiet the white population's collective anxiety. "We had heard how Gabriel, a leader in prayer-meetings, . . . plan[ned] [a] murder of all male whites, and a partition of the women and girl-children," the novelist recounted. "We had heard from the lips of eyewitnesses, scenes succeeding the Southampton massacre of every white within the reach of the murderous horde howling at the heels of the negro preacher whom his master had taught to read and write" (192–93).[9]

7. Mary Virginia Terhune to Virginia Eppes Dance, November 16, 1844, in Terhune Papers, Duke. For discussion of the Polk election and the Whig reaction see Eaton, *A History of the Old South*, 329–31.

8. One of Terhune's aunts actually sent her slaves to Liberia at her own expense and paid their way home when she learned of their profound unhappiness in Africa. For discussion of the Virginia debate over slavery in the wake of the Nat Turner rebellion, see Eaton, *A History of the Old South*, 345–51; and Alison Goodyear Freehling, *Drift Toward Dissolution: The Virginia Slavery Debate of 1831–1832* (Baton Rouge, 1982). Winthrop Jordan examines the philosophical origins of the Virginia debate on the perpetuation of race slavery in *White over Black: American Attitudes Toward the Negro, 1550–1812* (Chapel Hill, 1968).

9. The slave Gabriel's abortive rebellion in 1800, which included plans to capture the

The merest whisper of rebellion gripped Richmond with paralyzing fear. When, for example, in 1847 "there were indications of an organized conspiracy" that could be traced directly to the efforts of abolitionists in Henrico and Hanover counties, the city armed itself. "A double guard was on duty at the capitol, and a detachment of military from the armory paraded the streets all night," Terhune wrote breathlessly. "I was, I confess, somewhat alarmed, and not a little startled" (192). Although Samuel Hawes refused to believe that his slaves would revolt, his daughter was not as certain. "We knew them to be . . . passionate and unreasoning, facile and impulsive, and fanatical beyond anything conceivable by the full-blooded white," the novelist asserted. "The superstitious savagery their ancestors had brought from barbarous and benighted Africa, was yet in their veins. . . . We knew with what elements we should have to deal if the 'rising' ever took an organized form" (192).[10]

A series of murders of whites by blacks in Richmond in the summer of 1852 confirmed Terhune's opinion that slavery served a positive good in southern society. She was alone in her house with her servants on the night that the final episode of slaughter took place "within two squares," and later the young novelist recalled "the horror, the feeling of imminent danger that I had escaped—the loneliness—and then the full out gushing of thanksgiving." She wrote to a friend on July 20: "We need no prophet's eye to tell the unhappy consequences of such scenes, which have of late, been alarmingly frequent. A murder, a case of poisoning, and one of incendiarism . . . have taken place in our midst within a very short time, in each the coloured race were the aggressors, the whites the victims." Coming in the wake of a bout with a debilitating illness, the shock was particularly severe. "I feel as if I never cared to leave the bosom of my own family," Terhune lamented somewhat ironically, given the fact that unlike most white local slave owners, Samuel Hawes refused to

---

Richmond armory and kidnap the governor of Virginia, prompted Richmonders to exercise tighter control over the activities of both slaves and free blacks; nevertheless, residents continued to fear insurrection. See Marie Tyler-McGraw, "Richmond Free Blacks and African Colonization, 1816–1832," *Journal of American Studies*, XXI (1987), 207–24.

10. George M. Fredrickson discusses the specter of rebellion in *The Black Image in the White Mind: The Debate on Afro-American Character and Destiny, 1817–1914* (New York, 1971), 8–9, 53–54.

arm himself with anything more than a common carving knife (191).

Yet while Terhune declared in 1852 that "it is well understood here by both negroes and whites that a struggle for supremacy is at hand—this is but the beginning of the trouble," she refused to attribute southern problems solely to the abolitionist threat.[11] Unlike the first generation of southern domestic novelists, who especially after the publication of *Uncle Tom's Cabin* were inclined to view the deterioration of northern and southern relations as the direct result of the efforts of a small, highly visible enclave of antislavery advocates, Terhune characteristically sought out broader causes for sectional dissent. She believed that long before William Lloyd Garrison and his fellow travelers demanded the attention of literate white America, the North and the South had enjoyed an adversarial relationship; organized abolitionism only accentuated existing problems that were deeply rooted in the nation's complex social and political culture.[12] Thus, although Terhune and her publisher cultivated the notion that the novelist's work was identical to that of Gilman, Hentz, and McIntosh— Terhune, for instance, told McIntosh's biographer that "she owed to Miss McIntosh the strongest influences of her young life and those which had determined its bent and its development"—the younger writer's interpretation of and reaction to the contemporary political scene distinguished her work from that of the previous generation.[13]

Terhune's awareness of the broader causes of political conflict, the legacy of her father, led her to posit an alternative reason for northern and southern disharmony in her third novel, *Moss-side* (1857).[14] Enlarging upon themes introduced in *Alone* (1853) and *The Hidden Path* (1854), Terhune argued that the growing women's rights movement posed a more serious threat to national unity than did abolitionism.[15] Female activists, the novelist asserted, encouraged women to reject their divinely appointed

11. Terhune to Dance, July 20, 1852, in Terhune Papers, Duke.

12. See Hilldrup, "Cold War Against the Yankees," 370–84.

13. Terhune paraphrased in Colles, *Authors and Writers*, 174–75. See also Kate Sanborn, "Mary Virginia Terhune," in *Our Famous Women* (Hartford, 1884), 624–51; and Derby, *Fifty Years Among Authors*, 563–68.

14. Mary Virginia Terhune [Marion Harland], *Moss-side* (New York, 1857).

15. *Cf.* Terhune, *Alone* (Richmond, 1854), and *The Hidden Path* (New York, 1855). In both novels, Terhune uses strong-minded southern heroines to emphasize the importance of fulfilled domestic obligations in maintaining social equilibrium.

role of guardian of the home and hearth; they rewarded self-indulgence and selfishness and thereby threatened the fabric of American civilization. Surveying the feminist slate of reforms, Terhune recoiled in horror. First-generation novelists had expressed concern for the continued viability of northern domesticity as early as 1833; the list of demands circulated by women and some men above the Mason-Dixon Line suggested that their deepest fears had indeed become verifiable truth.

But while Terhune took rather grim pleasure in chronicling the demise of the northern home and family, she could not shake her apprehensions that southern domesticity was also threatened, endangered by the inexorable spread of northern ideas.[16] The women's rights movement, itself the outgrowth of organized abolitionism, seemed to bear out Terhune's suspicions that the variety of predominantly northern antebellum reform movements signaled the beginnings of widespread social upheaval.[17] Terhune's professed contempt for what one historian has labeled the "popular isms and ologies" of the North, an attitude she shared with many southerners, failed to disguise her terror that the hierarchical social structure of her native home was especially vulnerable to social unrest; her endless recital of the virtues of southern womanhood merely emphasized her reservations about the same.[18] In this particular context, Terhune's preoccupation with the destructive potential of northern feminism is understandable, because Terhune, like many male propagandists, recognized the vital link between the domestic sphere and the South's central institution of slavery.[19] Any perceptible change within the home and family, Terhune asserted, would have a deleterious impact on the South's larger social and economic structure with the possible consequence that the re-

16. See Terhune to Dance, October 18, 1855, in Terhune Papers, Duke. See also Hilldrup, "Cold War Against the Yankees," 370–84.

17. For examination of the integral relationship between antislavery activism and the drive for women's rights, see Dubois, *Feminism and Suffrage*, and Hersh, *The Slavery of Sex*.

18. See Brown's humorous discussion of the "popular isms and ologies" and their treatment in antebellum popular fiction in *The Sentimental Novel*, 181–200. Ronald Walters surveys the broad spectrum of northern reform in *American Reformers, 1815–1860* (New York, 1978).

19. Taylor, *Cavalier and Yankee*, 146–48, 162–76; Ruoff, "Southern Womanhood," 18–48; Jones, *Tomorrow Is Another Day*, 3–50. For contemporary articulation of this connection see Dew, "On the Characteristic Differences Between the Sexes."

gion (as she knew it) would be completely destroyed. Terhune's warning against northern feminism, which she viewed as the latest manifestation of northern aggression, was only part of her larger message: abolitionism was a minuscule portion of a comprehensive program of northern "reform" aimed at the decimation of the South.

Moss-side, which takes its name from its heroine's Virginia plantation, chronicles the struggles of a young southerner, Grace Leigh, to identify and accept her feminine destiny within the southern community. The story opens in New York City, where Grace, an intelligent, well-educated daughter of the Virginia aristocracy (whose background closely resembled Terhune's), has traveled to attend the wedding of Louise Wynne, a friend from school. Louise, who is skilled in the art of manipulation, has persuaded the somewhat reluctant Grace to exchange her "southern country home" for the "roar of a thronged city" by promising to include her in the wedding party and subsequent honeymoon trip.[20] "I knew nothing of her attachment to her successful suitor, or indeed that such a being existed, previous to her announcement of the anticipated marriage," Grace admits. Still, her curiosity bests her, and she decides to accept Louise's invitation (9).

Upon her arrival, Grace quickly forgets her reservations about the undertaking; she is overwhelmed by New York in general and by the Wynne family in particular. Not unfamiliar with luxury, Grace is nevertheless left gaping at the lavish display of her hosts' establishment. "The furniture of the apartment was splendid in comparison with that of my simple room at home," Grace observes. "Scattered everywhere were garments, that to my eyes were fit for the wear of royalty itself. . . . Glittering silver . . . jewel caskets, and [a] hundred nameless articles of bijouterie" litter Louise's chamber; the rest of the house is even more spectacular. Grace finds her fellow wedding guests, a horde of elaborately dressed people drawn from New York's fashionable circles, equally fascinating. Their elegant manners and lively conversation fill the "unsophisticated" southerner with envy. That Louise does not love her fiancé, David Evans, and that she marries merely to gain the freedom to pursue her own interests is, Grace comes to believe, a rather intriguing proposition. "I saw not

---

20. Terhune, *Moss-side*, 6. Hereinafter cited parenthetically by page number in the text.

an inch below the surface upon which the world might gaze," Grace rec-
ollects, and that limited perspective leaves her extremely dissatisfied with
her own circumstances (9).

The wedding trip to the White Mountains and Niagara increases
Grace's unhappiness. Surrounded by men and women of her own age, she
enjoys a degree of excitement and intellectual stimulation of which she
had previously only dreamed. "How vividly arises to my remembrance the
countenance and posture of each of our select company!" Grace reflects.
Louise's obvious indifference to her groom fails to arouse Grace's sympathies; if anything, Grace admires Louise's control. "If the heart were dead,
the intellect, with all its exquisite susceptibility to beauty, its grand capacities, its undying desire lived still," Grace enthuses, "and its expansion,
its longings . . . were painful in their intensity" (30). Once Grace returns
to Moss-side, she cannot stop thinking about her northern adventures and
drawing unfavorable parallels between her native environment and the
one she so briefly visited. "My Virginia home had no pretensions to ar-
chitectural elegance, nor was it imposing in size," Grace observes. "Mrs.
Wynne's placid orbs would have widened, and her aristocratic shoulders
executed the meaningful shrug, learned from the most stylish French mo-
diste of the day, at the sight of the humble abode." Bored with her companions, longing to discuss books and ideas, Grace woefully neglects her
domestic duties and throws her plantation community into disarray (66).[21]

Not until several years later, however, does Grace get the chance to
renew her acquaintance with Louise, who has, by this time, achieved considerable fame as a didactic writer. Death, disease, and unrequited love
have thrust Grace into deep despair; Louise's success merely accentuates
Grace's depression. Yet, when the family doctor prescribes a trip north to
lift her spirits, Grace hurries to comply, convinced that outside the stulti-
fying South her mood will improve. Instead, Grace encounters ideas and
attitudes that thrust her further into turmoil and ultimately cause her to
question the foundations of southern culture. Louise, her intellectual inspiration, has embraced the doctrine of women's rights and championed
the seditious ideology in an imposing philosophical treatise that has won
her the support of many northerners. "I have drawn down upon me a

21. Grace Leigh's failure to meet her domestic responsibilities parallels the trials of Ida
Ross in *Alone*. Both women endanger their respective communities through their inaction.

storm of abuse from the lordly sex and must submit resignedly to the fate and title of 'strong minded woman,'" Louise tells Grace. "But from the oppressed, the lowly slaves, to whom I have dared to preach freedom . . . I have had blessing and encouragement" (330–31).

Although Grace is warned against reading Louise's book on the grounds that it is "pernicious to morality, ruinous to the healthy content-ment of the mind," she ignores the advice and within minutes falls under Louise's spell. "Woman the slave; Society, Civilization and Religion as preached by Man, the enslavers; these were the texts insinuated . . . by the initial chapter," Grace recalls. "When the attention was enchained," the reader found herself confronted with a plan to transform society into nothing less than a matriarchy. Woman "should be enthroned, no lower than the angels, while he who had ruled her . . . should be well-pleased to occupy a subordinate place, and adore as queen and priestess the radiant Immaculate." Taken in by the northerner's powerful arguments, Grace marvels at the "pearls of fancy, diamonds of wit, the blood-red ruby of passion [that] gemmed the bowl, and dazzled [her] wavering perceptions of good and evil." She writes, "I drank in, never staying to question the source or the elements of the sparkling draught." By dark, she has finished reading Louise's book, and she is "miserable to wretchedness." Only a "dauntless spirit" able "to buckle on armor" could hasten the "millen-nium" that Louise described. "Too cowardly" to participate in "the cru-sade" herself and therefore destined to remain "one of the many million serfs portrayed—shackled, hand and foot, by despotism," Grace wonders, "What hope had I but in death?" (301–302).

Grace's seduction by Louise's theology of women's liberation pointed up Terhune's apprehensions concerning not only feminism but northern reform in general. Northern reformers, Terhune argued, were nothing more than highly educated, well-to-do men and women who fed off the ignorance and vulnerability of their intellectual and economic inferiors. Secure in their own wealth and power, these inveterate meddlers had no qualms about enjoining the less fortunate to question the time-honored structure of society. That they veiled their insidious plot to destroy society in esoteric logic and convoluted prose—Louise borrows heavily from the German idealism and its American distillation, Transcendentalism—and masked their intention to promote social unrest in the guise of moral re-form made the group and their self-proclaimed mission of social regeneration even more dangerous in Terhune's eyes.[22] For how could the "unsophisticated" southerners Grace Leigh represented resist those northerners so skilled in the art of deception? Louise Wynne, for example, the personification of the northern reform movement, exploits Grace's hunger for knowledge in much the same way the abolitionist exploited the slave's extreme religiosity.[23] Appealing to Grace's vanity, playing to her need for attention, Louise stealthily introduces the idea of rebellion into Grace's mind, with the intention of infecting the South with her subversive ideology and undermining its key institutions of home and family. Both feminist and abolitionist, Terhune implied, were dedicated to the destruction of southern society; both preyed on the unsuspecting, encouraged dissatisfaction, and endorsed rebellion as the means to a better world (303).

Although Grace is eventually reclaimed for the South through the tireless efforts of her sister-in-law, May—"I am not a slave, nor are you, and no sophistry should mislead us into making such a concession," May convinces Grace—her temporary seduction by northern doctrine issued a clear warning to Terhune's predominantly white middle- and upper-class audience, that segment of the female population Terhune believed would be most susceptible to ideological sedition (303). Grace's explanation for her transgression summarized Terhune's apprehensions about the limited moral capacity of southern women of privilege and also prescribed preventive measures: "Had I read fewer books; had introspection been less of a study with me; had I looked more into the hearts and lives of others; sued for information from those whose experience was superior to mine," Grace confesses regretfully, "the duration of my delusion would have been shortened." As it was, "an obstinacy" kept her attention focused on the North, on the artistic and the intellectual, to the detriment of her plantation community (179). Only when Grace realizes that Louise's continual immersion in French, Latin, and German classics as well as the writings of Goethe, Kant, and Fichte is "a species of dissipation" and "incom-

22. Terhune was not alone in this perception; many southerners were convinced of the seditious content of northern reform ideology. See Hilldrup, "Cold War Against the Yankees"; and Brown, *The Sentimental Novel*, 1. More recently, David S. Reynolds has discovered a darker side to the literature of northern antebellum reformers. See Reynolds, *Beneath the American Renaissance: The Subversive Imagination in the Age of Emerson and Melville* (New York, 1988).

23. *Cf.* Hentz, *The Planter's Northern Bride*, and McIntosh, *The Lofty and the Lowly*.

patible with the discharge of more sacred duties" does she find inner peace (119).

Certainly Terhune did not intend to come out against female education. Perhaps the best educated of the five southern domestic novelists—she boasted that her father instructed her tutor to educate her as if she were a boy preparing for college—Terhune viewed the expansion of women's intellectual opportunities as critical to the continued viability of southern institutions.[24] It was, rather, the sacrifice of "true affections" to "pure intellect" that Terhune deplored.[25] Predictably, once Grace accepts her femininity as defined by southern convention, she discovers it holds a wealth of potential for personal fulfillment. "A woman with a full, satisfied heart has no unhealthy thirst for pleasure, no haunting thoughts to flee," Grace concludes. "Nor is her intellect necessarily cramped because she has, in hackneyed parlance, 'no higher ambition.'" On the contrary, "the true woman . . . will cultivate every faculty, moral and mental" (118). In retrospect, Grace considers writing an appendix to Louise's book to rebut its dangerous argument: "Women! Sisters! in piling the blazing beacons that signal your resistance to thralldom old as the earth and time—take heed lest you trample out the fires upon your own hearth-stones" (334).

Terhune's repeated references to slavery were hardly coincidental; *Moss-side* serves simultaneously as a direct criticism of the despised northern reform movement of women's rights as well as an indirect defense of the South's peculiar institution. While Terhune, the dutiful daughter of Samuel Hawes, conscientiously confined her discussion of slavery to the abstract (the Whig party had banned discussion of slavery as early as 1840), as a self-styled defender of southern culture she could not let northern propaganda such as *Uncle Tom's Cabin* stand unchallenged. Grace's flirtation with women's rights provided Terhune with the perfect vehicle through which she could respond to charges leveled by antislavery activists without violating her inherited political principles; in describing the deleterious impact feminism exerted on the American home, Terhune appropriated a favorite argument of male propagandists,

24. Terhune, *Marion Harland's Autobiography*, 97.
25. This theme was central to Terhune's career, especially after the Civil War. See Florine Thayer McCray, "Marion Harland at Home," *Ladies' Home Journal*, IV (August, 1887), 3; and Sanborn, "Mary Virginia Terhune," 624–25. See also Terhune, "Domestic Infelicity," 312–20.

that in its purest form, southern slavery resembled nothing more than a well-ordered family.[26] Louise's "emancipation" from matrimonial bondage—she ignores her husband and allows a nurse to rear their child in order to pursue her literary career "unencumbered"—is suggestive of the chaos that would result on a national level should slavery be abolished; likewise, Grace's eventual realization that woman finds her greatest freedom through marriage reaffirms the distinctive organization of the South as that most conducive to social stability.[27] That Grace discovers the hidden strengths of dependence and recognizes the symbiotic relationship inherent within the bond of matrimony both acknowledged and reaffirmed Terhune's conservative attitude toward both male and female and black and white relations.[28]

To a great extent, Terhune's anxiety pertaining to the future of southern femininity hinged on her own experiences as a southern woman. Grace Leigh's battle for moral and intellectual independence, like that of all Terhune's heroines, was largely autobiographical. While there is no indication that Terhune was ever tempted to follow the example of fellow southerners Sarah and Angelina Grimké and join the ranks of northern reformers, her unpublished correspondence reveals an inner turbulence directly related to her domestic responsibilities.[29] "A man," Terhune wrote Virginia Eppes Dance in 1851, "goes into the broad open world to battle, stimulated by the presence and influence of his fellows, his every action has a witness and is censured or approved. . . . Woman finds her warfare within." Observers frequently failed to recognize "the battles agonizing and terrible" that women faced daily, Terhune told her "ever-dear" friend. "The victories" achieved within that "penetralia" were recorded only by "the angels who have seen and sympathized." When woman dies,

26. See Taylor, *Cavalier and Yankee*, 146–48, 162–76; Ruoff, "Southern Womanhood," 18–48; and Dew, "On the Characteristic Differences Between the Sexes."

27. *Cf.* Terhune, *Alone*, 226–30.

28. Terhune likened the matrimonial bond to "the old tale of the oak and the ivy": Man "the stalwart trunk, roughened by countless winters," and woman "the fragile creeper [who] loves the coarse bark upon which [she] fastens [her]self." Grace declares, "Let it be ivy to the last!" See Terhune, *Moss-side*, 429–30.

29. See Gerda Lerner's excellent biography, *The Grimké Sisters from South Carolina: Pioneers for Women's Rights and Abolitionism* (New York, 1967). Mary Kelley believes that Terhune's turmoil was generated by her frustration at being female. Kelley, *Private Woman*, 93–94.

Terhune mused, "the tide of selfish mortals rolls on," oblivious to the fact that "a martyr has gone from their midst."[30] Wallowing in sentimentalism, Terhune wondered out loud what point there was in carrying on.

Mary Virginia Terhune's melancholy was relatively short-lived; indeed, within that same anguished letter, she ridiculed her "rhapsodical" prose—"I laugh that one who knows human nature as well as I do, should have dared to put such nonsense upon paper," she confessed with some embarrassment. But she never forgot her dark night of the soul, and with characteristic solicitude, she took pains to ensure that her southern sisters might emerge from the inevitable period of self-doubt equally resilient.[31] Turning her hand to fiction in 1853, Terhune used her considerable skill to shore up the foundations of southern femininity, borrowing liberally from her own life and the lives of her friends in an effort to tell stories that would both amuse and inform. "My sympathy with young girls is so strong," Terhune wrote near the end of her career, "that I think with pain, of the chances that my mature matronhood may seem to them to put a barrier between us."[32]

Still, while Terhune managed to avoid the frustration suffered by many intelligent middle- and upper-class Victorian women by channeling her literary talents into an appropriate arena, she remained wary of the myriad temptations to shirk the "sacred obligations" of home and hearth that lesser women faced daily.[33] *Moss-side*, which warned of the dire consequences of feminine dissatisfaction, was written, not insignificantly, after Terhune first visited New York City and imbibed a heady draught of fame and fortune. "Since my arrival here," she wrote Virginia Eppes Dance in October, 1855, "I have had a succession of pleasures, as delicious as unexpected."[34] Ensconced in the home of her publisher, J. C. Derby, Ter-

---

30. Terhune to Dance, November 7, 1851, in Terhune Papers, Duke.

31. *Ibid.*

32. Mary Virginia Terhune to a friend, November 11, 1878, in Barrett Author Collection.

33. Catherine Clinton describes the frustration suffered by many aristocratic southern females in *The Plantation Mistress*, 36–86. While Clinton's study stops at approximately 1830, her observations are applicable to the subsequent decade. See also Scott, *The Southern Lady*, 3–44. Elizabeth Muhlenfeld profiles one of the more eloquent female representatives of the southern aristocracy in *Mary Boykin Chesnut*.

34. Terhune to Dance, October 18, 1855, in Terhune Papers, Duke.

hune had occasion to meet, among others, the poet Bayard Taylor, the juvenile author Samuel Griswold Goodrich, who published under the name "Peter Parley," and the journalist G. P. Morris. She went to her first opera accompanied by the domestic novelists Caroline Cheesbro' and Elizabeth Oakes Smith, attended several plays, and spent her mornings answering the flood of letters addressed to the author of *Alone* and *The Hidden Path*.[35] If Terhune had ever questioned her decision to embark upon a literary career, her "northern sojourn" laid her doubts to rest. "I may afford to rest now for a little while, from active labor, since my last book has already reached its fifteenth thousand and is still, as speculators say—'going up,'" she wrote Dance, observing that *Alone* had "received a new impetus from the success of its younger sister."[36]

Still, for all Terhune's fascination with her new milieu, she expressed grave doubts as to the morality of northern society. "I have gone hungry for weeks for a gospel sermon, loathing the whipped syllabubs and frosted sawdust of the essays dignified by the name of pulpit eloquence," she confessed to Dance. "I have had my ears filled with semi-infidel and Deistical discussions, heard the sneer of the skeptic and the ranting of the Spiritualist." The "hideous formalism, the hollow mockery of Unitarian theology" particularly galled the young southerner. "Out with speculation!" she proclaimed. "The whole truth and nothing but the truth." The dissipated climate of the North left the novelist "sick and weary at heart," clinging in desperation to "the noble and pure Belief" in which she had been nurtured. Yet though Terhune unequivocally condemned much of what she encountered above the Mason-Dixon Line, she was aware that she had to make some compromises if she were to maintain her popularity in the North, and that prospect disturbed her. "If ever, by deed or look I assent to a contrary opinion," she pledged somberly, "may thought and action be denied me until I acknowledge my sin."[37] The warnings against the seductive powers of northern society contained in *Moss-side*, the novel Terhune undertook immediately after her visit to New York, suggest that this was precisely what she was about.

35. Terhune, *Marion Harland's Autobiography*, 280–84.
36. Terhune to Dance, October 18, 1855, in Terhune Papers, Duke.
37. *Ibid.*

The same year Mary Virginia Terhune reveled in the hospitality of her "excellent friend and publisher" at his residence upon the Hudson, "a few miles from the great Babel of New York," Augusta Evans, a twenty-year-old from Mobile, Alabama, with whom Terhune would become closely identified, quietly issued her first novel, *Inez: A Tale of the Alamo*.[38] Unlike Terhune's first effort, however, which sold over fifty thousand copies and established its author as a leader within the field of popular literature, *Inez* failed to find an audience. While *Godey's* optimistically predicted that the novel would "doubtless have a good run during the present excited state of the public mind on the vexed questions of religious faith and observance," the *Southern Quarterly Review* offered a more typical response.[39] "There is not a natural character and scarcely a natural phrase in the whole volume," the anonymous reviewer stated flatly, and that assessment and others like it convinced many potential readers not to give the young southerner a hearing.[40] Marred by dense prose, an unrealistic setting, and a plot so complex as to be laughable, *Inez* contained few hints of its author's vivid imagination and natural storytelling ability. In fact, there is some suggestion that Augusta Evans' notable failure made it difficult for her four years later to market her second—and much better—novel, *Beulah*. J. C. Derby recalled that when Evans approached him with her manuscript in the summer of 1859, she admitted that she had offered the book to other publishers. "She had sent the manuscript some time previous from Mobile to the Appletons," and they had declined to take a risk on an author who had a reputation for limited sales.[41]

Contemporary criticism tends to confirm nineteenth-century opinion. On the rare occasions that *Inez* commands scholarly attention, it is as an example of the worst excesses of sentimental fiction rather than as an early indication of Augusta Evans' literary genius. Alexander Cowie, for example, called the novel "a crudely assembled story with little characterization, no humor, and inferior stylistic quality." He admitted, "Sentiment it contains, but much of the author's energy is drawn off into an account

38. *Ibid.*; Augusta Evans, *Inez: A Tale of the Alamo* (1855; rpr. New York, 1884).

39. Unsigned review of *Inez* in *Godey's* quoted in Nina Baym, *Novels, Readers, and Reviewers: Responses to Fiction in Antebellum America* (Ithaca, 1984), 219.

40. Review of Augusta Evans' *Inez* in *Southern Quarterly Review*, XI (1855), 541–42.

41. Derby, *Fifty Years Among Authors*, 389–99.

of the siege of the Alamo and tirades against Catholicism."[42] Evans' biographer William Fidler offered even harsher words in 1951: "The sheltered Puritan authoress was incapable of responding to the demands of
her story, particularly the love theme." Her inexperience resulted in
"stilted, self-conscious language" and a "zealous" tone reminiscent of a
"modern Red Cross Knight armed with reason."[43] More recently, Nina
Baym has lamented *Inez*'s failure to conform to the domestic genre: "It
begins as a conventional women's fiction but changes into a melodramatic
attack on Catholicism," Baym writes. Complicated by a bevy of heroines
instead of the usual one and a plethora of rather unconventional villains,
Inez is fatally flawed by its use of "scholarly dispute" as its climax. The
action "peaks in a fifteen-page debate" concerning "the doctrine of inter-
cession and other points of Catholic versus Protestant theology," render-
ing a potentially "exciting" novel a crashing bore.[44]

But in rejecting *Inez* on purely artistic grounds, modern scholars ignore the novel's infinite importance as a piece of proslavery propaganda.
Written in 1850, when Evans was fifteen and had just returned from a
four-year stint in San Antonio with her family, *Inez* affords an eyewitness
account of life in wartime Texas as well as a record of its southern settlers'
changing attitudes toward the North. Furthermore, *Inez* provides a window into the mind of one of the South's foremost female literary propagandists, foreshadowing the thematic concerns of the novelist's mature
work, most notably *Macaria; or, Altars of Sacrifice* (1864), and giving the
earliest articulation to the profoundly conservative view of society that
Evans promulgated throughout her lengthy career.[45] Stylistically less
sound than the work of first-generation southern domestic novelists or
even that of contemporary Mary Virginia Terhune—*Inez* incorporated
elements of the historical novel, the sermon, the epic poem, and the political tract—the novel represents one of the more creative and ambitious
interpretations of the causes of northern and southern hostilities found
not only in antebellum southern domestic fiction but in the whole of
southern literature.

42. Cowie, *The Rise of the American Novel*, 430–31.
43. Fidler, "Confederate Propagandist," 43.
44. Baym, *Woman's Fiction*, 281–82.
45. Augusta Evans, *Macaria: or, Altars of Sacrifice* (1864; rpr. New York, 1896). See
Fidler, "Confederate Propagandist," 32–44; and Fidler, *Augusta Evans Wilson*, 84–104.

For all its innovation, however, *Inez* projected a vision of the South wholly congruent with domestic convention. That Evans set her defense of southern culture in the West instead of the more typical Deep South, that she made her argument through historical analogy rather than senti-mental allegory, merely made her initial iteration of the domestic message all the more intriguing. The bookish Evans, who came to symbolize southern resistance to northern oppression, could hardly content herself with simply imitating her domestic forebears; on the contrary, she sensed from early on that she was destined to make an original contribution to southern history and culture. "I remember rambling about the crumbling walls of the Alamo, recalling all its bloody horrors," Evans explained in 1858. Watching "the last rays of the setting sun gild the hill-tops, creep down the sides, and slowly sink into the beautiful waves of the San Anto-nio River," surveying "the quietly beautiful valley, with its once noble Alameda of stately cottonwoods," Evans was overcome by emotion. "My heart throbbed," she told the writer Mary Forrest, "and I wondered if I should be able some day to write about it for those who had never looked upon [such] a scene." At that moment, atop "the moldering, melancholy pile" that symbolized the supreme sacrifice of Texas patriots, Evans real-ized the distinctive pattern of life below the Mason-Dixon Line and em-braced her future as a defender of southern culture.[46]

Personal experience and observation informed Evans's rather unusual perspective on northern and southern relations. Born into an aristocratic southern family in Columbus, Georgia, she grew up listening to tales of two of that town's most famous citizens, Mirabeau Bonaparte Lamar, who was elected president of Texas in 1838, and James W. Fannin, who was martyred by Santa Anna at Goliad in 1837.[47] In 1845, when her father, Matt Evans, a financially inept planter, proposed to follow his townsmen west in an effort to remake the fortune he had lost through a combination of economic depression and natural disaster, Augusta responded enthusi-astically. Years later, she recalled the excitement of the journey to Texas. "I seem, even now, to be winding once more through that lovely valley, holding my mother's hand tightly, as she repeated beautiful descriptions

46. Freeman, *Women of the South*, 329–30.
47. See William P. Fidler, "The Life and Works of Augusta Evans Wilson" (Ph.D. dissertation, University of Chicago, 1947), 5–6.

from Thomson's 'Seasons' and Cowper's 'Task,'" she told Mary Forrest in 1860. "Again I see the white flock slowly descending the hills, and bleating as they wound home."[48]

Upon reaching their destination, however, the Evans family, particularly the women, met with bitter disappointment. San Antonio in 1845 bore no resemblance whatsoever to Columbus; on the contrary, its unkempt population, filthy streets, and general air of decay was the very antithesis of the stable, hierarchical society the immigrants had left behind. Women wore revealing clothing, men drank heavily and fought in the streets, church attendance was irregular, and, perhaps most disconcerting, Mexicans consorted openly with blacks. While the peripatetic Frederick Law Olmsted found much to admire about "the first city of Texas" on his 1853 visit—"We have no city, except perhaps New Orleans, that can vie in point of picturesque interest that attaches to odd and antiquated foreignness with San Antonio," Olmsted wrote in 1857—evidence suggests that Evans' impressions paradoxically were more in keeping with those of the future mayor of San Antonio, Mexican aristocrat Juan Seguin, who once described San Antonio as "the receptacle of the scum of society."[49]

Matters were complicated for the new arrivals by the outbreak of war between the United States and Mexico. By the spring of 1846, San Antonio was occupied by U.S. troops and supply trains, at times swelling the prewar population of 2,500 to over 40,000. While some enterprising San Antonians managed to use the war to their advantage, selling supplies to U.S. forces at a considerable profit, Matt Evans with his usual flair for business failed to gain a single contract. Perhaps it was Evans' inability to prosper under the most auspicious of circumstances that convinced him that the West was not for him. Perhaps it was the realization that San Antonio's proximity to the Nueces made it unusually vulnerable to attack. The Mexican threat was accentuated by constant rumors of Indian uprisings, made all the more frightening by reports that the Indians, unlike the Mexicans, tortured women and children indiscriminately. For whatever

48. Freeman, *Women of the South*, 32.

49. Fidler, "Life and Works," 9. See also Frederick Law Olmsted, *A Journey Through Texas: or, A Saddle-trip on the Southwestern Frontier* (New York, 1859), 150–63. David Montejano describes territorial San Antonio in *Anglos and Mexicans in the Making of Texas, 1836–1986* (Austin, 1987), 24–49; Seguin is quoted on p. 27.

reason, in early 1849 Matt Evans again moved his family, this time to Mobile, Alabama, where he hoped to find work in the thriving cotton market. His wife and eldest daughter, who had long hungered for a return to the order and civility of the Deep South, greeted the move with enthusiasm.[50]

In *Inez*, Augusta Evans explored the roots of contemporary sectionalism against the backdrop of the 1836 Texas War for Independence from Mexico. Drawing an elaborate parallel between the circumstances leading up to the Battle of the Alamo and the current struggle between North and South over the expansion of slavery into the territories, she argued that in both instances innocent men and women fell victim to political treachery. In the first case, Evans asserted, noble settlers were forced to adopt the ideology of Mexico, specifically the Catholic religion, in order to be permitted to live in peace; in the second, southerners were being asked to surrender, or severely curtail, their right to perpetuate their indigenous institution of slavery. That Mexico was opposed to slavery in its possessions, that Texans intent on establishing a vigorous slave trade were in violation of territorial law, had no bearing on the precocious writer's belief that she had struck upon an important historical truth. Writing at a time and in a region where not a few southerners doubted the wisdom of secession, Evans became convinced of the essential similarity between 1836 and 1850 and held her findings out as a harbinger of the future.[51]

On one level, *Inez* records the trials and tribulations that the dispossessed southern aristocrats Florence Hamilton and her cousin Mary encounter at the hands of Mexican Catholics. Forced to leave the rarefied atmosphere of an exclusive boarding school upon the sudden financial ruin of Florence's father, the two girls must choose between moving in with less affluent relatives or accompanying Mr. Hamilton to Texas, where he optimistically plans to regain his fortune. Their spirit of adventure wins out; in what seems like a few weeks, Florence, Mary, Mr. Hamilton, a maiden aunt, and a handful of servants find themselves in a crude adobe dwelling overlooking the central plaza of San Antonio. No stranger to

50. Fidler, "Life and Works," 8–10. Evans' niece reported that Evans and her mother "persuaded Mr. Evans to return to Alabama because of the prevalence of immorality and violence in or near San Antonio."

51. See Potter, *The Impending Crisis*, 51–62, 86–107; and Don E. Fehrenbacher, *The South and Three Sectional Crises* (Baton Rouge, 1980), 25–44.

hard work, the girls toil diligently to wrest some semblance of comfort from the harsh Texas environment. After considerable effort, they replicate the ordered household they cherished back home. "A sideboard, covered with glass of various kinds, and a few handsome pieces of plate" stood in one corner; "a range of shelves, filled with books, . . . a pair of neat China vases, decked with brilliant prairie flowers" completed the furnishings of the front apartment. "How homelike, fresh, and beautiful it seemed!" Evans enthused. "An air of comfort, American, southern comfort pervaded the whole." [52]

But if Florence and Mary manage to subdue their private world, they are less successful in taming the world outside. Almost immediately after their arrival in San Antonio, the girls are menaced by Mexican Catholics seeking, among other things, to convert them to the false religion. The weak-willed Aunt Lizzy quickly falls victim to the incessant proselytizing of the wicked Father Mazzolin, the de facto ruler of San Antonio; her observance of fast days and other dietary restrictions throws the Hamilton household into an uproar. Still, even a casualty within the immediate family fails to alert Florence and Mary to the severity of the Catholic threat. They try to rationalize Aunt Lizzy's conversion as a matter of personal preference. "Aunt Lizzy has every opportunity of informing herself on this important question," Mary reasons. "Yet she prefers the easier method, of committing her conscience to the care of the priest; she has chosen her path in life, and determinedly closes her eyes to every other" (47).

As time passes, Florence and Mary come to realize that the Catholic church controls the very future of their community, dictating who is to marry whom, who shall be baptized, who will die in a state of grace or be condemned to eternal perdition. There is no shortage of stories concerning abuses perpetrated on both Catholics and Protestants. A fellow southerner, for example, tells the incredulous Florence that she fears Father Mazzolin will take her orphan ward from her if she fails to pay the priest his usual baptismal fee, even though the woman is a Protestant and intends to rear her ward in that faith (45–46). Another woman confesses that Mazzolin used spiritual blackmail to force her to marry her wealthy husband

---

52. Evans, *Inez*, 41–42. Hereinafter cited parenthetically by page number in the text.

in order that he himself might profit financially (60–62). When Mr. Hamilton falls gravely ill, the two girls learn the lengths to which Catholics will go to claim an additional southern soul. Over the course of Hamilton's illness, Father Mazzolin regularly sneaks into the sickroom and uses his wiles to convince the invalid of the evil of his ways. "You would usurp the prerogatives of Jehovah," Mary Hamilton tells the crafty priest, "but your threat is in vain. You cannot bless or damn my uncle at will" (140).

But while Mary Hamilton recognizes the palpable falsehood of Catholic doctrine, which she exposes with great enthusiasm, she is largely powerless to break its hold over the residents of San Antonio (113–27). When she and Florence open a school for the children of southern immigrants, Father Mazzolin shuts it down. Mazzolin is equally effective in preventing the immigration of a Protestant minister, one who could, according to Mary Hamilton, "effectually stem the tide of superstition and degradation that now flows unimpeded through this community" (46). Left without a means through which to "carry a light to this benighted race" of Catholics, Florence and Mary affirm their determination to "strive more and more earnestly to obtain perfect control" of themselves in hopes that they might then be better able to assist others; yet the two are increasingly convinced that their struggle is hopeless (47–48). Although they might well enjoin southern mothers to guard their children carefully, "for surrounded by these influences it will be difficult to prevent contamination," they realize that mere words are inadequate against a power that promises miracles (51).

Evans used the Hamiltons' personal struggle against Catholic tyranny to explore her broader concern: the relevance of the Texas War for Independence to the ongoing debate over slavery in the territories. Employing a rather simplistic formula that equated all Texans with southern expansionists and all Mexicans with northern antislavery forces, Evans argued that just as Texans rebelled against Mexico's attempts to subjugate them to the dominant Catholic ideology, so would southerners revolt against tyrannical abolitionism. General Santa Anna's "subversion" of the "liberal constitution of 1824," which, according to Evans, directly precipitated the Texas rebellion, had particular resonance to those southern expansionists who felt betrayed by President Zachary Taylor's failure to come out against the Wilmot Proviso, which threatened the future of slavery in the West.[53] Like the black-hearted Mexican, Evans implied, Taylor initially had promised to champion southern institutions, specifically slavery, against northern opposition. Like Santa Anna, the "arch-deceiver," Taylor had reversed his position for the sake of political expediency and instituted a tyrannical regime, and like Santa Anna, or so Augusta Evans believed, Taylor and his antislavery advisers had pushed southern patriots to the point of no return (52–53, 94). War "will most inevitably ensue," a friend of the Hamiltons warns, "for total submission [is demanded] by Santa Anna, and the Texans are not a people to comply with such conditions." Another concurs, "We will not submit to [Santa Anna's] crushing yoke" (53).

Ultimately, armed conflict proves the only solution to prevent continued Mexican oppression. In February, 1836, "the Alamo was garrisoned." On March 2, the Texans declared their independence and "girded themselves for a desperate conflict." "Mechanic, statesman, plowboy, poet, pressed forward to the ranks, emulous of priority alone," Evans wrote. "A small but intrepid band, they defied the tyrant who had subverted their liberties" (94). Learning that General Santa Anna is marching on San Antonio with up to eight thousand troops, the Hamiltons reluctantly evacuate the city, but not before Lieutenant Colonel William B. Travis and his band of volunteers have vowed to defend the church-fortress to the death. In phrases reminiscent of those she would later use to describe the battles of the Civil War, Evans depicted the tragedy: "The sun went down as it were in a sea of blood. . . . Black clouds rolled up and veiled the heavens in gloom. . . . Still the fury of the onset abated not: the Alamo shook to its firm basis. Despairingly the novel band raised its eyes to the blackened sky: 'God help us!' Then a deep voice rung clearly out, high above the surround din: 'Comrades, we are lost! Let us die like brave men!'" (242).

"When shall peace and good will reign throughout the world? When shall hatred, revenge, and malice die? And oh! when shall desolating war forever cease, and the bloody records of the past be viewed as monstrous distortions of a maddened brain?" the young novelist asked rhetorically. "When the polity of the world is changed . . . when statesmen cease their political . . . intrigues" (170–71). Yet Evans and much of her southern

---

53. See, for example, Fehrenbacher, *The South and Three Sectional Crises*, 25–44; and Potter, *The Impending Crisis*, 96. In *Inez*, Augusta Evans merely expressed the anxiety that permeated her surroundings.

audience believed that with the South's decreasing influence in national government, "the millennium" would never come. With a majority in neither the House nor the Senate, the South was at the mercy of antislavery interests, or so the argument went. Zachary Taylor's virtual silence on the issue of slavery in the West seemed part of a larger plot to render the South politically—and economically—impotent. Like Santa Anna's dastardly attempt to impose Catholic rule on the Protestant settlers of Texas, Taylor's inability or unwillingness to settle the "Negro question" once and for all was viewed by the politically astute Evans as the ultimate outrage, one that "true-hearted patriots" could not accept without compromising their "sacred honor."[54]

Ironically, in using Catholicism as a metaphor for northern abolitionism, Augusta Evans inadvertently subverted a line of argument that the anti-Catholic Harriet Beecher Stowe had once employed to criticize southern slavery. As Thomas Gossett notes in *"Uncle Tom's Cabin" and American Culture*, Stowe censured Catholicism in the same language and for the same reasons she condemned slavery: it was a hierarchical, legalistic system that denied the essential humanity of its adherents.[55] Comparing southern slaveholders with Catholic ecclesiastics, Stowe portrayed both as close-minded, manipulative, and fundamentally evil. In making her proslavery argument, Evans simply reversed the terms of Stowe's equation, asserting that Protestants (or southerners) were "the more tolerant of the two sects" (168). Catholics (or northerners) Evans averred, refused to tolerate any doctrinal deviation, to the detriment of their followers and the community at large. "I fear the extension of papal doctrines," Mary Hamilton asserts, "because liberty of conscience was never yet allowed where sufficient power was vested in the Roman Catholic clergy to compel submission. . . . Fierce, intolerable tyranny is . . . exercised where their jurisdiction is" (168).

"To preserve the balance of power in ecclesiastical affairs is the only aim of Protestants," Augusta Evans claimed, making indirect reference to the state of national politics. Arguing that Catholics (or antislavery activists) hopelessly prejudiced the masses against Protestant (or southern) in-

---

54. Potter, *The Impending Crisis*, 93.

55. Gossett, *"Uncle Tom's Cabin" and American Culture*, 55–56. In time, Gossett notes, Stowe became more tolerant of Catholics; ironically, so did Evans.

stitutions in order to advance their own greed and ambition, Evans claimed, "We but contend for the privilege of . . . flashing the glorious flambeau of truth into the dark recesses of ignorance and superstition" (168). The common man, if given a choice, would cast his lot with the South. It was because the Catholic hierarchy realized the precariousness of their hold over their followers that they appealed to their fears, using superstition to preempt any possible dissension. By predicting dire consequences and promising unremitting woe to those who contradicted Catholic doctrine, the Catholic clergy maintained its fragile hold over its communicants. "Begirt with darkening, crushing influence," Evans argued, Catholics were "effectually secluded from even a wandering ray of light." Even the writings of "the prince of novelists," Walter Scott, were forbidden to communicants, the young southerner wrote in horror. With such a dearth of information, it was no wonder that the "laity" accepted ecclesiastical dogma as truth (153).[56]

Undoubtedly, Evans' hostility toward the North was motivated in part by her father's repeated economic failure. In the mid-1830s, for example, the Evans family lived in one of the most outstanding homes in Columbus. Sherwood Hall, which came to be known as "Matt's Folly," boasted among its amenities solid mahogany doors with knobs of sterling silver. Less than ten years later, however, Evans lost his thriving mercantile business, the bank foreclosed on Sherwood Hall, and family possessions, including some thirty-six slaves, were sold at auction. Matt Evans was forced to go begging for employment. As William Fidler observes, the North was hardly responsible for all of Evans' problems; flood, fire, and the lowly boll weevil were equally important, although admittedly less appealing, precipitants of his financial ruin. Still, Evans himself placed more emphasis on the various economic "panics" of the late 1830s and early 1840s, asserting like many similarly affected southerners that the prolonged depression, which caused cotton prices to plunge from fifteen cents to a little over three cents per pound in seven years, was directly attributable to northern greed and corruption. In this scenario of victimization, Evans' inability to get a contract to supply the U.S. Army in Texas, an occurrence that Fidler credits to his incompetence, was but another example of a

---

56. Catholics were forbidden to read Scott, Evans argued, because he portrayed the Roman Catholic church as the corrupt institution it was.

northern conspiracy to ruin the South.[57] Augusta Evans' preoccupation with Catholic conspiracy in *Inez* is instructive: at the novel's end, Florence discovers that Father Mazzolin has agreed to betray his own flock to General Santa Anna in return for absolute control over San Antonio and the right to marry a Protestant, or southern, sympathizer against her will (264–65).

A series of four articles that Evans wrote on northern and southern literature for the Mobile *Daily Advertiser* in October and November, 1859, suggests that she was not immune to her father's line of thinking.[58] Although she professed to feel no animosity toward the North about the poor reception of *Inez*—she told J. C. Derby that she "was not discouraged" by the failure of her first novel to make the equivalent of the modern best-seller list, because she herself was dissatisfied with *Inez*—her discussion argues otherwise, indicating that she, like Maria McIntosh, viewed what she perceived as northern aggression in deeply personal terms.[59] Considering the "difficulties and embarrassments" of the southern writer, which she remarked were "far more numerous and harder to surmount than are to be found impeding the progress of an author who happens to reside in any other part of the civilized world," Evans singled out the North for blame. "The North," Evans wrote, "believes that no good can come out of the Southern latitudes, and will not read anything to which a Southern odor attaches." While Evans argued that southerners should not restrict their literary efforts to their region (literature "in the production of which there is no higher object in view than that of contributing to a literature purely local," she maintained, was almost always of inferior quality), she admitted that this "approach" held particular appeal in these days of unbridled northern hostility. "If we are not cautious," Evans continued, "a mass of Southern literature will have accumulated, before many years shall have passed away, which will not only do no credit to the South, but of which Southerners themselves will be ashamed."[60]

"If a book, paper or periodical is not read," Evans asserted bravely in

57. See Fidler, "Life and Works," 3–5

58. See Evans, "Northern Literature," Mobile *Daily Advertiser*, October 11 and 16, 1859, and Evans, "Southern Literature," Mobile *Daily Advertiser*, October 30 and November 6, 1859; Fidler, "Confederate Propagandist," 33–35.

59. Derby, *Fifty Years Among Authors*, 389–90.

60. Evans, "Southern Literature," Mobile *Daily Advertiser*, October 30, 1859.

her November 6 installment of the newspaper series, "the fact itself is a pretty sure indication that it is not worth reading." Still, the domestic novelist who waited four years before she peddled her second volume, immediately qualified her generalization. In the first place, she argued, southerners typically did not embrace the offerings of their fellows with the unconditional enthusiasm that the southern writer might have desired: "An acquaintance with [southern literature] is not sought, nobody has a thought for it, or if so, the thought is expressed in some remark such as 'Well, what a *pity* it is that the South cannot support a Southern literary newspaper or monthly, while the North has scores of them.'" In the second place, Evans continued, northern critics more often than not failed to apportion their praise or censure judiciously. "We have seen much Northern criticism of Southern production written evidently in view of the favorable effects which flattery is likely to make," she sniffed, adding that the "appeals" to southern "vanity have in some instances been followed by the cry of triumph which they were intended to draw out." But while Evans concluded that it was bad form for a writer to chastise the unresponsive public—"Let a public speaker . . . denounce his audience for not attending to his eloquence, and two reasons immediately spring into existence for neglecting him, where only one existed before"—she could not shake the feeling that somehow or other her work had been sabotaged.[61]

But if Evans' 1859 series betrayed her frustration with her moribund literary career, it also revealed her growing talent for political propaganda.[62] In her four newspaper articles comparing northern and southern literature, Evans skillfully reworked the conspiracy themes she had introduced in *Inez* to make a convincing argument that the North was using its literary hegemony to reduce the South to "provincial status." By encouraging southerners to write exclusively "southern" literature, northern publishers consciously repressed the development of southern genius and ensured that the South would remain inferior to the North in the world of national and international letters. "We desire that what proceeds from Southern pens shall be read wherever the English language is spoken and read," Evans declared. "We desire that our histories shall be written in

61. *Ibid.*, October 30, November 6, 1859.
62. Fidler, "Confederate Propagandist," 33–35.

language whose style will fall under the most severe rules of literary taste." Directing her readers to recognize attempts by the "degenerate" northern press to engage the South in heated debate over "insane" matters as an obvious attempt to divert southern talent from meaningful literary endeavor, Evans called her fellows to action.[63] "Could a Southern writer be more patriotically engaged," she wondered, than one who rose "above special pleading and wr[o]te for the people who speak the English language?" Could anything be more disconcerting to the North than for the South to resist its "insane attempts" to subjugate the collective consciousness of the southern people?[64] Clearly, Evans thought not.

Antisouthern sentiment within the northern publishing community, however, was only one of Evans' concerns; she was equally disturbed by what she believed was the North's concerted effort to undermine southern institutions, particularly slavery, through the circulation of sensational literature. What "daily floats over the country from northern sources, is a disgrace to its authors and insulting to the intelligence of the American people." Northern writers, the novelist continued, were concerned not with the truth but with what would sell: "periodicals are filled with startling, distorted, and in many instances, utterly untruthful details."[65] In "the Dead Sea" of northern literature, Evans remarked, the "bruiser and the Senator are raised to a political equality" and the "low sensual African is dragged up from his normal position and violently thrust into an importance which the Creator has denied him by indications as strong as physical inferiority and mental incapacity could make them. . . . The demons of pandemonium are actually prowling through the Northern States, making efforts to tear down fabrics which genius, guided by the wisdom and experience of past ages, has erected," Evans continued, citing a "*family* newspaper containing the photograph of a distinguished statesman on the same page with that of an African murderer" as evidence of the North's diabolical plan to abolish racial segregation.[66] If distinctions between blacks and whites were not upheld in literature, Evans reasoned,

63. Evans, "Southern Literature," Mobile *Daily Advertiser*, November 6, 1859.
64. *Ibid.*, October 30, 1859.
65. Evans, "Northern Literature," Mobile *Daily Advertiser*, October 10, 1859.
66. *Ibid.*, October 16, 1859.

soon they would be similarly ignored in reality to the detriment of national harmony. "No attentive reader," she wrote piously, "can fail to see [northern literature's] decided tendency toward evil."[67]

"What excuse can possibly be given for deluging the world with such monstrous trash?" Evans queried. "What sort of . . . literature is that which seeks to render all classes of society dissatisfied with their normal condition?"[68] Surveying the spectrum of southern society, the novelist found little to criticize and much to extol. Unlike the chaotic North, the South enjoyed a high degree of social stability generated and reinforced by its indigenous institutions; northern writers who clamored for social equality might take notice. "Next to the British aristocrat, we know of no position in the world more desirable than that of the Southern planter," Evans wrote indignantly. "That class of citizens," which the northern press regularly represented as nothing more than cruel taskmasters, was, in fact, "the most enlightened of any in the country," Evans stated. "There is no other class which at present can . . . attend properly to the interests of the country. From the sons of our planters we must again look for the talents, learning and statesmanship" that were so markedly absent from contemporary politics.[69] As things currently stood, everything was misdirected. "We of the South are drifting unconsciously into the wake of a vessel which, if it continues its course, will soon dash to fragments and all on board will be involved in a common destruction."[70]

Invoking the names of Washington, Jefferson, Madison, and "that entire line of [southern] statesmen to Calhoun and Clay," Evans lamented the state of national politics. Without the "conservative" influence of the South, she argued, the nation was easy prey for northern greed and corruption. The "extraordinary dearth of intellect, or rather total lack of intellectual culture now pervading national politics," was symptomatic of the insidious disease that threatened the future of the South and the whole American civilization; politicians' "every breath infuses some deadly poison into the vitals of the nation [they] claim to represent," with the end result being the destruction of the Republic. Only the South's resumption

67. *Ibid.*, October 10, 1859.
68. Evans, "Southern Literature," Mobile *Daily Advertiser*, November 6, 1859.
69. *Ibid.*, October 30, November 6, 1859.
70. Evans, "Northern Literature," Mobile *Daily Advertiser*, October 10, 1859.

of complete control over the mechanism of national politics could avert disaster, Evans implied, though she seemed to realize that this was an impossibility; there was no viable candidate to restore the South's former greatness.[71] "Ah! how the Titans of this century are falling away, sinking from the crested wave of Time, into the vast, echoless depths of Eternity," she wrote wistfully shortly after her passionate denunciation of the North. "In one brief year how many glory-crowned heads have been placed beneath monumental marble. . . . The brightest constellation of the 19th century blotted from our sky."[72]

Augusta Evans' persistent attempts to identify the larger issues of sectional dissent paralleled those of Mary Virginia Terhune and pointed up the conceptual differences between first- and second-generation southern domestic novelists. Like Terhune, Evans believed that the causes of contemporary political debate were deeply rooted in America's social and political culture; like Terhune, Evans refused to attribute the escalation of tensions between North and South solely to the activities of antislavery activists; and like Terhune, Evans used personal experiences and observations as the foundation of her unique political analysis. Whether the danger was of fairly recent origin, emanating, as Terhune would have it, from the various permutations of the northern reform movement, or whether, as Evans opined, it was the logical culmination of a decades-long drive to subjugate the South politically and culturally, they concurred that the South faced a clear and present threat from the North that demanded a unified response from its people. When the two women met in the publishing offices of J. C. Derby shortly after Evans' stunning success with *Beulah* (1859), they found many points of agreement.[73] "I confess I was fascinated by a sort of 'bonhomie,' indescribable but irresistible," Evans wrote in 1862. "She impressed me as a genial, impulsive, noble-souled, warm-hearted Southern woman, par excellence."[74] For her part, Terhune was equally impressed.

71. Evans, "Southern Literature," *ibid.*, November 6, 1859.
72. Augusta Evans to Rachel Lyons, January 21, 1860, in Rachel Lyons Heustis Papers, Southern Historical Collection, University of North Carolina.
73. Derby took Evans under his wing and introduced her to the northern literary community much the same way he had sponsored Terhune four years earlier. See Fidler, *Augusta Evans Wilson*, 72–74.
74. Evans to Janie Tyler, March 14, 1862, in Fidler, *Augusta Evans Wilson*, 88.

Years later, she remembered Evans as "quietly refined in manner and speech, and incredibly unspoiled by the flood of popular favor that had taken her by surprise."[75]

The relatively sophisticated political perspective of the two younger domestic novelists reflected both their superior education and their heightened political awareness.[76] Although Terhune's political philosophy reflected the elitist leanings of Samuel Hawes, whereas Evans' drew directly from Matt Evans' militant expansionism, both writers were convinced that the South and its distinctive culture held the key to national stability. For this reason, they dedicated their efforts to combating what they perceived as northern attempts to undermine the domestic structure of the South, using their pens to protest northern oppression as well as to alert their southern readers of the myriad dangers they faced at northern hands. That their efforts failed to provoke an immediate response from their audience did not deter them. Augusta Evans' persistence in pursuing the publication of her writing in spite of her inauspicious debut is telling. Trying to convince Derby of *Beulah*'s marketability, Evans assured him that "she now thought she had written a story which the public would read, if she could find a publisher."[77] If Derby rejected the manuscript, Evans implied, she would simply offer it to a competitor; she had no intention of returning to Mobile without a contract that would ensure her access to the audience she was determined to reach.

Yet for all the thematic differences between literary generations, the domestic tradition remained remarkably intact. The persistence of the earlier arguments against *Uncle Tom's Cabin*, albeit in revised form, in the antebellum fiction of Mary Virginia Terhune and Augusta Evans is but one indication that all five southern domestic novelists agreed on the fundamental nature of the South and feared that that essence was menaced by an external force. That Terhune and Evans identified that force differently—they viewed Harriet Beecher Stowe's brain child as symptomatic

75. Terhune, *Marion Harland's Autobiography*, 285.

76. Kelley calls Terhune the best educated of the twelve domestic novelists she studies in *Private Woman*, 93. Contemporaries repeatedly remarked upon Evans' vast knowledge; on more than one occasion, she was accused of having "swallowed" an encyclopedia. Freeman, *Women of the South*, 329–30. Fidler speculates that the novelist had a photographic memory. Fidler, *Augusta Evans Wilson*, 21.

77. Derby, *Fifty Years Among Authors*, 389–90.

of the disease rather than the disease itself—is less a challenge to Caroline Gilman, Caroline Hentz, and Maria McIntosh than an affirmation of their collective wisdom. For while the two later writers did indeed rework the agenda set by their domestic forebears to reflect both their individual interests and their particular talents, the vision of a benevolent South they promulgated through their fiction remained wholly congruent with what had come before. Bringing renewed energy and freshness of vision to the problems that polarized the nation, Terhune and Evans transformed southern domestic fiction, first, into an assertion of southern independence and, later, into a panegyric to a lost cause. Still, their faithful adherence to the standards set by their elders ensured the future of the domestic novel as an effective ideological tool and a compelling evocation of a region and its people.

In the months immediately preceding the Civil War, the prospect of armed conflict was the furthest thing from Augusta Evans' mind; although she had greeted the secession of her beloved Alabama with something akin to glee, she had never once considered that this move brought war one step closer.[78] Since achieving some degree of financial security with her second novel, Evans had been carefully planning a trip to Europe, which she hoped to make with her friend Rachel Lyons in the summer of 1861. "From early childhood I have been singularly anxious to make myself acquainted with the wonders of the Old World," Evans wrote an admirer in late 1859. "As the years roll their waves over my head, the desire increases." Hoping "to arrange matters so that I can spend the winter in Rome and Florence, and give the summer months to Germany," she nevertheless insisted that sight-seeing was hardly a priority: "If I go it will be to *study*."[79] As 1860 unrolled, Evans continued to maintain the fiction that in the next year she would realize her cherished dream. "Do adhere to the determination of a European trip," she wrote Lyons in 1860. "Just imagine us both, safely landed in Rome; once there we could place ourselves under the protection of Elizabeth Barrett Browning, and her scarcely

78. Augusta Evans to L. Virginia French, January 13, 1861, in *Alabama Historical Quarterly*, III (1941), 65–67.
79. Augusta Evans to Colonel Seaver, December 31, 1859, in Augusta Evans Wilson Collection (#8293), Clifton Waller Barrett Library, Manuscripts Division, Special Collections Department, University of Virginia Library.

less illustrious Lord, Robert." If her companion had some objection to the "Poets of Parnassus," Evans assured her, other arrangements could be made easily. "We could doubtless prevail on Charlotte Cushman or Harriet Hosmer to *chaperon us*," Evans wrote confidently. "I see they have rented a house and are living together."[80] Yet while Evans resolutely held out hope for a European tour until the last minute, reality ultimately prevailed. On April 12, 1861, General P. G. T. Beauregard fired upon Fort Sumter. Shortly thereafter, Augusta Evans postponed her trip indefinitely.

80. Evans to Lyons, January 21, 1860, in Heustis Papers.

5

Altars of Sacrifice

*I*n the fall of 1865, Augusta Evans mourned the passing of the Confederacy. Closeted in the small room over her father's Mobile store that she had occupied over the course of the Civil War, the thirty-year-old novelist eloquently translated her pain and humiliation into words. "I believe I loved our cause *as a Jesuit his order*," Evans wrote to her long-time confidant, the Confederate congressman J. L. M. Curry, on October 7, "and its utter ruin has saddened and crushed me, as no other event of my life had power to do." Having lost all her property (slaves and Confederate bonds) during the war, Evans explained that she was confronted with a variety of responsibilities for which she had little aptitude and even less interest: cooking, cleaning, and caring for her "desperately wounded" brother Howard left her no time to pursue her intellectual interests. "Sometimes I shudder at the bitter, bitter feelings I find smoldering in my heart," she confessed to the former statesman. "God help me to be patient under this coarse national trial!" But while Evans freely admitted, "I feel that I have no country, no home, no hope in coming years, and I brood over our hallowed precious past, with its chrism of martyr blood," she wondered what had happened to make that declaration necessary. What had propelled the American people toward war? Why had the "sacred cause" foundered? Drained by the myriad demands she faced as the de facto head of her household, exhausted by "the question of bread & butter," Evans' mind raced on, replaying the events of the past four years in an effort to understand.[1]

In the Newark, New Jersey, parsonage where she had lived with her minister husband for some six years, Mary Virginia Terhune shared Evans' determination to put the Civil War into context. Forced to choose be-

1. Augusta Evans to J. L. M. Curry, October 7, 1866, in Curry Papers, Library of Congress.

tween her northern husband and her family of origin, Terhune had spent the war years in a state of near hysteria. Although she dutifully echoed her husband's prayers for the Union army, she "had no personal interest in one [Union] soldier"; her heart was instead with her "best-loved brother [who] was in the fiercest of the fight down there, in the State dearer to me than any other could ever be," as well as the "cousins by the score, and friends and valued acquaintances by the hundred" who fought for the Confederacy. "My situation was peculiar, and, among my daily associates, unique," she recalled long afterward, comparing her trials with the "test of rack and flame as the martyrs of old endured." While Terhune channeled her nervous energy into the variety of benevolent organizations that sprang up across the Northeast, she found that the psychological relief the "domestic, literary, religious, charitable and patriotic" activities afforded her was only temporary. "When—as happened almost daily—our paper published lists of the killed and wounded in Lee's army, my hand shook so violently in holding the sheet, that I had to lay it on the table to steady the lines into legibility, my heart rolling over with sick thuds, while my eyes ran down the line of names," she recalled.[2] Although she regained a degree of emotional equilibrium upon the conclusion of the conflict, she could not forget the exquisite torture of 1861–1865; it lived on in her memory.

That the two southern domestic novelists were obsessed with explaining the immediate past is hardly surprising. The respective authors of two of the most popular novels of the late antebellum period, *Alone* (1854) and *Beulah* (1859), Terhune and Evans owed no small part of their fame to their southern heritage. Their publisher, J. C. Derby, had relentlessly promoted them as daughters of the South, apparently acting under the assumption that northern readers would purchase a southern novel if for no other reason than to demonstrate symbolically a commitment to national conciliation.[3] "Foster this gifted daughter of the South, . . . let Virginia produce a few more such writers, and the cry that the South has no literature is silenced forever!" wrote one critic Derby hired to praise, or "puff," Terhune's second novel, *The Hidden Path*. Proclaiming Terhune's effort one that "North or South, East or West, may point to with the finger of honest pride," the puffer predicted that the novel would lead to the "great

2. Terhune, *Marion Harland's Autobiography*, 396–97.
3. See Derby, *Fifty Years Among Authors*, 389–99, 563–68.

goal of eternal peace."⁴ Terhune herself endorsed Evans' *Beulah*: "I pronounce it the best work of fiction ever published by a Southern writer. . . .
No American authoress has ever published a greater book."⁵ But while the
two southern domestic novelists had found their regional identities an
asset before the Civil War, they were by no means certain that their popularity above the Mason-Dixon Line would continue in its aftermath.
Northern readers might well summarily reject the efforts of a southern
author as an unpleasant reminder of the war, even one who, like Terhune,
ultimately had sided with the North, and since northern readers were the
only group in the depressed postwar economy with the purchasing power
to rejuvenate languishing literary careers, their good opinion was vital.
Under these circumstances, it was no wonder that Terhune and Evans
subjected the war years to careful scrutiny, interpreting and reinterpreting
recent history. Unless they managed to present the war in a commercially
acceptable manner, their loyal readers might desert them.

Still, in spite of these very real financial considerations, the intensity
with which Evans and Terhune pursued their past—Evans tirelessly solic-
ited recollections of Confederate statesmen and military leaders among
others for inclusion in a proposed history of the glorious cause, while
Terhune collected personal correspondence and transcribed prewar and
wartime conversations with fanatical detail—suggests that their activity
was motivated by more than simple economics.⁶ The youngest of five
antebellum southern domestic novelists who had devoted their careers toward establishing the moral benevolence of the South, the two had inherited a set of assumptions about their native region that informed not only
their personal vision of the South but also its expression in their literature;
in the aftermath of national tragedy, they were necessarily concerned that
this image of the South so integral to their consciousness be upheld. With
the retirement of Caroline Gilman around 1852, the death of Caroline
Hentz in 1856, and, with the notable exception of *Two Pictures; or, To
Seem and To Be* (1863), the virtual silence of Maria McIntosh after 1854,

4. Anna Cora Ritchie quoted in Derby, *Fifty Years Among Authors*, 565.

5. Mary Virginia Terhune, Review of Augusta Evans' *Beulah*, Mobile *Register*, October 7, 1859, in Augusta Evans Wilson File, Alabama Department of Archives and History,
Montgomery.

6. See especially Evans to Curry, October 7, 1866, in Curry Papers, Library of Congress; Terhune, *Marion Harland's Autobiography*, 374.

the perpetuation of the antebellum literary defense of southern culture had devolved upon Augusta Evans and Mary Virginia Terhune; the Civil War had merely affirmed this transfer of power. Thus, where Gilman and McIntosh were able to get on with the business of living, Evans and Terhune were imprisoned by their individual and collective southern past. "Like the mourning Carian Queen, I shall spend my life in building an historic mausoleum which will never hold the sacred ashes of the darling dead," Evans predicted dramatically.[7] The more pragmatic Terhune speculated that she would direct her attention toward reuniting her scattered family.[8]

In their struggle to maintain the antebellum literary tradition that had portrayed the South as the North's moral superior by virtue of its distinctive institution of slavery, Evans and Terhune simultaneously acknowledged their debt to their literary predecessors as well as their determination to claim the genre of southern domestic fiction as their own. Both *Macaria; or, Altars of Sacrifice* (1864), Evans' wartime tribute to the Confederate ideal, and *Sunnybank* (1866), Terhune's literary overture toward national conciliation, incorporated themes central to the southern domestic novel as inaugurated by Caroline Hentz in 1833 and defined over the subsequent two decades by Hentz, Gilman, and McIntosh. That these two novels were born of different historical moments goes without question; two years and any number of experiences separated *Sunnybank* from *Macaria*. Nevertheless, the similarities between these two novels are ultimately more important than their differences, highlighting the personal and political concerns of Terhune and Evans as well as the constraints of their chosen literary genre. Both novels, for example, attempted to present the South as a bastion of stability, a stronghold of republican virtue; both featured strong-minded southern heroines from the planter class who learned through a series of misadventures to serve as the center of their immediate and extended communities; and both exaggerated the better aspects of relationships between southern blacks and whites in an attempt to illustrate the positive good of slavery. Yet while first-generation writers were able, with a reasonable degree of credibility, to portray the South as preyed upon by the North, after 1861 the second generation no longer

---

7. Evans to Curry, October 7, 1866, in Curry Papers, Library of Congress.
8. Terhune, *Marion Harland's Autobiography*, 408.

had that luxury. The guns of Fort Sumter exerted a profound impact on the southern domestic novel, forcing its practitioners to confront a new set of questions and to formulate a satisfactory explanation for the South's perceived aggression.

Evans' all-consuming need to put the turbulent times in which she lived into historical context was hardly a postwar phenomenon; as early as January, 1861, she had ventured the first in a series of explanations for the political polarization of America.[9] "For fifteen years, we of the South have endured insult and aggression; have ironed down our just indignation, and suffered numberless encroachments, because of our devotion to the 'Union,'" Evans proclaimed to another writer, L. Virginia French, in the wake of Alabama's secession. Although "patriotic men of both sections" had struggled mightily to resolve the growing sectional conflict, ultimately northern "fanaticism" in the form of abolitionism had prevailed and now "threatened to pollute the sacred precincts of the 'White House.'" Under these circumstances, the novelist asserted, it was impossible for right-minded southerners to support the Union. "The present attitude of the Republican party" and the "desperate and unscrupulous character of its leaders" held out no hope for "satisfactory redress" of southern grievances," Evans argued. "'The Union' has become a misnomer and rather than witness the desecration of our glorious Fane, we of the South, will Sampson-like, lay hold upon its pillars, and if need be, perish in its ruins." Comparing the South's collective response to northern oppression with that of the thirteen colonies that "cut the chains of Great Britain to regain their birth-right," Evans reiterated her conviction with almost schoolgirl fervor that the South was the national stronghold of republican virtue.[10]

Evans' simplistic interpretation and hysterical tone were hardly the expert political analysis she intended, but any superficiality was relatively short-lived. Almost immediately after her passionate outburst to French, Evans set about familiarizing herself with the circumstances of the current

9. Evans anticipated much of her argument in her 1859 series of editorials on southern literature for the Mobile *Daily Advertiser*. See Evans, "Northern Literature," Mobile *Daily Advertiser*, October 11 and 16, 1859; and Evans, "Southern Literature," *ibid.*, October 30, November 6, 1859. See also Fidler, "Confederate Propagandist."

10. Augusta Evans to L. Virginia French, January 13, 1861, in *Alabama Historical Quarterly*, III (1941), 65–67.

crisis, using her celebrity as the author of *Beulah* to gain access to people and places that otherwise would have been beyond her reach. In February, 1861, for example, she traveled from Mobile to Montgomery to witness the swearing in of Jefferson Davis as provisional president of the Confederate States of America; while in the capital, she managed introductions to a number of Confederate leaders and wangled an invitation to tea with a former professor and Alabama congressman, Henry W. Hilliard.[11] Although Evans probably did not make the sort of lasting impression that she would have liked—for example, Georgia delegate Thomas Cobb, whom Evans later eulogized as "the pride, the crowning glory of his state," commented only that Evans was "very young-looking, though not pretty and very loquacious"—she nevertheless made headway in establishing the web of friendships with influential Confederates she would draw upon to inform her subsequent political opinions.[12]

As 1861 unfolded and it became clear that war was inevitable, Evans stepped up her efforts to gain perspective on the coming conflict. In late June, she traveled beyond her beloved Alabama to inspect the Confederate fortifications at Norfolk, Virginia, where her two brothers were stationed. Although the battle Evans had hoped to witness failed to materialize—"I think there will be no trouble here, for a while at least," she wrote Rachel Lyons with disappointment—she effortlessly managed to precipitate a minor skirmish. Visiting some Georgia friends encamped upon Sewell's Point, she wandered onto an "exposed point to take a look at Fortress Munro [*sic*], immediately opposite." Northern troops quickly pointed "the immense Rifle Cannon" in her direction, sending two and then three "missles of death" into the field behind her. Mesmerized, Evans stood her ground until the officers almost forcibly removed her from the line of fire; even so, she continued to exult in her near brush with death. "I longed for a secession flag to shake *defiantly* in their teeth at *every fire*: and my fingers fairly itched to touch off a *red hot ball* in answer to their *chivalric civilities*," the self-styled paragon of southern femininity boasted to Lyons.[13]

11. See Fidler, *Augusta Evans Wilson*, 84–104.

12. Evans to Curry, December 20, 1862, in Curry Papers, Library of Congress. See also Fidler, "Life and Works," 22n.

13. Augusta Evans to Rachel Lyons, June 26, 1861, in Heustis Papers.

Evans apparently found danger addictive. The day after her perilous promenade, she persuaded Confederate General Huger to permit her to accompany a number of northerners who had requested sanctuary at "Fortress Munro" to their destination. Sailing under "a *flag of truce*," Evans and three friends thus gained "a fine view" of the fortress and "all other points of interest." "We lay for three hours right under the 60 guns of the Flag ship 'Minnesota' and were very near the traitorous Cumberland, Monticello, Anacostia and others," her letter to Lyons continued. While the southerners were engaged in transporting the "precious cargo of renegades," Union General Butler chose to reopen fire on Sewell's Point, and Evans was again confronted with her own mortality. "We stopped on our return to the City, and sent a boat ashore to know whether any injury was effected," she told Lyons, "but 'Nobody hurt' was shouted back, amid bursts of *laughter* from the gunners. . . . The day was one of the most eventful of my life, and I think I shall never forget it."

But if Evans used her Norfolk visit to prove her personal courage, she also increased her store of knowledge about the state of Confederate preparedness. In addition to pronouncing their defenses "very complete and formidable," she inspected the local hospital, which she predicted would be full "as warm weather advances," and "with an officer of great intelligence" she toured the navy yard. She observed so much in the "machine shops and laboratories," Evans assured Rachel Lyons smugly, that she felt "very, very tired." She declared, "Of the future I know nothing." Still, her speculation that "I may leave any day" suggested that her months in Norfolk had served their purpose. Summarizing her findings in a missive that she readily admitted did not contain the whole of her adventures—"you must pardon my brevity," she wrote—may well have convinced her that she was ready to continue her investigation elsewhere.[14] The ambitious novelist determined to use her entrée into military and political circles to what she convinced herself was her country's advantage.

Evans' privileged position enabled her to learn more about the war effort than Confederate officials may have expected. Ordinary men and women, the backbone of the fledgling nation, poured out their hearts to the unimposing "Miss Evans," who obviously took such great interest in

14. *Ibid.*

their circumstances.[15] That Evans in reality was interested in yeomen and poor whites only inasmuch as their stories helped secure her position on the fringes of the Confederate hierarchy was not apparent to the novelist's less sophisticated audience. In 1862, she traveled to Mississippi to survey the extent of southern losses at Corinth. She arrived in Chickamauga, Georgia, in 1863 on the eve of battle; wrapped in her dressing gown, she serenaded Confederate troops with a rousing version of "Maryland, My Maryland."[16] In early 1864, however, it seemed as if Evans' standing "passport" might have run its course. Flushed with her sense of mission, Evans decided to violate standing orders from Confederate General Maury prohibiting noncombatants from traveling into and out of Mobile and journeyed the length of Alabama to assess the mood of her beleaguered state. To complicate matters further, in her arrogance Evans included two girlfriends in her party, assuring the provost marshal who objected to her plan that she "would make all things satisfactory to Gen'l Maury." Although the trip was relatively uneventful, upon the party's return their train was subjected to repeated stops, and while Evans' pass "proved 'open sesame'" for all at the first two stops, at the third, "the charm ended." Evans and her companions were forced to disembark and spend a night waiting for a "telegraphic pass" from General Maury. If Maury's delay in sending his permission was meant to signify his disapproval of her flagrant disobedience, it failed to discourage her. While Evans admitted to Rachel Lyons that she had "encountered almost as many difficulties as Ulysses," her spirits remained high, and her commitment to pursuing the truth was undiminished.[17]

"The present crisis is so replete with interest, the questions involved

15. There is some evidence that Evans was able to influence minor military decisions through a carefully placed word. See Fidler, *Augusta Evans Wilson*, 103; and Fidler, "Confederate Propagandist." See also T. C. Deleon, "Biographical Reminiscences," in Augusta Evans Wilson, *Devota* (1907; rpr. New York, 1913), 125–97.

16. See Fidler, *Augusta Evans Wilson*, 97–99; and Deleon, "Biographical Reminiscences." See also T. C. Deleon, "'Maryland' by Moonlight," Mobile *Daily Register*, November 21, 1906; "Mrs. Wilson in War Times," unidentified clipping dated May 10, 1909, in Augusta Evans Wilson File, Alabama Department of Archives and History.

17. Augusta Evans to Rachel Lyons, February 8, 1864, in Augusta Evans Wilson Papers, Hoole Special Collections Library, University of Alabama.

so vital, the ties that link us as a people so inexpressibly dear, that I find
no leisure for my studies," Evans confided to her friend Janie Tyler in
1862. "While a nation's history is daily being written, page by page, in
characters of blood, one has little thought for the dusty records of the dim
bygone." Actually she told her women friends little; her comments to Tyler, which echoed her comments to Lyons, were less an apology for her
infrequent letters than an affirmation of her value to the Confederacy. But
she went to great lengths to cultivate the good opinion of highly placed
men, offering the feeblest of excuses to renew introductions she had en-
gineered in Montgomery and elsewhere. When, for example, General
Beauregard, the hero of Fort Sumter, sent Evans his personal pen, via an
aide-de-camp, in recognition of her outstanding service, Evans hastened
to thank the general directly. "With a heart throbbing with pleasure, and
surely pardonable pride, I avail myself of the very earliest opportunity to
attempt an expression of my earnest, cordial thanks," Evans enthused.
"I can imagine no compliment more delicate and valuable, than that,
which you have so unexpectedly paid me." "Inexpressibly gratified" by the
"priceless token of a friendship, I had not sufficient presumption to hope
for," Evans assured her benefactor of her extreme devotion. "I shall place
your pen in the Kaaba of memory, whence, daily pilgrimages shall yield
me reminiscences infinitely dearer and more valuable." [18]

Evans' relationship with Congressman Curry followed much the same
pattern. In early 1861, when she met Curry in Montgomery, Evans borrowed a book, which she then used as the pretext for a lengthy correspondence. "Permit me to tender my sincere thanks for the *speeches*, you
kindly sent me some weeks since, and which afforded me *much pleasure*,"
Evans wrote in the fall of 1862. Apologizing for her tardiness in expressing
her "grateful acknowledgments," Evans explained that an unusual amount
of sickness in her family and neighborhood had kept her "constantly nursing for some weeks past." She said nothing about the contents of the volume, nor when she planned to return it, information that could justify
one, if not two, more letters. Instead, she apologized "for this wretched

18. Augusta Evans to Janie Tyler, January 18, 1862, in Fidler, *Augusta Evans Wilson*,
87–88; Augusta Evans to General P. G. T. Beauregard, March 17, 1863, in *Heroines of Dixie:
Spring of High Hopes*, ed. Katherine M. Jones (New York, 1974), 224–28.

brown paper," explaining that only "the stringency of the blockade" would have precipitated such a grievous social blunder.[19]

Flattery and cajolery aside, Evans' penetrating observations on the conduct of the war turned warriors and statesmen into regular correspondents. Her assortment of public opinion on leading issues of the day ensured their timely reply.[20] To Curry's concern about the exemption bill, which provided for paid military substitutes, Evans responded in 1862: "You have doubtless become to some extent acquainted with the spirit of insubordination and disaffection which is rife in our armies, and which has attained in this section of the Confederacy, melancholy and alarming proportions." Soldiers "almost daily" received letters "in which their families implore them to come home at *every hazard* and save them from the pinching penury that scowls at their threshold." Evans related, "One wife exhausted all other means of subsistence, and had just sold her *two last extra dresses*, to purchase at an exorbitant price, meal enough to satisfy her children's hunger."[21] Everyone she consulted, Evans told Curry, blamed such doleful circumstances on the exemption bill and predicted that unless Congress rescinded this favor to the wealthy at the expense of the poor, the situation would only get worse. Paradoxically, the same men Evans cultivated used her as a sounding board, voicing ideas and opinions that they were forced by necessity to keep confidential. Apparently Evans was unaware of this practice among her correspondents and leaked a sensitive letter from Senator Benjamin Hill to the Columbus [Georgia] *Sun* in which Hill was clearly identified. The senator was greatly embarrassed.

By 1863 Evans had learned enough about the Confederate effort that she felt qualified, if not obligated, to put her analysis before her countrymen. *Macaria; or, Altars of Sacrifice* (1864), which took its name from the Greek heroine who cast herself into a sacrificial fire in order to save her country, grew out of Evans' relentless pursuit of information and experience. Drawing heavily upon her correspondence with her high-ranking friends—Evans based her account of Manassas on Beauregard's field notes, and she transcribed paragraphs of her letters to Beauregard and

19. Evans to Curry, November 10, 1862, in Curry Papers, Library of Congress.

20. In her extensive network of highly placed Confederates, Evans resembled another woman writer, Mary Chesnut. See Muhlenfeld, *Mary Boykin Chesnut*.

21. Evans to Curry, December 20, 1862, in Curry Papers, Library of Congress.

Curry into her text word for word—she painted a compelling picture of a nation in the throes of war; with deliberate strokes she conveyed the heroic behavior of the men and women of the Confederacy. Furthermore, with customary assurance and more than a little arrogance, Evans promulgated her opinions on the conduct of the war, using her large cast of southern characters to judge, usually favorably, the ideas and activities of those in power.[22]

"It is not my privilege to enter the ranks, wielding a sword, in my country's cause," Evans had explained to General Beauregard early on. "Debarred from the tented field" by reason of her gender, she confessed that she frequently "felt disposed to lament the limited circle of action, the insignificant *role* assigned [women] in the mightiest drama that ever rivetted the gaze of the civilized world." Still, for all Evans' envy of her "dauntless immortal namesake of Saragossa," she took consolation in her "feeble, womanly pen." All she could contribute to "the consummation of our freedom," she told the general, she had "humbly, but at least faithfully and untiringly *endeavored* to achieve." Reflecting that "after all, woman's sphere of influence might be like Pascal's, 'one of which the centre is everywhere, the circumference nowhere,'" Evans assured Beauregard that "the cause of our beloved, struggling Confederacy may yet be advanced through the agency of its daughters," particularly, she implied, if the daughters in question would but follow her own example of selfless devotion.[23] Over time, Evans came to view the actual writing of *Macaria* as illustrative of her total immersion in the war effort. "Scribbled in pencil while sitting up with the sick soldiers in the hospital attached to 'Camp Beulah,'" *Macaria* contained, so Evans told J. C. Derby, the essence of her soul: "my *very heart beat in its pages*, coarse and brown though the dear old Confederate paper was."[24]

Whether Evans immediately sensed the symbolic significance of her multifaceted activity—the youthful best-selling novelist, nursing the mortally wounded in a facility named in her honor, eulogizing the South on paper in moments snatched from her life-saving ministrations—or, more

22. See Fidler, "Life and Works," 21n.
23. Augusta Evans to General P. G. T. Beauregard, August 4, 1862, in *The Alabama Confederate Reader*, ed. Malcolm L. McMillan (Tuscaloosa, 1963), 353–55.
24. Derby, *Fifty Years Among Authors*, 393. See also Sidney Phillips, "The Life and Works of Augusta Evans Wilson" (M.A. thesis, Alabama Polytechnic Institute, 1937), 56–57.

likely, recognized its propaganda value only afterward, she went to great lengths to embed that particular image of herself in America's imagination; both her private and public accounts describe the war years as an excruciating period of personal sacrifice.[25] In spite of the appeal of those postwar recollections, however, her contemporary correspondence with Rachel Lyons suggests that in fact her sufferings were of rather a different sort. In March, 1864, for example, Evans complained to Lyons that she had been besieged by Confederate officers to the point where she had no time to sleep, much less answer Lyons' letters. "If you only knew how constantly I am interrupted by company," Evans wrote. "Morning, noon and night my ears are greeted with the sound of '*Miss Gusta somebody is coming up the walk.*'" Intoxicated by an inordinate amount of attention and, on one occasion, the champagne a caller had procured from a blockade runner, Evans enumerated her various "tribulations" freely. Would Selden's battery return to Camp Beulah "before long?" ("I hope so at least, for I shall miss Mr. Lovelace very much indeed.") Would the unseasonably cold weather freeze the geraniums that Major Polk Johnston and Captain Cox had spent an entire day helping her transplant? Would "Godfrey, the Captain of the 'Denibigh,'" fulfill his promise to bring her the "finest gold pen in *Cuba*?" "Oh! torture beyond all the refined cruelties," Evans declared in a telling observation, "to be sleepy in a room full of company!"[26]

Ten days later, Evans wrote Lyons in much the same vein. "Your letter arrived two days ago and I should have answered it immediately but for a rush of company which left me no leisure whatever," the novelist explained grandly. She had spent a great deal of time with both General Quarles—"we have become most excellent friends," she boasted—and General Shoup, who had insisted upon paying his compliments before he left Mobile to take command of General Johnston's artillery. She had visited assorted family members: "Mr. Evans had a little son . . . Alice Vivien has had the measles and I hear the mumps!" She had also managed, she reported proudly, to help along Lyons' long-standing romance with the dashing Dr. Heustis. "I have known him long and well, and understand

25. See Phillips, "Life and Works of Augusta Evans Wilson," 61.
26. Evans to Lyons, March 18, 1864, in Wilson Papers, University of Alabama.

his character better than anyone else beside his own family," Evans asserted with customary dogmatism. "Dr. Heustis loves you sincerely, and I shall not forgive you if you do not make him the happiest man in the Confederacy." It was only in passing that Evans mentioned that "that chronic nuisance yclept *Macaria* will probably make its bow before the 'dear people' next week." Evans' tribute to the Confederacy at the time paled beside the novelist's burning interest in how long it would be before Lyons came to Mobile to live.[27]

Whatever Evans' later exaggeration of her wartime sufferings, *Macaria* memorialized "a nation of laboring, nimble-fingered, prayerful-hearted, brave-spirited women, and chivalric, high-souled, heroic men, who had never learned that Americans could live and not be free"; what more than one critic regards as "the best novel to come out of the Civil War from either side" reveals Evans at the height of her powers as propagandist.[28] Although in its basic outline Evans' mature conceptualization of the sectional crisis resembled her 1861 analysis—the Civil War as the result of the South's effort to redeem the failed promise of the American Revolution—*Macaria* reflected not only Evans' deepened understanding of contemporary politics but also her broader range of experience. Thus, while *Macaria* retained the same sort of obscure literary and historical allusions that had prompted critics to label *Inez* and *Beulah* "pedantic," it escaped a similar fate by its accuracy of detail and liberal use of eyewitness testimony.[29] Ironically, though Evans herself recognized that her third novel was her best, she failed to recognize the reasons why. "The book is on the whole, superior to '*Beulah*,'" Evans told Congressman Curry, but, she apologized, "it contains less philosophic lore, and no metaphysical disputation."[30] That notwithstanding, *Macaria* was quite popular above and below the Mason-Dixon Line. At least one Union general was forced to ban the book among his troops, and several southerners later claimed that the novel saved their lives by deflecting bullets or bayonets.

27. Evans to Lyons, March 28, 1864, *ibid.*

28. See Fidler, *Augusta Evans Wilson*, 105–14; and Fidler, "Confederate Propagandist." See also Lively, *Fiction Fights the Civil War*, 85–86; Muhlenfeld, "The Civil War and Authorship," 182.

29. See Fidler, "Life and Works," 28n.

30. Evans to Curry, July 15, 1863, in Curry Papers, Library of Congress.

In testifying to the strength and endurance of a people under siege, *Macaria* signaled the end of traditional southern domestic fiction. Unlike the antebellum southern domestic novel as defined by Gilman, Hentz, McIntosh, Terhune, and Evans herself, which had succeeded because they buried their criticism of the North under dense prose and convoluted plots, Evans' wartime revision was overtly partisan.[31] Whereas before the war Gilman, Hentz, and McIntosh and to a lesser extent Terhune and Evans had managed to find some redeeming features in northern society and thereby appeal to a national audience, Evans now made no concessions to northern sensibilities even though she still sought northern publication. By thrusting political conflict into the center of her story, by subordinating the requisite romance to explicitly political commentary, and, more important, by subverting the traditional ending in favor of one she deemed more realistic, Evans upset the conventions of the southern domestic novel. In adapting the antebellum genre to contemporary needs, she ensured that it would not survive the war.

Macaria dramatized the shattering impact of the Civil War on individuals and the community through chronicling twenty years in the lives of three young southerners. The story opens in a small Georgia town in the middle 1840s where Russell Aubrey, a poor boy of noble character, his orphaned cousin Electra Grey, whose artistic temperament closely resembled Evans' own, and Irene Huntingdon, heiress to one of the largest plantations in the South, are busy preparing for lives of service. Russell is intent upon becoming a lawyer. Having grown to young manhood under a cloud—his father was unfairly convicted of murder and committed suicide in prison— he is anxious to redeem his family's honor. Electra plans to elevate the moral tone of society by her painting. Irene's ambitions are no less modest. The southern beauty, whose financial resources are exceeded only by her virtue, hopes to realize the domestic ideal for aristocratic southern females: to serve as the center of her immediate and extended community.[32]

31. *Cf.* Evans, *Inez* and *Beulah*. See also Fidler, "Confederate Propagandist."
32. Augusta Evans, *Macaria; or, Altars of Sacrifice* (Richmond, 1864), 38–48. Hereinafter cited parenthetically by page number in the text.

Secure in the protected environment of the antebellum South, the three friends negotiate the hurdles of youth with considerable success. Russell and Electra, for instance, who are excruciatingly poor, find patrons who provide them with the means and encouragement to realize their dreams. Russell studies law; Electra develops her artistic talents. Irene solicits attention of a different kind. Deprived of her mother since birth, she must find an appropriate substitute if she is to develop the particular sort of moral and intellectual independence deemed essential to productive southern womanhood. Given her father's selfish desires to turn her first into a society belle and later into the fashionable wife of her degenerate cousin Hugh, Irene's struggles to ally herself with a sympathetic female are doubly imperative. In the long run, however, these efforts toward self-improvement are useless, for while Russell, Electra, and Irene are laboring to become productive citizens, the region that has nurtured and sustained them is being relentlessly undermined by dissolute northern politicians (55, 64–66, 68–71).

Russell is the first to sense the impending crisis. On a trip to New York City, he attends a political meeting, and what he sees and hears fills him with terror. Masses of European immigrants who are "utterly ignorant of [American] institutions" are being used by the Republican party to sway the vote against the South. Victims of northern demagogism, that "hydra-headed foe of democracy," this class of "paupers" already had influenced the outcome of elections in northern and western states, and unless the South put up a vigorous resistance, "the crude foreign vote" would eventually determine "who will sit in the presidential chair and how far the constitution will be observed." As Russell asserts, "It requires no extraordinary prescience to predict that the great fundamental principles of this government will become a simple question of arithmetic"; the South will "lie at the mercy of an unscrupulous majority." He warns, "The surging waves of Northern faction and fanaticism already break ominously against our time-honored constitutional dikes . . . If the South would strengthen her bulwarks there is no time to be slept or wrangled away." Russell's region proves receptive to his message of imminent danger; almost immediately after he reports his findings, he is elected to Congress on a platform of suffrage "reform" that he believes will ensure the South political parity: a restricted foreign vote, a reinstated property qualification, life terms for the judiciary, extended presidential terms, and, most critical, fewer popular elections (246).[33]

Up until this point, *Macaria* closely resembled any number of antebellum southern domestic novels, at least on a superficial level. Maria McIntosh's *The Lofty and the Lowly* (1854), for example, focused on the moral and intellectual development of financially and emotionally impoverished southern males and females. Both novels portrayed the South as the exclusive province of national virtue; both argued that the region was threatened by northern greed and corruption. Finally, both sent their respective heroes to Congress to redress southern grievances. But while McIntosh ends her novels on that resolutely optimistic note, Russell Aubrey's election to the Senate occurs only slightly more than halfway through *Macaria*. More important, when Aubrey, a hero conceived in the throes of civil war, raises his voice in defense of the South, as did the southern delegation he represents, he fails to prevent the coming of war.[34]

Certainly, Evans' decision to confront divisive sectional issues and developments was influenced by the decade that separated *Macaria* from *The Lofty and the Lowly*; by 1863 it was painfully obvious that the statesmen to whom the South had entrusted its defense had failed to fulfill their sacred responsibilities. While McIntosh in the early 1850s clearly was aware of the lack of southern leadership, she was more inclined to blame disruption of national harmony on the activities of a single northerner: Harriet Beecher Stowe. Yet McIntosh's repetition of her 1854 ending in *Two Pictures* (1863) suggests that there was something more at issue than a simple disagreement over the assignment of blame. In sending her hero to Congress and leaving him there, McIntosh upheld the literary tradition of indirect political expression; she criticized the state of current affairs but avoided explicit political discussion that might impinge upon the promised sectional conciliation. Conversely, by integrating the substance of contemporary political debate into the very heart of her narrative, Evans necessarily altered the shape of the southern domestic novel.

33. Evans enumerates the same reforms in a letter to Curry. See Evans to Curry, July 15, 1863, in Curry Papers, Library of Congress.

34. See Hentz, *Marcus Warland*, 287; and McIntosh, *The Lofty and the Lowly*, 321. In those novels, the heroes are confident that they can sway politics in the South's favor. In *Macaria*, Evans is not so optimistic.

Evans' synopsis of Russell Aubrey's brief tenure in public office illuminated the novelist's evolving interpretation of the coming of the war and of the historical relationship between North and South. Elected to Congress in 1856, the year after Evans indicted the North for crimes against the South in *Inez*, Russell perceives, like Evans herself, that "the period was rapidly approaching when the Southern states, unless united and on the alert, would lie bound at the feet of an insolent and rapacious Northern faction." Southerners "slept on the thin heaving crust of a volcano, which would inevitably soon burst forth," Russell realizes; it was imperative that they awaken and assert their rights (256). Still, in spite of Russell's best efforts to curb the power of the North, he is overwhelmed by the sheer magnitude of the northern political machine. "Faction, fanaticism, demagogism, held high revel" in halls of national government, making it impossible even for one motivated by "purest patriotism" to remain optimistic about the continued viability of the Union (336).

Time bears out Russell's suspicions. Over the course of the next several years, "Seward cantered toward Washington on the hobby-labeled Emancipation, dragging Lincoln at his heels," and the "faithful guardians" of the South lifted "their warning voices" and pointed to the "only path of safety" to no avail (336). By the time the Democratic party met in Charleston, South Carolina, to select its 1860 presidential candidate, "the die was cast" (337). Recognizing that "through the demoralization of the Northern wing of Democracy, Lincoln would be elected," Russell joins with that other "sleepless watchman on the tower of Southern Rights," William Lowndes Yancey, "to prepare the masses for that final separation which he foresaw was inevitable" (336). "The gauntlet had been thrown down by the South at Charleston," Evans wrote, but the North "sneered at the threat" that the election of "a sectional president" would be "the signal for separation." "Abolitionism, so long adroitly cloaked, was triumphantly clad in robes of state—shameless now, and hideous" (337). Resigning from office in disgust, Russell returns to Georgia to prepare for war.

"The 6th of November dawned upon a vast populous empire, rich in every resource, capable of the acme of human greatness and prosperity, claiming to be the guardian of peaceful liberty," Evans intoned ominously. "It set upon a nation rent in twain, between whose sections yawned a bottomless, bridgeless gulf where the shining pillars of the temple of Con-

cord had stood for eighty years" (337). Almost immediately, South Carolina, "ever the *avant courier* in the march of freedom," seceded in protest;
"seven sovereign states" followed in quick succession. While a provisional
government founded on the "fundamental doctrine" that all "just govern-
ments rest on the consent of the governed" tried valiantly to negotiate a
peaceful "separation," its efforts were in vain (339). By April 12, 1861,
relations between North and South had degenerated to the point where
armed conflict could no longer be avoided. "The discharge of the first gun
from Fort Moultrie crushed the lingering vestiges of 'Unionism,'" Evans
wrote, "and welded the entire Confederacy into one huge homogeneous
mass of stubborn resistance to despotism" (339). It was "Act I of a long
and bloody civil war," Irene Huntingdon observes, "but it was forced upon
us. . . . God is witness that we have earnestly endeavored to avert hostilities—that the blood of this war rests upon the government at Washington;
our hands are stainless" (340).

Yet while Evans personally challenged both social and literary convention in her explicit discussion of contemporary politics in *Macaria*, she
continued to endorse a traditional, albeit considerably expanded, gender
role for her predominantly female audience. Electra Grey and Irene
Huntingdon, southern heroines par excellence, wholly conform to the
feminine ideal advanced through antebellum southern domestic fiction.
Intelligent, independent, and supremely competent in meeting their responsibilities to their social and economic equals and inferiors before the
war, Electra and Irene heed Russell's early warnings that the South "must
prepare to pay the invariable sacrificial dues which liberty inexorably demands," and by April 12 they have made significant headway in mobilizing
their community for battle (339). "You and I have much to do, during
these days of gloom and national trial," Irene tells Electra, "for upon the
purity, the devotion, and the patriotism of the women of our land, not less
than upon the heroism of our armies, depends our national salvation." By
guarding southern "homes and social circles from the inroads of corruption," by keeping "the fires of patriotism burning upon the altar of the
South," by cheering on those who were "wrestling" for the South's "birth-
right of freedom," southern women could "hasten the hour" when peace
would "again make her abode" below the Mason-Dixon Line (339). "Rise,
woman rise!" Evans ordered through her fictional heroines, as if the sheer
force of her rhetoric could force her literary constituency to fall in line.

"Henceforward, rise, aspire, / To all the calms, and magnanimities . . . /
To which thou art elect for evermore" (469).

"Though we are very properly debarred from the 'tented-field,'" Irene
declares on another occasion, "I have entire confidence that the cause
of our country may be advanced, and its good promoted, through the
agency of its daughters" (416). Unlike their northern counterparts, Irene
contends, southern women had "no desire to usurp the legislative reins."
They were instead content to "mould the manners and morals of the nation," to check "the wild excesses of fashionable life and the dangerous
spirit of extravagance" (416). Most important, "statesmen" were "trained
up around the mother's arm-chair, and she [could] imbue the boy with
lofty sentiments, and inspire him with aims which [would] lead him in
congressional halls to adhere to principles, to advance the Truth" (417).
Still, as Irene, Electra, and the host of southern women they represented
ultimately discover, intense familial involvement, which in peacetime provided the "true Southern woman" with a sense of self-worth and social
purpose, guaranteed heartbreak in time of war. Across the South, Evans
wrote, "mothers closed their lips firmly to repress a wail of sorrow," "fond
wives silently packed their husbands' knapsacks," and "sisters with tearless
eyes, bent by the light of midnight lamps over canteens" (348). For Irene,
who has only just acknowledged her love for Russell, the emotional strain
is almost unbearable. "I cannot, like Macaria, by self-immolation redeem
my country; from that great privilege I am debarred; but I yield up more
than she ever possessed," Irene laments. "I give my all on earth . . . to our
beloved and suffering country. My God! accept the sacrifice, and crown
the South a sovereign, independent nation!" (372). "Another adjective
than 'Spartan' must fleck with glory the pages of future historians," Evans
predicted (348). The sacrifices of southerners in general and southern
women in particular, the novelist asserted, quite simply exceeded those
heretofore known to man.

The final chapters of *Macaria* enlarge upon that theme of self-
abnegation, as Russell dies "gloriously" at the Battle of Malvern Hill and
Irene and Electra dedicate the remainder of their lives to the "sacred
cause" of southern freedom (358). There was no time to waste mourning,
Evans argued. "The spirit which actuates the North—the diabolical hate
and fiendishness which its people have manifested" toward the South
made it imperative that all southerners, regardless of the extent of their

personal losses, immediately spring to the aid of their country (412). "The precious blood of a sacrifice" does not "unsettle the holy foundation of the altar," Irene reflects upon learning of Russell's ultimate sacrifice. "Rather would I have men, women, and children fill one wide common grave, than live in subjection to, or connection with a people so depraved, unscrupulous, and Godless" (412). And, lest some disenchanted readers argue that the price of liberty came too high, Evans had her heroines reassert the wisdom of righteous revolution at the moment of their bereavement. "The ultimate result can never affect the question of the right and propriety of Secession, though it may demonstrate the deplorable consequences of our procrastination," Irene tells Electra. "I am more than ever convinced of the correctness of my views, and the absolute necessity of the step we took" (412). "A long dark vista stretches before the Confederacy," Evans concluded, "a vista lined with the bloody graves of her best sons; but beyond Freedom—Independence" (411).

Repeatedly and relentlessly Evans struggled to imprint the ideal of sacrifice and service upon the hearts and minds of her readers, enjoining men and women throughout the South to follow her example and answer the call of their country. Drawing upon her extensive reading and correspondence, she patiently rehearsed the ideological foundations of the sectional crisis, phrasing her argument in words and images designed to reach the broadest possible audience. Refining and, to a limited extent, revising the existing model for feminine behavior, Evans challenged her southern sisters to meet the standard of excellence that she and her fellow southern domestic novelists had prescribed over the previous two decades. But though *Macaria* faithfully reiterated the central premise of antebellum southern domestic fiction, that southern women could protect their immediate and extended community from northern aggression if they would but realize moral and intellectual independence, it differed significantly from what had come before. For in a literary tradition that was conceived as an outlet for indirect political commentary, *Macaria* was overtly political. In a tradition designed to resolve sectional conflict through emphasizing similarities between northerners and southerners, *Macaria* argued that compromise was impossible. In a tradition that depended upon an ending with the heroine's marriage and assumption of conventional women's roles, *Macaria* ended with its hero dead, its heroines unmarried.

Augusta Evans' inability to conform to the conventions of antebellum

southern domestic fiction in 1863 was undoubtedly influenced by her dis-
satisfaction with the current direction of southern politics. Her letters to
Congressman Curry dating from the period during which she published
Macaria reveal the novelist's deep pessimism about the future of her beloved region and provide a partial explanation for the stresses and strains
that permeate her third novel. In her letter of July 15, 1863, for example,
Evans suggested that Curry lecture upon the broad topic "Political and
Social Quicksands of the Future" to "popularize the remedies" to what
she believed was growing political unrest. "In casting our national horo-
scope, my heart is weighed down with ceaseless apprehensions," Evans
confided, "and I feel that here, on the threshold, warning tones would be
heard and warning hands lifted toward the moldering mournful ruins,
which blacken the *past of Republics*." "Corruption stalks through the
land," she told the congressman—although she failed to specify exactly
what kind—and if it were not "speedily vanquished," southerners might
as well give up all hope of a *"permanent republic."* It was, after all, to
secure liberty that the South had seceded, Evans continued; southerners
would do well to remember precisely what that commitment to freedom
entailed. "All the evils which History proves inherent in Democratic Republics, now threaten us in aggravated form; and to point the people to
them, pleading for reform, seems the *imperative* duty of our Statesmen."
Perhaps anticipating a suggestion from Curry that she address that issue
in her fiction, Evans immediately disqualified herself. "My courage fails
me, I am not competent to the noble task," she demurred. "The mantle
of Tacitus or Xenophon would ill-become my shoulders."[35]

Yet the reforms of which Evans spoke were hardly democratic; on the
contrary, in her recommendations to Congressman Curry, the woman
who had cultivated the common man and woman reaffirmed her identification with the planter class. Proposing to restrict suffrage—"the masses
must be trained and elevated to a *higher stand point*" before they were
allowed to cast a ballot—Evans expressed her concern that "even after
obtaining our independence," the South would be "plunged into hopeless
anarchy, or crushed under the iron heel of despotism" as a result of widespread ignorance and inexperience.[36] Although Evans did not elaborate,

35. Evans to Curry, July 15, 1863, in Curry Papers, Library of Congress.
36. *Ibid.*

she probably had in mind the growing disaffection of yeomen and poor whites with a government that, as the war progressed, addressed fewer and fewer of their social or economic needs. By early 1864, Evans' anxiety had intensified. "Mankind plunges into cruel wars, into internecine conflicts, in defense of *principles* which during the revolution they permit to slip through their fingers," she wrote Curry on January 27. Applying ideas cribbed from the historian H. T. Buckle, Evans asserted that "three years of struggling" had "singularly modified" the opinions of southerners; she was "pained and astonished" to discover how many of her countrymen were willing to "glide unresistingly" into a "*dictatorship*" or, still worse, "a state of *Colonial dependence* with *gradual emancipation* as a condition of foreign intervention." She warned, "The people *are rocking* from their former firm faith in *democratic republicanism* and liable at any moment to sink into *absolutism.*"[37]

Paradoxically, Evans "forgot" her profound distrust of the southern masses after the South's defeat; indeed, immediately after the Civil War, she began to emphasize her kinship with the common man. "I feel as if my heart were inured with my country's flag, and my people's freedom," she wrote a friend on June 20, 1866. "I am not reconciled, I am not philosophically, or religiously resigned—and I never shall be!" Seeking to make sense of "a struggle" that she described as robbing her life of meaning—"all my hopes were involved, and *crushed*"—in the depths of her despair, Evans reached out across the lines of class that she had so diligently struggled to reinforce only months earlier.[38] Besieged by responsibilities, burdened by circumstances beyond her control, Evans slowly began to cultivate the larger myth of her wartime sacrifices, portraying herself, like the men and women she eulogized in *Macaria*, as a martyr to a holy cause. It was with no small pleasure that she (with General Beauregard's permission) refused the writer John Esten Cooke's request for information about the late Mrs. Beauregard to include in his proposed tribute to southern women. Mrs. Beauregard had done nothing "in any way for the advancement" of the Confederacy except to profess her undying

37. Evans to Curry, January 27, 1864, in Curry Papers, Library of Congress.
38. Evans to [?], June 20, 1866, in Augusta Evans Wilson Collection, Clifton Waller Barrett Library. See also Derby, *Fifty Years Among Authors*, 193–94; Deleon, "Biographical Reminiscences"; Manly, "Augusta Evans Wilson," 5842; and Elizabeth Brown Pryor, *Clara Barton: Professional Angel* (Philadelphia, 1987).

loyalty to her country on her deathbed, Evans told Cooke with relish. Although the novelist purported to be quoting the general, her language was revealing: "What are *words* compared to the acts of those noble-hearted women, who devoted their time and labor to assisting and caring for the sick and wounded, besides encouraging the faint-hearted who almost despaired of the Republic?" And lest Cooke, who was himself not above exaggeration, miss the subtext of her letter, Evans tactfully reminded him of her own contributions. The closing paragraph thanked one of the South's more popular male novelists for the "friendly words of encouragement which you so generously bestow on my little books."[39]

Evans was no less self-serving in responding to any number of letters from Confederate veterans and widows, regularly implying that she had made as many, if not more, sacrifices than those southerners who importuned her for assistance in reconstructing their shattered lives.[40] On February 3, 1866, for example, Evans wrote a Mrs. J. H. Chrisman that her own "grief deepens day by day—grows more poignant. . . . All my hopes, aims, aspirations were bound up in the success of our holy precious cause; its failure has bowed down and crushed my heart as I thought nothing earthly had power to do." While Evans did acknowledge indirectly that Chrisman's lot was difficult, the novelist insensitively asked her correspondent if she would "willingly recall" her husband "from the cradling arms of glory." Evans instructed, "Mourn not that your darling was called to his eternal rest before the land of his birth went down in a starless night of degradation and slavery"; rather, be grateful that he did not survive to see "that synagogue of Satan"—New England—triumph over the South. "Human sympathy" was "inadequate" for "affliction such as yours," the novelist assured the widow perfunctorily, and with characteristic aplomb—"I shall attempt no words of consolation"—she dismissed the plea for help.[41]

Evans' decision to cling to the past—she planned to abandon popular fiction and write a comprehensive history of the Confederacy—left her

39. Evans to John Esten Cooke, October 30, 1866, in P. G. T. Beauregard Papers, Library of Congress.

40. See, for example, Evans to Mrs. Chrisman, February 3, 1866, and "A Chat with Mrs. Wilson," New York *World*, November, 1878, both in Augusta Evans Wilson File, Alabama Department of Archives and History.

41. Evans to Mrs. Chrisman, February 3, 1866, *ibid.*

markedly unsympathetic to those who accepted defeat and moved on with their lives. "I regret exceedingly, my valued friend, that you are *compelled to ask for pardon*," Evans wrote Congressman Curry in late 1865. "I had hoped that you would not apply for it, but quit the country, which is *no longer our own dear sunny South*, our happy land of civil and religious freedom—but a crushed, mutilated degraded—'Niobe of Nations.'" She herself had no intention of acknowledging the legitimacy of the Reconstruction government; she could not believe that one as instrumental as Curry had been in charting the course of the Confederacy could so quickly foreswear his allegiance to his homeland. "Nothing but the desire to save my brother's life would have induced me to visit a section, which it is probably unnecessary to tell you I cordially detest," she declared, making reference to her recent visit to New York City.[42]

Still, although Evans clearly believed that Curry had gone too far, she managed to excuse her political mentor's impetuosity. There was, after all, no point in alienating the congressman whose favor she had courted so assiduously. Curry's considerable talents might well afford him a place in the new regime, and Evans knew how helpful powerful men could be. On a more practical level, Evans would need access to the "valuable *congressional documents*" contained in Curry's library if she were to write her history. "The truths of history crystallize slowly [and] it will be a gigantic task to eliminate them from the *debris* of falsehood and exaggeration," the would-be historian complained. She hoped that she could count on Curry to help her sort out her "data."[43]

If Evans was prepared to make an exception in Curry's case, however, she held her friend and colleague Mary Virginia Terhune to more exacting standards. In 1862, she had branded as a traitor the novelist who had been so lavish in her praise of *Beulah*; she never changed her opinion.[44] "It was with painful emotions of mingled shame and indignation that I learned that 'Marion Harland,' the boast and ornament of Virginia literature, had

42. See Evans to Curry, October 7, 1865, in Curry Papers, Library of Congress. Her brother Howard never recovered from his wounds. Fidler, *Augusta Evans Wilson*, 122–23, 146.

43. Evans to Curry, October 7, 1865, in Curry Papers, Library of Congress.

44. See Terhune, Review of *Beulah*, in Augusta Evans Wilson File, Alabama Department of Archives and History.

deserted the cause of her native state, of the bleeding South, who had felt so proud of her genius," Evans wrote. Outraged that Terhune "remained at the North, living contentedly among the oppressors of the *only free* people left upon the American continent," Evans struggled to explain the writer's behavior: "I have been told her husband voted for Lincoln; but I am amazed that she ever for one instant suffered his abolition views to distort and discolor her own." Recollecting the positive impression Terhune had made when the two women first met in J. C. Derby's New York office, Evans seemed to take Terhune's decision to cast her loyalty with her northern husband as a personal affront. "I am totally unprepared for the announcement that she chose to side with the Philistines at this great crisis. I am mortified that a Southern woman should thus disgrace her section."[45]

Whether or not Terhune ever learned of Evans' censure remains open to question. The publishing firm of Derby and Jackson, which at one time had held Evans and Terhune under contract, failed in 1861, and although Derby continued to correspond with both writers after his enforced retirement, there is no indication that he ever again sought to bring together the two women whose friendship he had nurtured.[46] On the other hand, as late as 1903 Terhune assured a biographer of her abiding affection for "Mrs. Wilson," remarking that they had been friends for many years; Terhune's 1910 autobiography provides much the same information.[47] One thing is certain. Evans' characterization of Terhune as a turncoat was neither fair nor accurate, for the domestic novelist, who since her early twenties had identified her personal and professional interests with that of her native South, could not so easily forget her past, even as she resolutely linked her future with that of a minister from the North in 1856. "Here, in the home of my girlhood, where everything is unaltered, and I seem welded as it were into the household chain, I cannot believe that my place

45. Evans to Janie Tyler, March 14, 1862, in Fidler, *Augusta Evans Wilson*, 88.

46. See Fidler, *Augusta Evans Wilson*, 88. In an interview for the New York *World* in 1878, Wilson praised Terhune as one of New York's most gifted writers, but she made no effort to renew their acquaintance. See "A Chat with Mrs. Wilson," in Augusta Evans Wilson File, Alabama Department of Archives and History.

47. See Francis Whiting Halsey, "Marion Harland," in *Women Authors of Our Day in Their Homes: Personal Descriptions and Interviews*, ed. Halsey (New York, 1903), 24; and Terhune, *Marion Harland's Autobiography*, 285.

is so soon to be vacant," Terhune wrote her best friend, Virginia Eppes Dance, shortly before the wedding ceremony. "Brain and heart are both so full of crowding thoughts and emotions that I wonder how I preserve a composed manner." Never for one instant had she doubted her choice, Terhune told Dance, "or contemplated this life-long union except with happy hope." Nevertheless, the bride-to-be admitted to "many and solemn thoughts that come to me in hours of solitary reflection," not the least of which was, undoubtedly, the wisdom of marrying a northerner.[48]

That Terhune would permit her marriage vows to take precedence over her sectional loyalties apparently was beyond Evans' comprehension. As part of Evans' postwar effort to portray herself as a real-life heroine, she proudly asserted that she had rejected her only serious suitor, the editor James Reed Spaulding, when she realized that Spaulding's pro-Union sympathies were incompatible with her own; in her eagerness to impress the "poor crippled soldiers, asking me to find them employment," Evans was unwilling to make a distinction between her situation and Terhune's.[49] For her part, Terhune, who in a later incarnation as a domestic adviser repeatedly asserted the primacy of the marriage bond in defining a woman's existence, believed that her choice was clear. "What more does a woman's heart crave," the novelist asked rhetorically, than a "worthy" mate, "one whom she loves and who loves her?"[50] Yet while Terhune assumed her husband's political views publicly as a matter of course, privately her loyalties remained with the land of her birth. While she could appreciate her husband's "staunch feelings of fidelity to the government," unlike the New Jersey–born and –educated Edward Payson Terhune, she found it difficult to sever her "romantic and tender" attachment to the "brave old days that were . . . the poetry of domestic and social life."[51] Thirty years of residence above the Mason-Dixon Line failed to alter Terhune's regional identity. "As a Virginia woman, I am your debtor for the words of kindly appreciation," Terhune wrote an enthusiastic reader in

48. Mary Virginia Terhune to Virginia Eppes Dance, August 16, 1856, in Terhune Papers, Duke.

49. Evans to Curry, May 7, 1866, in Curry Papers, Library of Congress. See also Deleon, "Biographical Reminiscences," 148–49; and Fidler, "Life and Works," 19n.

50. Terhune to Dance, November 8, 1857, in Terhune Papers, Duke.

51. Terhune, *Marion Harland's Autobiography*, 388.

1886. "Unwittingly you have touched me on a spot where I am most vulnerable to praise. I love my native State!"[52]

Terhune's efforts to adopt her husband's Republican world view were greatly facilitated by her highly politicized childhood. Under the expert tutelage of her father, Samuel Hawes, a Whig party stalwart, Terhune had come to view the fortunes of the South as inextricably tied to those of the country as a whole. Hawes, a slaveholder who believed slavery more a necessary evil than a positive good, had campaigned hard against expansionism; he argued that the peculiar institution must be allowed to die a natural death if the Union were to remain intact. While Terhune later took exception to her father's position on slavery—she came to believe that slavery was the only way to civilize a dangerously savage race—she accepted his contention that the Union was sacred. Thus, whereas Evans, the daughter of a militant expansionist, held that Unionism and southern rights were, by definition, mutually exclusive, Terhune could recognize that was not necessarily the case. Still, with the escalation of sectional tensions in the years immediately preceding the Civil War, Terhune found it more and more difficult to view the situation from a purely intellectual standpoint; her emotions kept intruding. Although she could and did deny her southern partisanship in the late 1850s much the same way Caroline Gilman, Caroline Hentz, and Maria McIntosh did a decade before, as the country moved ineluctably toward armed conflict, Terhune, like the first generation of southern domestic novelists, found the tension between what was and what ought to be almost unbearable. Ironically, the "internecine conflict" that had provided Evans with any number of previously unknown pleasures drained every ounce of Terhune's existing happiness.

In the early years of her marriage, Terhune was not required to subordinate her affection for her region to her feelings for her husband; in fact, her private correspondence and public recollections suggest that during this period her loyalty to the South grew even stronger. The Reverend Mr. Terhune had been called to the "rambling hamlet" of Charlotte Court-House, Virginia, less than a day's drive from his bride's former Richmond residence but a world apart in its myriad "historical associations." It was in "Charlotte C.H.," for example, that Terhune furthered

52. Mary Virginia Terhune to Mrs. Early, July 2, 1886, in Barrett Author Collection.

her appreciation of colonial history and began collecting the "genealogical details" and "tales of real life and happenings" that she would later publish as *Some Colonial Homesteads and Their Stories* (1899); it was there that she made the lasting acquaintance of Patrick Henry's grandson and biographer Wirt Henry and John Randolph's nephew and heir St. George Randolph.[53] "Every other name mentioned in my hearing was interwoven with recitals of deeds of valor and of statesmanship performed by the fathers of American history," Terhune marveled. "The very earth was soaked" in history. Situated in her "white cottage, a story-and-a-half high, fronted and backed by wide porches," Terhune had merely to look out the window to see the courthouse designed by Thomas Jefferson in 1823 and its less auspicious but equally significant predecessor where both Patrick Henry and John Randolph had bade their "adoring constituents" farewell upon their retirement from public life. In Terhune's mind "the Past, with its tender and hallowed memories," and "the Present with calm, real pleasures," converged in the sleepy "shiretown" she called home for some three years, and it was precisely this sense of the past in the present that the novelist took with her into "the bright although vague future."[54]

If Terhune's residence in Charlotte Court-House broadened her understanding of the South's critical role in the building of the nation, it also confirmed her positive opinion of its peculiar institution, for although the new bride willingly accepted her husband's refusal to own slaves, she found it difficult to run her household without them. Her mother, Terhune recalled, had been a "good housekeeper," but her ability to keep "the wheels of her machine in smooth ruts" depended more upon the efforts of her "old and competent servants" than her native ability: "I doubt if she had ever swept a room, or roasted a piece of meat in her life." Terhune herself had been "considered to have a turn, if not a talent for housewifery" in her father's house; she was thus confident of her ability "to navigate the unknown seas that looked calm and bright from the shore" (334). Yet the primarily supervisory skills that had won her accolades before her

53. Terhune's *Some Colonial Homesteads and Their Stories* (New York, 1899) was followed by *More Colonial Homesteads and Their Stories* (New York, 1899), as well as a series of historical biographies. See also Halsey, "Marion Harland," 28.

54. Terhune to Dance, August 16, 1856, in Terhune Papers, Duke; Terhune, *Marion Harland's Autobiography*, 313–14. The latter work is cited parenthetically in the text by page number in the remainder of this section of this chapter.

marriage were poorly suited to her current circumstances. The parish did provide a cook, Emily, "one of the superfluous 'hands' who were hired out from year's end to year's end," but she proved to be completely incompetent as well as "shiftless and indifferent." Furthermore, Emily was not above "stealing" from the larder. Terhune could not release Emily from her "contract" on the grounds of her incompetence—hands "were not warranted as first-class workers"—and neither could she effectively discipline the woman, because she did not own her. Virtually alone in the kitchen of the "prosperous county parish" parsonage, where "liberal hospitality was the law of daily living," Terhune confronted her domestic limitations (334). "I was as unlearned as the babe unborn in everything that a practical housekeeper should know," the minister's wife remembered with chagrin, but significantly, she kept her troubles to herself. "If my cook did not understand her business," Terhune resolved, "I would not confess it"—as if admitting her inability to "manage" the clearly unmanageable Emily were somehow a poor reflection on her aristocratic southern heritage (338).

In the spring of 1858, Terhune's idyll in "the nest beneath the oaks" threatened to come to an end. Her father-in-law, Judge John Terhune, had long advised his son to seek a city parish to advance rapidly. Much to the novelist's consternation, her husband finally took his father's words to heart and initiated a search for an alternative pastorate. The church at Charlotte Court-House was "eminently respectable in character, and honorable in all things pertaining to church traditions," Terhune wrote somewhat defensively fifty years after the Reverend Mr. Terhune had resigned his post, but it was undeniably in "the backwoods" of Virginia and thus unlikely to provide any "hope of preferment." In view of the minister's superior "talent and education" as well as his ever-increasing family, this was a very real concern (351). Still, while Terhune reminded herself that she had promised "of her own free will and accord" before her marriage never to attempt to "sway" her husband's judgment "in anything relating to his profession," she was hard-pressed to keep her resolutions, especially when he expressed interest in a pulpit in the North over that of the Third Presbyterian Church in Richmond. "I wanted to go to Richmond *horribly*," she remembered. "Family, friends, ties of early association, strengthened by nearly fifteen years of residence at the formative period of life" called her "back home." But in spite of Terhune's longing to rejoin her "brothers, sisters, and true and tried intimates," "letters bearing Northern postmarks ... flutter[ed] down" with invitations that her husband ultimately found more attractive than those issued by any parish in his wife's native region. Although Terhune "prayed with strong crying and tears, that God would send us to Richmond," her husband chose a pastorate in Newark, New Jersey. "I needed Spartan firmness of will and stoical reticence," she recollected, but even that could not stop her frustration at the injustice of it all. The yearlong ordeal, full of "perplexity, puzzle, and pain" was to culminate in her removal from her beloved South and relocation to the hated "Yankee land" (353).

By the time the Terhunes broke up their household in Virginia, the novelist had reconciled herself to her fate, her "high revolt" replaced by "a fair show of cheerfulness." What else, she queried, could "a sensible, God-fearing woman" do other than "make the very best of what no human power could avert?" (354). In later years Terhune came to look upon the move to Newark as divinely ordained—"I see so clearly the working out of a benign and merciful design," she wrote in 1910, "that I cannot say whether humility or devout gratitude has the ascendancy in my thoughts." Yet her acceptance at the time was predicated less on faith than on an elaborate web of self-denial and deceit (354). By the time Terhune had packed her "Lares and Penates" and prepared to journey north, she had nearly convinced herself that she was moving not to the dreaded region she had so effectively portrayed in her fiction but to an altogether different place. It was, she remembered, in response to repeated demands for "defense of the reasons for tearing ourselves up by the tender roots and transplanting the tender vine" that she first came to make the distinction between the Middle Atlantic states and "Yankee land" that would prove so critical to her subsequent psychological survival. Disquieted beyond belief by her relatives' gloomy predictions about life in the North, anxious to remove some part of the "burden of explanation" from the shoulders of the "worn and harassed man of the hour," she inadvertently became "an honest defender of her husband's home state as an entity distinct from the North" and, apparently through simple repetition, almost came to believe her own rhetoric (356). Still, as the February departure date drew nearer, the arguments that had seemed so persuasive in Richmond became less and less convincing, and the Reverend Mr. Terhune's failure to recognize the significance of his wife's protestations that they were not in fact traveling to his native region did nothing to bolster the novelist's confidence.

Terhune's "contradistinction" between the North and the Middle Atlantic states enabled her to retain her identity with her native region without violating her primary loyalty to her husband; it also helped her reconcile herself to her extensive duties as a minister's wife on "alien soil" (356). Clearly, the woman who once remarked that "the importance of such a trust as the happiness of another" was enough to make her "tremble" recognized the potentially damaging impact that her well-known southern partisanship could have on her husband's Newark congregation, just as she realized the challenge she faced working among a people she had long regarded as hopelessly corrupt. In choosing to locate herself geographically and, more important, psychologically in what she perceived as the nation's politically temperate middle zone rather than the incendiary North, Terhune simultaneously freed herself from any sense of hypocrisy and, at least superficially, reunited her divided self: the bride who, upon the eve of marriage, had shuddered at the thought of "impairing" her husband's "usefulness" and "clouding his life with disappointment" and the novelist who had regularly portrayed northerners, especially northern women, as slaves to money and fashion could under these circumstances coexist in relative peace. "I never before knew and felt my own deficiencies as I do now," Terhune had written Virginia Eppes Dance in 1856; by the spring of 1859, the novelist's awareness of her own limitations was all the more acute.[55] But while Terhune's position was undeniably difficult—she was, after all, far from home and family—her conscientious struggle to mute her partisanship eventually paid off. Both she and her husband were "petted and made much of," and after a time the crucial "contradistinction" became automatic (357).

Yet Mary Virginia Terhune's struggle to reflect well upon her minister husband was not without personal cost. Beginning in the spring of 1859, the novelist's immersion in her various church activities left her little occasion to write, much less to indulge in another favorite pastime of speculating on the direction of contemporary politics. Whereas in Charlotte Court-House Terhune's status as a newlywed had freed her from many obligations, in Newark she could claim no such exemption (357). Teaching

55. Terhune to Dance, August 16, 1856, in Terhune Papers, Duke.

Bible class, chairing committee meetings, and running a household with nothing more than "white servants" took up much of her time. Visits to New York City, where "the best libraries and shops in the country" afforded "numberless means of entertainment and education," occupied whatever hours remained (358). In fact, Terhune's involvement in her New Jersey parish was so complete that, if her 1910 autobiography is to be believed, the crucial presidential election of 1860 took her completely by surprise. "So much for so little!" she recalled commenting at the time, professing total mystification as to why men were marching in the streets. Pronouncing the spectacle "ingenious and amusing," she nevertheless dismissed it as just so much bombast: "The President will be elected, as other Presidents have been, and as maybe a hundred others will be, and there the farce will end" (360).

Still, although the novelist's lack of leisure cannot be disputed, it is not sufficient explanation for her purported unfamiliarity with those same political issues that had previously informed her fiction and provided her with an endless source of amusement. The writer who as a young girl had flaunted a medal with Clay's image on one side and the slogan "PROTECTION AND UNION" on the other merely to "spite sundry fiery democrats or *Polkats*" at her school would hardly lose interest in the vital questions of her day, particularly when the future of her native South was under discussion.[56] It is far more likely that Terhune's "ignorance" was the result of a conscious or unconscious decision to deny the severity of the growing rift between the North and South, to direct her attention toward less disturbing matters. Under these circumstances, Terhune's assertion that she realized the significance of the presidential race only after her husband explained it to her gains credence. For although Terhune the southern propagandist clearly needed no one to tell her that the sky was "red and lowering in the South" and that there was no telling "what the rabble may do" given the poor quality of leadership above and below the Mason-Dixon Line—she had been arguing much the same thing for a number of years—Terhune the southerner married to a northerner could not afford to entertain such disturbing ideas (360). Thus, when confronted with her husband's decision to cast his ballot for the "low-born" Mr. Lincoln, who had "no pretensions to breeding" to recommend him, Terhune pretended

56. Terhune to Dance, November 16, 1844, *ibid.*

not to understand; the alternative was simply too much for her psyche to bear (361).

Terhune's fifth novel, *Nemesis* (1860), reflected the tension that permeated the novelist's private and public life. A tale of injury and betrayal across three generations, *Nemesis* was set in postrevolutionary Virginia, a time and a place that Terhune apparently believed best symbolized the moment when northern and southern interests were in closest accord. Chronicling the troubled relationship between two families—northerners Mark and Bessy Hale and their infant daughter, Kitty, and their wealthy landlords, the Malcolm Argyles—*Nemesis* illustrated how seemingly insurmountable difficulties could be resolved over the course of history. Arguing that no offense was too great to be forgiven, that no mistake was irreversible, the novel, which gained an air of credibility from Terhune's repeated references to her antiquarian research in Charlotte Court-House, articulated its author's fervent hope that with proper guidance and encouragement, the North and the South could regain the sense of shared purpose that had characterized their early union. "I do not pretend today that my tale is a literal transcript of the lives of the various personages introduced, or that I have not interpolated characters and events," Terhune stated in her introduction to the novel, insisting that if she had told the literal truth, no one would have believed it. Whatever the balance between fact and fiction, Terhune's message was clear: as she put it in her autobiography, "The good Ship of State has been driving straight on to the rocks" since time immemorial, and despite all indications to the contrary, it had not struck yet.[57]

The story opens with the Hales' arrival in tidewater Virginia from Massachusetts. Mark Hale, a veteran of the Revolution, suffers from the double burden of poor health and humble means; he has traveled south in hopes that the temperate climate and flourishing economy might improve his lot. Yet, in spite of Hale's numerous advance preparations—he makes arrangements through a local land agent to rent a cottage and a small plot of land from the wealthy but prejudiced Malcolm Argyle—his plans to cobble shoes and farm are destined for failure. The rental property is in poor repair, the land is unsuitable for the kind of farming with which Hale

57. Terhune, *Marion Harland's Autobiography*, 360.

is familiar, and, most important, there is no market for shoes, since slaves produce whatever footwear the planter community requires. Bessy Hale's attempts to assist her husband in making a living are similarly frustrating. Seeking employment as a seamstress or maid of all work, Bessy quickly finds that there is no demand for her services. Slaves perform all routine maintenance, she is told, and even if there were a need to hire outsiders, free black labor would be preferable to white. Matters are further complicated by the Hales' uncanny ability to offend their new neighbors by their unwillingness to ask for, much less to take, advice; the northerners' natural independence, a product of their New England heritage, is interpreted in the South as rudeness and pretension. Were it not for the benevolence of Miss Barbara Brook, the chatelaine of Ben Lomond, the Argyle estate, the transplanted northerners would have starved.

Winter comes, and the Hales' lot only gets worse. Mark Hale falls seriously ill as the result of too little food and too much worry, and Bessy and young Kitty can do nothing to assuage his misery. On the contrary, Bessy's pride drives off those who would have helped her. Although Barbara Brook continues to provide whatever assistance she can, her generosity reaches its limit. All household expenditures must be approved by the Argyle business manager, Mr. Sancroft, and that "money-worshipping hypocrite" is determined to put a halt to the housekeeper's charity.[58] The Argyle children are equally unresponsive to their tenants' growing desperation. Malcolm, Jr., heir to Ben Lomond, is away at college; he assumes that the New Englanders are adjusting to their new environment. His sister Jessie whose besetting sin is laziness, does not bother to inform him otherwise; having enjoyed ridiculing the northern family's pretenses to gentility, she now applauds their rapid decline. Malcolm's older sister, Eleanor, who is completely heartless, goes out of her way to hasten the Hales' demise. Acting upon the widely held opinion that the Hales were "vulgar, pushy people" who "ought to be taught where their level was," the elder daughter denies Bessy Hale's tearful supplications for an extension on her overdue rent and ensures that the family will be prosecuted to the fullest extent of the law (133). "I am not my father's man-of-business," Eleanor declares. "I never interfere in such matters" (151–52). By the

---

58. Mary Virginia Terhune [Marion Harland], *Nemesis* (New York, 1860), 91. Hereinafter cited parenthetically by page number in the text.

time Malcolm, Jr., learns of his sister's cruelty, Mark Hale has died in prison and his wife and daughter have disappeared.

Years later, Bessy Hale returns with Kitty to Ben Lomond in order to avenge her husband's death. Having married into wealth and power, Bessy, now known as Mrs. Rashleigh, is pleased to discover that the Argyles have fallen upon hard times. Malcolm, Jr., is a lonely bachelor; Jessie has lost her beauty and her health; Eleanor is married to an inveterate gambler. But although Bessy quickly achieves many of her objectives—she manages to involve Eleanor's husband in a scandal and expose the diabolical Mr. Sancroft as a forger—things do not work out exactly as she had hoped. Notably, Kitty, now known as Katherine, who for some unexplained reason has no memory of her past, falls in love with Malcolm in spite of the vast difference in their ages, and Mrs. Rashleigh's attempts to put a halt to the courtship are unsuccessful. Thus, while Bessy can take great satisfaction in rejecting Eleanor's pleas on her husband's behalf, using the identical language Eleanor herself used so long ago, Bessy's love for Kitty ultimately prevents her from exacting total retribution (475–79). In fact, once Kitty and Malcolm have married, Bessy decides to let matters stand and dedicates the remainder of her life and fortune toward philanthropic works in the community that had scorned her in an earlier incarnation. (A severe blow to the head seems to have influenced Bessy's actions, although the connection between the accident and Bessy's subsequent good works is not altogether clear.) The story ends with the birth of Bessy's grandchild, Mark Hale Argyle, the embodiment of the best qualities of the New England artisan class and the southern aristocracy, and the living symbol of the union between North and South.

Terhune's curious narrative incorporated many themes favored by the first generation of southern domestic novelists. *Nemesis* argued that difficulties between the North and South resulted from unfamiliarity with regional customs rather than inhabitants' fundamental incompatibility and that with proper education sectional dissension could be wholly eliminated.[59] For example, Mark Hale fails primarily because he is ignorant about southern labor and agriculture, not because he is ill-suited to the region. He and his family flounder because they inadvertently alienate

---

59. Hentz's *Lovell's Folly* and McIntosh's *Two Lives* are also excellent examples of this argument.

their community, not because that community, with the obvious exception
of several members of the Argyle clan, is uncaring. That Barbara Brook
and Malcolm, Jr., continue to blame themselves for the Hales' tragedy
long afterward suggests that the inhumanity the northerners experience
was more a question of individual rather than regional depravity. Even in
these most extraordinary of circumstances, Terhune implied, neither
North nor South was wholly to blame. If nothing else, Bessy Hale's mis-
spent life illustrated how destructive holding a region and a people responsible for the immorality of a few could be, an idea that had particular
resonance for the times in which Terhune herself lived. "The mills of the
gods grind slowly," Terhune admitted, but it was not for man or, for that
matter, woman to attempt to accelerate their progress.[60]

But while Terhune continued publicly to express her optimism that
North and South would long endure, privately she suspected the worst.
For all her professions of political ignorance in the fall of 1860, she was
thoroughly convinced that the Constitutional Union party's presidential
ticket of Bell and Everett was the only choice for "lovers of peace and
concord," and when that party, which seemed to Terhune "to represent
the sanest element in this mammoth muddle," failed to win the election,
she knew that it was only a question of time. Although the novelist continued to put up a brave front, her applause for her young son's attempt to
cool a South Carolinian's temper by filling his hat with ice water and her
laughter over "gloomy predictions" that the Confederate cavalry would
be stabled in Fanueil Hall "inside of three months from the day of the
inauguration of the 'Springfield Ape'" did little to reduce her tension and,
in fact, may have accentuated her feelings of helplessness.[61]

Years later, she recalled "the awful awakening" from her self-
constructed "fool's paradise of incredulity and levity" with nothing less
than horror, particularly when she realized the danger in which she had
placed her family. For in a final act of denial, Mary Virginia Terhune had
insisted on following through with plans for a southern vacation in early
April, 1861, even though she knew that the Confederates had laid siege to
Fort Sumter. Two weeks into her trip, reality came crashing down. On
April 14, the "good Ship of State" ran aground in Charleston Harbor.

60. Terhune, *Nemesis*, epigraph.
61. Terhune, *Marion Harland's Autobiography*, 361, 366.

Terhune's diary captured her anguish. "For two days," she wrote from
Richmond, "the air was thick with rumors of war and bloodshed. . . . For
two days, thousands and hundreds . . . cried mightily unto our country's
God to avert this last and direst trial . . . [but] under the whole expanse of
heaven, there was no answer to those prayers, except the reverberation of
the cruel guns." As men and women poured into the streets to celebrate
the Confederate "victory," Terhune stood motionless. "As in a baleful
dream, I comprehended, in the sick whirl of conflicting sensations, what
Rebellion, active and in arms, would mean in hundreds of homes on both
sides of the border."[62]

Terhune's premonition proved accurate. In her immediate family
alone, four noncombatants fell victim to the devastating effects of war,
including her young son; her sister Alice, who suffered from a chronic
lung ailment that worsened during an enforced stay in the North; her
father, whose well-known pro-Union sympathies before the war led to
wartime persecution; and her grandmother, who was the wife and mother
of Revolutionary War veterans. Those who survived suffered as well. One
of Terhune's brothers, a lieutenant in the Richmond Howitzers, was captured and imprisoned for a year at Fort Delaware; another brother, a minister in a "country parish," endured repeated raids by the Federals and was
menaced at least twice by "cavalry dashes under leaders whose names were
a terror throughout southern and central Virginia"; still another brother,
"an utter stranger to physical fear in any shape whatsoever," enlisted at
the age of fourteen and courted danger "as a courier under Lee's own
eye." During that dreadful interval, Terhune recalled, "we were to need
all the fullness of consolation that could be expressed from divining grace
and human friendships."[63]

In her final domestic novel, *Sunnybank* (1866), Terhune challenged
herself to examine what she believed was the senseless violence of four
years past. Drawing heavily from her experiences and those of her southern friends and family, Terhune used her unique perception as a southerner in the North to inform her exploration of the causes and consequences of sectional strife. Resurrecting the genre that had served her well
before the war, Terhune sought to convey the pain and anger she suffered

62. *Ibid.*, 368–69, 371.
63. *Ibid.*, 389, 397.

as a daughter of the South who opposed war on moral grounds and to come to terms with her grief. But just as Terhune misjudged the immediacy of war in 1861—"So foolish was I, and ignorant of the excesses to which sectional fury can carry individuals and nations," she remarked—in 1866 she miscalculated the capacity of her chosen vehicle for catharsis.[64] For the literary form that had been designed over the antebellum period to minimize sectional conflict through championing the cause of the South did not lend itself to Terhune's postwar expressions of disgust and horror. Attempting to explain a war she could not begin to comprehend, Terhune predictably seized upon the familiar medium of domestic fiction only to find that that medium, like everything else, had been irrevocably altered by civil war.

In *Sunnybank* Terhune sought out the familiar, returning to the characters and the setting of her first and most successful novel, *Alone*. Picking up the story of the trials and tribulations of the ever-popular Ida Ross some twenty years after Ida had married her youthful sweetheart, Morton Lacy, and retired to her plantation to mother a new generation of morally and intellectually independent southerners, *Sunnybank*, which took its name from Ida's ancestral home, evoked a world of comfort and ease that Terhune clearly believed was a thing of the past. At Sunnybank, where violets always bloomed earlier than they did "anywhere else north of the James River" and "crocuses, jonquils, and snowdrops" burst forth in a riot of color, Ida, her husband, their children, Elinor, Ross, and Lynn, and their ward, Agatha Lamar, "lineal descendant[s] and honorable representative[s] of one of those most famous ornaments of our Republic—the first families of Virginia"—lead exemplary lives.[65] In this magical community where hospitality was the order of the day, men and women intuitively recognized their responsibilities to their social and economic equals and inferiors; master and mistress labored alongside their devoted slaves. Questions, political or otherwise, were resolved amicably, for the community was as one. The life-style *Sunnybank* represented was, in short, the nearest thing to perfection that mortal man had ever achieved, and it

64. *Ibid.*, 370.
65. Mary Virginia Terhune [Marion Harland], *Sunnybank* (New York, 1866), 7. Hereinafter cited parenthetically by page number in the text.

was with regret that Mary Virginia Terhune, who had enjoyed its arcadian splendor, recorded its passing.

Terhune's decision to go full circle and resume the Ida Ross story was influenced in part by her reduced economic circumstances. The failure of her publishers, Derby and Jackson, in 1861 had cut off the "sure and certain source of revenue" provided by her "good sellers," and the Terhunes who until this point had "never known the pinch of financial 'difficulties,'" found it hard to adjust.[66] The war itself exacerbated the existing strain because Terhune found herself ostracized by a significant portion of her audience. Southerners, as onetime friend Augusta Evans quickly pointed out, held Terhune's marriage to a northerner and continued residence on "alien soil" against her; what could be tolerated before the war as a mere lapse in judgment was simply unacceptable during wartime. Northerners, too, were suspicious of Terhune's apparently divided loyalties; the nostalgic tone of *Nemesis* could not compensate for the overt partisanship of Terhune's previous novels. As a result, Terhune's fourth book, the mediocre *Miriam* (1862), and a halfhearted volume of short stories, *Husbands and Homes* (1865), found few readers above or below the Mason-Dixon Line. By returning to the tried and true, Terhune doubtlessly hoped to revive her flagging popularity and settle her financial problems once and for all.

Yet Terhune's resumption of the story that had launched her career reflected more than her craving for economic security; her desire to impose some sort of order on her personal past was of even greater consequence. In *Sunnybank*, which opened at approximately the same time Terhune made her final journey South before the "four long years" between 1861 and 1865, the novelist essentially relived the war, incorporating many of her contemporaneous words and actions into her text.[67] The correspondence between the events of *Sunnybank* and Terhune's later factual account is striking, particularly in the novel's opening scenes where the potential for national conflict is scrutinized. For example, in the first chapter of the 1866 novel, Elinor Lacy, who, like Terhune, is in love with a northerner, listens to her father, brothers, and close male friends debate the

66. Terhune, *Marion Harland's Autobiography*, 363.
67. *Ibid.*, 382–87.

question of secession. "We, who uphold the right of Secession," Rolf Kingston, a brash young planter, asserts, "declare that each State is a complete living system in itself; that separated from one or all of the rest, it could exist and act freely as before" (65). The "unequal, grievous and oppressive" Constitution, he continues, was designed to keep the South in a permanent state of subordination. Having encouraged "the domination of the manufacturing and commercial section over the agricultural [and] burdensome taxation without adequate representation" from its incipiency, the "doctrine of consolidation" now proved the "chief obstacle to the independence of the South." In view of the "numberless encroachments of the North upon the prerogatives of the South," right-minded southerners had no other alternative than to seek out a more congenial system of government. "It is not in the nature of Southerners to submit to impertinent dictation, to interference with their property and opinions," the aristocratic youth declares (62). "The time is very near at hand when every brave son of the South may be . . . [a] 'hero in the strife'" (69).

Elinor's father, the very image of Samuel Hawes, recoils: "A bleeding dismembered Republic! a body of death, crumbling and falling apart, in place of a glorious, united indissoluble Nation!" Surely no "words of horror and grief" were "too strong" with which to describe the "calamity" that was "the plaything of a thousand flippant tongues!" (65). The South had "lived and prospered" under the Constitution "for more than seventy years," Morton Lacy argues. "Hers have been the chief places in our national councils, and the most lucrative offices in the gift of the government" (63). Dismissing Kingston's contention that "oppression, robbery and the threatened subversion of cherished liberties" made secession a necessity as "the clap-trap of thwarted politicians, ravening after the loaves and fishes upon which they have fattened for so many years," Lacy reiterates his conviction that the "Federal Union is the essence of national life" (56–61, 63).

Terhune's 1910 autobiography recalled the same occasion, albeit on a different date. On the evening of April 14, the novelist wrote, "two or three visitors dropped in" at her father's house in Richmond, and "the talk of the evening" turned toward "the Great Controversy": both sides were "brought forward, temperately, but with force born of conviction." Her brother-in-law, John Miller, "opened the ball" by voicing his hope that "the North was now convinced that the South was in earnest in maintaining her rights." An unnamed youth concurred. "The dissatisfaction of the South," he comments, was "as old as the Constitution itself." At that time, a "farsighted statesman" had "prophesied" that "the consolidation policy taught in the Constitution" would be found "unequal, grievous, and oppressive." The prophet had foreseen that "the manufacturer of the North would dominate the agriculturist of the South; that there would be burdensome taxation without adequate representation; in short, that there would be numberless encroachments of the North upon the prerogatives of the Southern slaveholder." "For more than seventy years, the South has prospered under the Constitution," the Reverend Mr. Terhune interjects. "Hers have been the chief places in our national councils and the most lucrative offices in the gift of the government." At that point, Mrs. Hawes, like her fictional counterpart, Ida Ross Lacy, changes the subject.[68]

"If I go somewhat into the details of the conversation," Terhune wrote apologetically in 1910, "it is because I would make clear the truth that each party in the struggle we feared might be imminent, believed honestly that justice and right were at the foundation of faith." Having written down "the substance of the memorable discussion" just as she recorded other incidents of the "ever-to-be-remembered era, while it was still in the making," she could state with certainty that she gave the story correctly. Still, for all her insistence upon its accuracy, Terhune's later account of her reaction to the coming of war differs significantly from her more immediate recollection, suggesting that the novelist's perception of herself, and consequently her attitude, had changed over time. In *Sunnybank*, for example, Terhune's alter ego, Elinor Lacy, listens intently to the menfolks' political exchange, but neither she nor her mother intervenes; they are, quite simply, too confused to offer an opinion. Conversely, in Terhune's autobiographical description of the identical scenario, she reports that she took vigorous exception to the notion of secession. "There has been no madness equal to Secession since the swine ran violently down a steep place into the sea," she "retorted flippantly," predicting that "the choking in the waves" would come later.[69] Terhune's probable 1910 revision of the incident to give herself a voice emphasized both the enormity of the psychological task she set for herself during the immediate postwar

68. *Ibid.*, 374–76.
69. *Ibid.*

period and the relative difficulty with which she met the self-imposed demands. For in publicly recording her supposedly long-standing reservations about the Confederacy while at the same time professing undying
loyalty to her native region, Terhune indicated that she had come to terms
with her divided loyalties privately. Almost fifty years after she had initiated her quest for psychic wholeness, Terhune found inner peace.

In *Sunnybank*, Terhune began to formulate the argument that would
later allow her to deny any inconsistencies in her simultaneous support of
the Confederacy and the Union. Drawing a distinction between Virginia
and the South as a whole in much the same way she had separated the
Middle Atlantic states from the North, Terhune portrayed her beloved
state as the victim of political treachery, a pawn in the hands of unscrupulous southern statesmen. Virginia secedes only because "an overstrained
and false sense of honor" compels it to spring to the aid of its inferiors;
undone by the very code of chivalry it has struggled to uphold, the "gal-
lant Commonwealth" succumbs to the "flattering lures of specious politicians." The unhappy rupture between North and South is "a spectacle
so monstrous in ghastliness of woe as to wring from every patriot . . . a
cry of bitterness like that which rent the Saviour's heart as he wept over
Jerusalem the doomed." Superior in all things to "her southern sisters,"
Virginia sacrifices "her bravest sons" for an allegedly "condemned and
abhorred" cause (57–58).

As the war progresses, Virginia continues to suffer at the hands of
what Terhune refers to as the "far-off South." "Bow down to us as your
saviors and masters," the "arrogant far-Southerners" demand. Determined to punish Virginia for hesitating in seceding, Confederate politicians require "the once proud Old Dominion" to engage in acts of con-
trition. "Treat us well," they warn, "or we will withdraw from your
defenses, and you will be swallowed, at a gulp, by the ravenous Yank."
With this sort of ultimatum, the Lacys' ward, Agatha Lamar, wonders,
"What is poor, cheated famishing Virginia to do, but bow her hoary, dis-
crowned head in base subjection, and, clinging to the gray skirts of her
new masters, implore them not to leave her in the lurch?" (305). Across
the state, Agatha observes, "want stares in the face of those who prior to
the war lived in luxurious ease" (328). Stripped of its foodstuffs, livestock,
and able-bodied men, Virginia testifies to the infinite greed of the Deep

South that Mary Virginia Terhune's chief rival and critic, Augusta Evans, called home.

Clearly, Terhune's portrait of Virginia immediately before the war reflects her Whig antecedents. Her assertion that Virginia was manipulated into secession by the Deep South, that only the "rabble" of society supported the April 17 ordinance that irrevocably linked the novelist's birthplace with the Confederacy, says much about the prevalence of Unionist sentiment in the antebellum Upper South, particularly within Terhune's social and economic milieu. Yet Terhune's discussion contained an element of wishful thinking, for while it is incorrect to suggest that all Virginians supported secession, it is equally incorrect to imply that secession was forcibly imposed.[70] Terhune's implication that planter-class Virginians were victims of Deep South conspirators reveals more about what the pacifistic Terhune wanted to believe than what actually happened. Even the behavior of her own father, Whig party regular Samuel Hawes, failed to bear out her postwar interpretation of the events leading up to secession. Although Hawes initially repudiated secessionism, he quickly came to support the Confederacy and willingly sent food, supplies, and at least two of his sons into battle; there was no force involved.

Terhune's failure to include in *Sunnybank* her eyewitness accounts of the celebrations in Richmond on April 14 and again three days later, then, seems to indicate that while she was not unaware of the widespread support for secession, she was as yet unable to acknowledge it; certainly it was not from unfamiliarity with the circumstances. At the news of Fort Sumter's surrender, she wrote in 1910, the streets "were alive with men, women and children. Firecrackers, pistols and guns were discharged into the throbbing air . . . secession flags blossomed in windows and from roofs; were waved from doors and porches by girls and women." In Capitol Square, "the grounds were filled with a tumultuous crowd," and as the "crowd cheered itself mad over a fresh demonstration of popular passion," Terhune noticed the object of its jubilation: "The rebel flag had been run up from the peak of the Capitol roof!"[71] Terhune's virtual silence in 1866

70. See Daniel W. Crofts, *Reluctant Confederates: The Upper South Unionists in the Secession Crisis* (Chapel Hill, 1989).

71. Terhune, *Marion Harland's Autobiography*, 371, 373.

on the near-riot in Richmond—the Lacys learn the details of Virginia's secession through a messenger—suggests that she realized on some level that her assertions of Virginia's innocence were unfounded. By 1910, she had, through years of repetition, eliminated the inconsistencies in her argument, at least to her satisfaction. In the immediate aftermath of war, however, she recognized the disjunctions in her interpretation and only through careful editing avoided the most obvious contradictions.

Ironically, it is in her description of the innumerable deprivations that southerners suffered as a consequence of war, experiences she did not know firsthand, that Terhune made a more lasting contribution to postwar literature. "Coffee was no more an every morning institution, nor has tea the aromatic flavor that used to greet the olfactories," Agatha Lamar complains. Sugar is "whitey-brown," and its growing scarcity results in a "corresponding decrease" in "cakes, preserves, and the like sweets" (122). While the Lacy women experiment with a variety of substitutes—roasted and ground black-eyed peas take the place of coffee beans and crushed berries and fruit syrup stand in for sugar—the results are far from satisfactory. "A step toward the achievement of southern independence," Agatha marvels as she spins yarn for the family's winter wardrobe, but Ida Ross Lacy demurs: "A retrogressive step!" she tells her ward. "For this is inferior to that made on the plantation forty years ago, when manufacturers were in their cradle" (329–30). As long as milk and butter are in plentiful supply and the poultry is free from blockaders, there is no danger of starvation at Sunnybank, but as the years pass and the plantation is subjected to repeated raids, the outlook becomes increasingly grim.

The Lacys' imposed isolation from their spiritual community accentuates their physical discomfort. The "neat house of worship" that provided succor to Ida Ross Lacy in the troubled years before her marriage and afterward facilitated the religious instruction of her black and white family has been "twice used as a hospital"; by 1863, it is a barracks, "the seats torn out for firewood and the window sashes dashed from their frames." With neither building nor pastor, "the little flock that gathered in the beloved sanctuary are as sheep scattered abroad" (259). In desperation, Mrs. Lacy turns to the family's faithful retainer Uncle Will for spiritual leadership. Uncle Will, whose ministrations were directly responsible for Ida Ross Lacy's realization of the domestic feminine ideal, leads the white southerners in powerful prayer: "Have mercy upon us, O Lord!

have mercy upon us! for our soul is exceedingly filled with the scorning of those that are at ease, and the contempt of the proud." The "quavering accents of the aged slave, untaught save by the Spirit of . . . God," simultaneously reaffirm the primacy of the master-slave relationship and provide the larger Lacy family with courage to continue their struggle to survive (326–27).

The Lacys' tribulations, Terhune asserted, were "part of the never-to-be-written history of the rebellion," the story of the men and women who were left behind (144). Still, in spite of the valuable insight Terhune's narrative afforded concerning the conditions of the home front, her focus on the harsh realities of the wartime South directly contradicted the highly romanticized version of plantation life that featured prominently in earlier southern domestic fiction and signaled the end of that literary genre. Her portrayal of Virginia as a place unto itself, like her depiction of the South as polarized by the conflicting interests of the planter class and the uneducated masses, was at odds with the standard depiction of that region as a harmonious and, most crucially, homogeneous community. For almost three decades, southern domestic novelists, Terhune herself included, had argued that the South was morally superior to the North by virtue of its indigenous institutions; Terhune's fifth and final volume suggested that this was not the case, that the South was, in fact, neither better nor worse than its northern rival.

That Terhune's divided loyalties impelled her toward this conclusion is clear. Torn between her affection for the South and her deference to her husband, she could only hope that the day would not come when she was forced to choose. For a time, she was able to reconcile her conflict through an elaborate process of denial, convincing herself that there was, in fact, no sectional crisis. Even after the fall of Fort Sumter, she held out hope for rapid reconciliation, using her familiarity with the divisive Clay-Polk election as her point of reference.[72] In *Sunnybank*, Terhune blamed the South, in particular Virginia, for the personal torment she and the thousands she represented were forced to endure. If Virginia had assumed the role of "the Great Pacificator" and had held out the "olive-branch of compromise" to the North and the South, men and women across America would not have been called upon to sacrifice their all (58). "Mar-

72. See *ibid.*, 152–61.

tyrs in the cause of truth" had always stood up "valiantly for the right," Terhune wrote bitterly (305). Why could not Virginia have held firm until the country regained some symptoms of sanity? Using her pen to defuse some portion of her anguish, Terhune translated her grief into domestic fiction and in the process destroyed the genre she had helped to create.

Certainly, Terhune did not consciously challenge the terms of the southern domestic novel; in the midst of her assault, she employed several of its most salient features. For example, in *Sunnybank*, as in all southern domestic fiction, northerners remain the primary villains while southerners possess the preponderance of virtue. The Federals regularly raid the Lacy estate, helping themselves to whatever they can find and encouraging the slave population to run away. Although Uncle Will's influence keeps the servants "miraculously faithful"—Will obeys his "heavenly Marster first!" and his "earthly marster Next!" and requires similar devotion from his brethren—the Lacys hear plenty of horror stories (387). At one nearby plantation, for example, a marauding band "smashed the china and mirrors, split up the piano and bureaus into kindling-wood for their camp fires, carried off and destroyed provisions and clothing, beside pocketing all the silver" and opening a "newly-made grave . . . in quest of plate." "I was a Union man once," a Confederate officer confesses, but the "fiendish spirit" of the invaders has converted him. He is convinced, along with "every intelligent Southerner," that "His Satanic Majesty had his birthplace north of the Mason & Dixon's Line, and . . . holds now his highest court in the city of Washington" (164–65).

The ending of *Sunnybank* likewise illustrated Terhune's efforts to conform. Unlike Evans, who rejected the conventional ending in favor of one she deemed more realistic, Terhune closed the Lacy saga with the marriage of northerner to southerner. Immediately after Appomattox, Harry Wilton marries Elinor Lacy, and together the two prepare to rebuild that which war has destroyed. Still, even in this most conventional of endings, Terhune challenged domestic tradition. For whereas in antebellum fiction northerner married southerner (after having been convinced of the superiority of southern civilization) to give birth to a new generation capable of transcending sectional differences, Harry Wilton weds Elinor Lacy to cement the North's triumph over the South. In the postwar world, Harry's culture will replace Elinor's; he is no longer required to subordinate his materialistic interests to those of the plantation community.[73] In this context, the happy ending was not really happy at all; rather, it was an admission of defeat and, at least for the single remaining southern domestic novelist, an acknowledgment of failure. In spite of her concerted efforts to reclaim the past, Terhune could not regain the world she had lost; neither could she, at least in 1866, exorcise her anger.

In its manipulation of established literary tradition to suit its author's personal needs, *Sunnybank* closely resembled Evans' effort of three years before. Like Evans, Terhune used her own experiences to inform her novel, incorporating her particular opinions and prejudices into the heart of her story. Like Evans, Terhune ventured a unique interpretation of the coming of the war, and like Evans, she despaired as to the continued viability of the aristocratic southern way of life with which she rightly or wrongly identified. In many respects, the final chapters of *Sunnybank* serve as a more realistic conclusion to *Macaria*. For in acknowledging the triumph of the North, *Sunnybank* confirmed Evans' suspicions that the baser elements of society had eroded the South's will to prevail. *Macaria*'s dual heroines, Irene Huntingdon and Electra Grey, paragons of southern virtue, might well vow to remain single in order to defend their culture from northern aggression, but many women would be forced by circumstances, among them economic survival, to accept "Yankee rule" as the inevitable consequence of southern defeat and to make the best of the tragic situation. In pledging her heroines to celibacy, Evans legitimized her own choice, but at least in this instance she probably vastly overestimated the "patriotism" of her countrywomen.[74]

On some level, both Terhune and Evans recognized that the southern domestic novel, as defined before the war, had run its course. Although the genre, which had been used by Caroline Gilman, Caroline Hentz, and Maria McIntosh in the 1830s and 1840s to minimize sectional conflict by stressing the essential similarity of North and South, had survived the

73. Terhune did not believe that some degree of what she called "mercantilism" was necessarily a bad thing. Early in the novel, she anticipates the day when "commercial princes will rule the land" and argues that for this reason "gentlemen, intelligent, cultivated men should enter a profession which has been too long given up to the illiterate or self-educated toilers after wealth for wealth's sake." Terhune, *Sunnybank*, 11.

74. Evans herself married the wealthy Mobilean Lorenzo Madison Wilson in 1868. See Fidler, *Augusta Evans Wilson*, 149.

challenge of a new generation in the middle 1850s, it could withstand no further revision. The initial transformation of southern domestic fiction from a medium of conciliation to one of protest had involved little more than a change of emphasis; conversely, Evans' and Terhune's wartime and immediate postwar endeavors revealed significant—and largely unresolved—ideological divisions. Unable to decide upon the fundamental character of the southern people, much less to explain the South's decision to enter into war, Evans and Terhune compromised the quality of their fictional defense of southern culture to such an extent that at times it was unrecognizable. Evans' decision to write a history of the Confederacy even after acknowledging that *Macaria* was her best book so far was revealing.[75] The most outspoken of the five southern domestic novelists was the first to realize that the southern domestic novel provided an inadequate explanation of the recent past and to seek out an alternative means of expression.

It was not that the southern domestic novel could not accommodate political discourse; on the contrary, antebellum southern domestic fiction was replete with political commentary, articulating an extremely conservative view of southern society while prescribing a greatly expanded role for southern women. But whereas first- and second-generation writers before the war agreed on the benevolence of the plantation South and identified specific literary images and plot devices with which best to defend their region and its institutions against external, or northern, aggression, after the war these conventions were not necessarily respected. Part of the problem arose from the inescapable realities of civil war: it was next to impossible to write a story of an aristocratic southern girl's moral and intellectual development that culminated in her marriage to an enlightened northerner and a subsequent reduction of sectional tensions when, in fact, northerners and southerners were locked in mortal combat. Certainly, lack of realism had never troubled southern domestic novelists; indeed, domestic fiction in general gave new meaning to the concept of the willing suspension of disbelief. But before April, 1861, there had always been a possibility that the characteristic happy ending could be realized on a national scale; with the advent of war, that possibility vanished.

75. Augusta Evans to J. L. M. Curry, July 15, 1863, in Curry Papers, Library of Congress.

The demise of southern domestic fiction was further hastened by its authors' inability to resolve their own feelings toward their war-torn region. For Evans, war had provided significant personal and professional benefits. Having established herself as a liaison between the common man and woman and the Confederate hierarchy—apparently on false premises—Evans enjoyed an enviable amount of respect and attention. Her pleasure in her newfound authority, however, was undermined by her increasing apprehension that the same southern masses that had originally brought her fame might betray the "holy cause" and return her to private life; this contradictory attitude toward the majority of the South's population resonates throughout *Macaria* and points up Evans' personal and professional uncertainty.[76] Terhune's ambivalence was even more pronounced. Forced to distinguish between her loyalties to her northern husband and to her southern home, she blamed unscrupulous leaders for placing her in an untenable position, reserving her harshest criticism for her dearly beloved Virginia. In *Sunnybank* Terhune attempted the impossible: she tried to defend the South while holding it responsible for the Civil War. Terhune's determination to have it both ways involved her in any amount of self-deception and denial, yet ultimately her efforts were in vain.[77] Lacking the conviction in the South's moral superiority, which had previously been accepted as an article of faith, the wartime and immediate postwar southern domestic novel could not sustain the narrative demands Evans and Terhune tried to impose.

But if the southern domestic novel had run its course, its influence lingered well into the twentieth century. Thomas Nelson Page, for example, drew upon its well-defined setting and characters and clearly articulated race relations in his numerous turn-of-the-century celebrations of plantation life; Page's novels, which served as the literary centerpiece for the Cult of the Lost Cause, exerted a tremendous impact on literary and historical interpretations of the Old South. More important, successive generations of southern women writers, among them Ellen Glasgow and Mary Johnston, took inspiration from the southern domestics and their work, using their example as professional writers as models for their own careers. Before the advent of southern domestic fiction, southern lit-

76. See Fidler, "Confederate Propagandist."
77. Terhune states her dilemma clearly in the preface to *Sunnybank*.

erature boasted only a handful of women writers; after the Civil War, that number began to increase and continued to grow as readers of domestic fiction began to explore the notion of the southern woman's proper place, which had first found discussion in the southern domestic novel. As Anne Goodwyn Jones has brilliantly illustrated, Margaret Mitchell's Scarlett O'Hara can trace her lineage directly to Beulah Benton and a host of antebellum southern domestic heroines. The lives and work of Gilman, Hentz, McIntosh, Terhune, and Evans may have been wholly forgotten, but their ideas and imaginations continue to shape perceptions of the South and its people, its past, and, to some extent, its present.[78]

With the passing of the southern domestic novel in 1866, the remaining domestic writers turned their attention toward other pursuits. After the publication of *Sunnybank*, Mary Virginia Terhune embarked upon a second career as domestic adviser, plying her female audience with cookbooks, etiquette guides, and child-care manuals. Late in life she would return to southern themes, although in the form of historical biographies.[79] Augusta Evans channeled her energy into memorializing the dead; in 1866, she started a subscription drive to erect a monument to the heroes of what she was already calling the "Lost Cause." Evans' most successful work, *St. Elmo*, was yet to come, but its theme, as well as those in her subsequent works, transcends sectional concerns. Not until 1892 would she again make mention of the Civil War in her fiction and then in an overtly conciliatory manner.[80] Maria McIntosh returned to work, but as a teacher, not as a writer; after advancing her idea of the causes of the Civil

78. See Gaines, *The Southern Plantation*; Muhlenfeld, "The Civil War and Authorship," 178–87; and Mackethan, "Plantation Fiction," 209–18. See also Gaines M. Foster, *Ghosts of the Confederacy: Defeat, the Lost Cause, and the Emergence of the New South, 1865–1913* (New York, 1987); Jones, *Tomorrow Is Another Day*; and Elizabeth Fox-Genovese, "Scarlett O'Hara: The Southern Lady as New Woman," *American Quarterly*, XXXIII (1981), 391–411.

79. As "Marion Harland," Terhune launched her "Common Sense" series with *Common Sense in the Household: A Manual of Practical Housewifery* (New York, 1871). The volume was so popular that Terhune's daughter, Christine Herrick, was asked to revise it for gas and electricity fifty-five years later.

80. Augusta Jane Evans, *St. Elmo* (New York, 1867), and Evans, *A Speckled Bird* (New York, 1902). For discussion of the monument drive, see Augusta Evans to J. L. M. Curry, April 15, May 7, and June 22, 1866, in Curry Papers, Library of Congress. See also Augusta Evans to the Mayor, Board of Aldermen, and Common Council of the City of Mobile, June 20, 1866, in Augusta Evans Wilson File, Alabama Department of Archives and History.

War in 1863, McIntosh wrote no more domestic novels.[81] Although Caroline Hentz had died in 1856, her children carried her legacy. Two sons, Thaddeus and Charles, served in the Confederate army, and one daughter, Julia, joined the community of southern emigrés who sought to reestablish a slave society in South America. Hentz's work continued to be read well into the Reconstruction era.

And in 1866 Caroline Gilman, the first successful southern domestic novelist, prepared to travel north. Exiled to Greenville, South Carolina, in 1863, where she endured Sherman's march and countless privations, Gilman returned to Charleston to find a cannonball lodged under her stairs; she was convinced that nothing she might encounter on a visit above the Mason-Dixon Line could disconcert her. "Since my decision to meet you 'face to face,'" Gilman wrote her daughter Eliza on December 19, "I have lost my interest in writing. Letters seem so unfinished, so inarticulate compared with kind voices." Concerned that Eliza, who had supported the Union in the recent struggle, was apprehensive concerning her mother's politics, Gilman hastened to reassure her: "What I desire is that no restraint shall be put on any one's political opinion on my account in my presence." She added, "I have always been accustomed to look on both sides of the question and try still to look truth in the face." There was no need to worry that she would deliberately seek out controversy, the elderly novelist emphasized; she was interested only in reaffirming family ties. "I shall never argue or even express an opinion on National topics in the U.S. That time has gone by, & indeed my interest in the matter has gone by."[82] Caroline Gilman had laid the issue to rest.

81. For discussion of McIntosh's activities after the war, see Colles, *Authors and Writers*, 174–76; and Hornberger, "Maria Jane McIntosh," 468–69.
82. Caroline Gilman to Eliza [Webb], December 19, 1866, in Caroline Howard Gilman Papers.

Bibliography

UNPUBLISHED PRIMARY SOURCES

Alabama Department of Archives and History, Montgomery
Wilson, Augusta Evans. File.
Boston Public Library
Griswold Papers.
City Museums of Mobile, Ala.
Wilson, Augusta Evans. Papers.
Clifton Waller Barrett Library, Manuscripts Division, Special Collections
Department, University of Virginia, Charlottesville
Barrett, Clifton Waller. Author Collection (#9040).
Wilson, Augusta Evans. Collection (#8293).
Fidler, William Perry, Tuscaloosa, Ala.
Private collection.
Hay Library, Brown University, Providence, R.I.
Beauregard, P. G. T. Papers.
Historic Mobile Preservation Society, Mobile, Ala.
Wilson, Augusta Evans. Papers.
Historical Society of Pennsylvania, Philadelphia
Gratz, Simon. Collection.
Hoole Special Collections Library, University of Alabama, Tuscaloosa
Wilson, Augusta Evans. Papers.
Huntington Library, San Marino, Calif.
Hentz, Caroline. Papers.
Terhune, Mary Virginia. Papers.
Wilson, Augusta Evans. Papers.
Library of Congress, Washington, D.C.
Curry, J. L. M. Papers.

Beauregard, P. G. T. Papers.
Wilson, Augusta Evans. Papers.
Massachusetts Historical Society, Boston
  Bellows Papers.
  Dwight Papers.
  Norcross Papers.
New York Public Library, New York City
  Berg, Henry W. and Albert A. Collection.
Perkins Library, Duke University, Durham, N.C.
  Beauregard, P. G. T. Papers
  Curry, J. L. M. Papers.
  Hayne, P. H. Papers.
  Terhune, Mary Virginia. Papers.
Schlesinger Library, Radcliffe College, Cambridge, Mass.
  Terhune, Mary Virginia. Papers.
South Carolina Historical Society, Charleston
  Gilman, Caroline. Autobiographical Essay.
  Gilman, Caroline Howard. Papers.
South Caroliniana Library, University of South Carolina, Columbia
  Gilman, Samuel. Papers.
Southern Historical Collection, University of North Carolina,
  Chapel Hill
  Hentz, Caroline. Diary.
  Hentz, Dr. Charles A. Unpublished Autobiography.
  Hentz Family Papers.
  Heustis, Rachel Lyons. Papers.
  Wilson, Augusta Evans. Papers.
Special Collections Library, Barnard College, New York
  Overbury Collection.
Virginia Historical Society, Richmond
  Hawes Family Papers.
Woodruff Library, Emory University, Atlanta
  Beauregard, P. G. T. Papers.
  Candler, Warren A. Papers.
  Seydell, Mildred. Papers.
  Stephens, Alexander H. Papers.

PUBLISHED PRIMARY SOURCES

Caruthers, William Alexander. *The Cavaliers of Virginia.* 1834; rpr. Ridgewood, N.J., 1968.

———. *The Knights of the Golden Horseshoe.* 1844; rpr. Chapel Hill, 1970.

Chesnut, Mary Boykin. *Mary Chesnut's Civil War.* Edited by C. Vann Woodward. New Haven, 1981.

Cooke, John Esten. *Henry St. John, Gentleman.* New York, 1859.

———. *Lord Fairfax; or, The Master of Greenway Court.* New York, 1896.

Cummins, Maria. *The Lamplighter.* Edited by Nina Baym. 1854; rpr. New Brunswick, N.J., 1988.

Deleon, T. C. "Biographical Reminiscences." In *Devota,* by Augusta Evans. 1907; rpr. New York, 1913.

———. "'Maryland' by Moonlight." Mobile *Daily Register,* November 21, 1906.

Derby, James C. *Fifty Years Among Authors, Books, and Publishers.* New York, 1884.

Dew, Thomas. "Abolition of Negro Slavery." *American Quarterly Review,* XII (1832), 189–265. Reprinted in *The Ideology of Slavery: Proslavery Thought in the Antebellum South, 1830–1860,* edited by Drew Gilpin Faust. Baton Rouge, 1981.

———. "On the Characteristic Differences Between the Sexes, and on the Position and Influence of Woman in Society." *Southern Literary Messenger,* I (May, 1835), 493–512; (July, 1835), 621–23; (August, 1835), 672–91.

Evans, Augusta. *At the Mercy of Tiberius.* New York, 1887.

———. *Beulah.* New York, 1859.

———. *Devota.* 1907; rpr. New York, 1913.

———. *Inez: A Tale of the Alamo.* 1855; rpr. New York, 1884.

———. *Infelice.* New York, 1875.

———. Letter to L. Virginia French, January 13, 1861, in *Alabama Historical Quarterly,* III (1941), 65–67.

———. *Macaria; or, Altars of Sacrifice.* Richmond, 1864; rpr. New York, 1896.

———. "The Mutilation of the Hermae." *Gulf City Home Journal* (Mobile, Ala.), November 9, 1862.

————. "Northern Literature." Mobile *Daily Advertiser*, October 11 and 16, 1859.

————. *St. Elmo*. New York, 1867.

————. "Southern Literature." Mobile *Daily Advertiser*, October 30, November 6, 1859.

————. *A Speckled Bird*. New York, 1902.

————. *Vashti; or, Until Death Do Us Part*. New York, 1867.

Fitzhugh, George. *Sociology for the South; or, The Failure of Free Society*. 1854; rpr. New York, 1965.

Gilman, Arthur. *The Gilman Family*. Albany, N.Y., 1869.

Gilman, Caroline Howard. *A Gift Book of Stories and Poems for Children*. New York, 1850.

————. *Love's Progress*. New York, 1840.

————. *Oracles for Youth*. New York, 1852.

————. *Oracles from the Poets*. New York, 1854.

————. *The Poetic Fate Book*. Boston, 1874.

————. *The Poetry of Travelling in the United States*. 1838; rpr. Upper Saddle River, N.J., 1970.

————. *Recollections of a Housekeeper*. New York, 1834.

————. *Recollections of a New England Housekeeper*. 1834; rpr. New York, 1852.

————. *Recollections of a Southern Matron*. 1838; rpr. New York, 1852.

————. *The Sibyl*. New York, 1852.

————. *Tales and Ballads*. Boston, 1839.

Glasgow, Ellen. *Virginia*. 1913; rpr. Garden City, 1929.

Halsey, Francis Whiting. "Marion Harland." In *Women Authors of Our Day in Their Homes: Personal Descriptions and Interviews*, edited by Francis Whiting Halsey. New York, 1903.

Helper, Hinton Rowan. *The Impending Crisis of the South: How to Meet It*. New York, 1857.

Hentz, Caroline. *Aunt Patty's Scrap Bag*. 1846; rpr. Philadelphia, 1872.

————. *The Banished Son and Other Stories of the Heart*. Philadelphia, 1856.

————. *Courtship and Marriage; or, The Joys and Sorrows of American Life*. Philadelphia, 1856.

————. *Eoline; or, Magnolia Vale*. Philadelphia, 1852.

————. *Ernest Linwood*. Boston, 1856.

————. *Helen and Arthur; or, Miss Thusa's Spinning Wheel.* 1853; rpr. Philadelphia, 1856.

————. *Linda; or, the Young Pilot of the Belle Creole.* Philadelphia, 1850.

————. *Love After Marriage and Other Stories of the Heart.* Philadelphia, 1857.

————. *Lovell's Folly.* Cincinnati, 1833.

————. *Marcus Warland; or, The Long Moss Spring.* Philadelphia, 1852.

————. *The Planter's Northern Bride.* Edited by Rhoda Ellison. 1854; rpr. Chapel Hill, 1970.

————. *Rena; or, The Snowbird.* Philadelphia, 1851.

————. *Robert Graham.* 1855; rpr. Philadelphia, 1856.

————. *Wild Jack; or, The Stolen Child and Other Stories.* Philadelphia, 1853.

Hentz, Nicholas Marcellus. *Spiders of the United States: A Collection of the Arachnological Writings of N. M. Hentz, M.D.* New York, 1875.

Holloway, Laura C. *The Woman's Story.* New York, 1889.

Holmes, George Frederick. "Review of *Uncle Tom's Cabin.*" *Southern Literary Messenger*, XVIII (1852), 721–31. Reprinted in *Slavery Defended: The Views of the Old South*, edited by Eric L. McKitrick. Englewood Cliffs, N.J., 1963.

Hundley, Daniel R. *Social Relations in Our Southern States.* New York, 1860.

Johnston, Mary. *Hagar.* Boston, 1913.

Kennedy, John Pendleton. *Swallow Barn; or, A Sojourn in the Old Dominion.* 1832; rpr. New York, 1962.

McCray, Florine Thayer. "Marion Harland at Home." *Ladies' Home Journal*, IV (August, 1887), 3.

McIntosh, Maria. *Charms and Counter Charms.* New York, 1848.

————. *Evenings at Donaldson Manor.* New York, 1851.

————. *A Letter on the Address of the Women of England to Their Sisters of America in Relation to Slavery.* New York, 1853.

————. *The Lofty and the Lowly; or, Good in All and None All-Good.* New York, 1853.

————. *Two Lives; or, To Seem and To Be.* 1846; rpr. New York, 1865.

————. *Two Pictures; or, What We Think of Ourselves and What the World Thinks of Us.* New York, 1863.

————. *Violet; or, The Cross and the Crown.* New York, 1856.

————. *Woman an Enigma*. New York, 1843.

————. *Woman in America: Her Work and Her Reward*. New York, 1850.

Martineau, Harriet. *Harriet Martineau's Autobiography*. 2 vols. Edited by Maria Chapman. Boston, 1877.

Nott, Josiah. "The Natural History of the Caucasian and Negro Races." In *The Ideology of Slavery: Proslavery Thought in the Antebellum South*, edited by Drew Gilpin Faust. Baton Rouge, 1981.

Olmsted, Frederick Law. *A Journey Through Texas; or, A Saddle-trip on the Southwestern Frontier*. New York, 1859.

Parton, Sara [Fanny Fern]. *Rose Clark*. New York, 1856.

————. *Ruth Hall: A Domestic Tale of the Present Time*. Edited by Joyce W. Warren. 1854; rpr. New Brunswick, N.J., 1986.

Peterson, Merrill D., ed. *The Portable Thomas Jefferson*. New York, 1975.

Sedgwick, Catharine. *Home*. Boston, 1835.

————. *Hope Leslie*. Edited by Mary Kelley. 1822; rpr. New Brunswick, N.J., 1987.

————. *The Linwoods; or, "Sixty Years Since" in America*. 2 vols. New York, 1835.

————. *Married or Single?* 2 vols. New York, 1857.

————. *A New England Tale*. New York, 1822.

————. *The Poor Rich Man and the Rich Poor Man*. New York, 1837.

Simms, William Gilmore. *Woodcraft*. New York, 1854.

Southworth, E. D. E. N. *The Hidden Hand*. Edited by Joanne Dobson. 1859; rpr. New Brunswick, N.J., 1988.

————. *Self Raised; or, From the Depths*. New York, n.d.

Stowe, Harriet Beecher. *The Key to "Uncle Tom's Cabin."* 1853; rpr. New York, 1969.

————. *The Minister's Wooing*. 1859; rpr. Cambridge, Mass., 1896.

————. *My Wife and I; or, Harry Henderson's History*. 1871; rpr. Cambridge, Mass., 1896.

————. *Oldtown Folks*. 1869; rpr. Cambridge, Mass., 1966.

————. *The Pearl of Orr's Island: A Story of the Coast of Maine*. 1862; rpr. Cambridge, Mass., 1896.

————. *Pink and White Tyranny: A Society Novel*. 1871; rpr. Cambridge, Mass., 1896.

————. *Uncle Tom's Cabin; or, Life Among the Lowly*. Edited by Kennith S. Lynn. 1852; rpr. Cambridge, Mass., 1981.

Terhune, Mary Virginia [Marion Harland]. *Alone.* Richmond, 1854.
————. *The Carringtons of High Hill.* New York, 1919.
————. *Common Sense in the Household: A Manual of Practical House-wifery.* New York, 1871.
————. "The Domestic Infelicity of Literary Women." *Arena*, II (1890), 313–20.
————. *Eve's Daughters.* New York, 1885.
————. *Helen Gardner's Wedding Day.* New York, 1870.
————. *The Hidden Path.* New York, 1855.
————. *Husbands and Homes.* New York, 1865.
————. *Husks.* New York, 1863.
————. *Jessamine.* New York, 1873.
————. *Judith.* New York, 1883.
————. *Miriam.* New York, 1862.
————. *Marion Harland's Autobiography: The Story of a Long Life.* New York, 1910.
————. *More Colonial Homesteads and Their Stories.* New York, 1899.
————. *Moss-side.* New York, 1857.
————. *Nemesis.* New York, 1860.
————. *Phemie's Temptation.* New York, 1897.
————. Review of *Beulah*, by Augusta Evans. Mobile *Daily Register*, October 7, 1854.
————. *Some Colonial Homesteads and Their Stories.* New York, 1899.
————. *Sunnybank.* 1866; rpr. New York, 1867.
————. *Where Ghosts Walk.* New York, 1910.
Tutwiler, Julia. "Southern Women in New York." *Bookman*, XVIII (February, 1904), 624–34; XIX (March, 1904), 51–58.
Warner, Susan. *The Wide, Wide World.* Edited by Jane Tompkins. 1850; rpr. New York, 1987.

SECONDARY SOURCES

Aaron, Daniel. *The Unwritten War: American Writers and the Civil War.* New York, 1973.
Ammons, Elizabeth. "Heroines in *Uncle Tom's Cabin.*" *American Literature*, LIX (1977), 161–79.

Amos, Harriet E. "'City Belles': Images and Realities of the Lives of White Women in Antebellum Mobile." *Alabama Review*, XXXIV (1981), 3–19.

Appleby, Joyce. "Reconciliation and the Northern Novelists, 1865–1880." *Civil War History*, X (1964), 117–29.

Bakker, Jan. "Caroline Gilman and the Issue of Slavery in the *Rose* Magazine, 1832–1839." *Southern Studies*, XXIV (1985), 273–83.

Bartlett, Irving H., and C. Glenn Cambor. "The History and Psychodynamics of Southern Womanhood." *Women's Studies*, II (1974), 9–24.

Baym, Nina. "Melodramas of Beset Manhood: How Theories of American Fiction Exclude Women Authors." In *The New Feminist Criticism: Essays on Women, Literature, and Theory*, edited by Elaine Showalter. New York, 1985.

———. *Novels, Readers, and Reviewers: Responses to Fiction in Antebellum America*. Ithaca, 1984.

———. *Woman's Fiction: A Guide to Novels by and About Women in America, 1820–1870*. Ithaca, 1978.

Berdan, Alan. "Caroline Lee Hentz: Northern Defender of Southern Tradition." M.A. thesis, St. John's University, 1948.

Berg, Barbara J. *The Remembered Gate: Origins of American Feminism*. New York, 1978.

Berkin, Carol Ruth, and Mary Beth Norton. *Women in America: A History*. Boston, 1979.

Blassingame, John W. *The Slave Community: Plantation Life in the Antebellum South*. New York, 1979.

Bode, Carl. *The Anatomy of Popular Culture, 1840–1861*. Berkeley, 1959.

Bolton, Sarah K. *Successful Women*. Boston, 1888.

Boydston, Jeanne, Mary Kelley, and Anne Margolis, eds. *The Limits of Sisterhood: The Beecher Sisters on Women's Rights and Woman's Sphere*. Chapel Hill, 1988.

Branch, E. Douglas. *The Sentimental Years, 1838–1860*. New York, 1934.

Bratton, Mary Jo. "'Marion Harland': A Literary Woman of the Old Dominion." *Virginia Cavalcade*, XXXV (1986), 136–42.

Brown, Herbert Ross. *The Sentimental Novel in America, 1789–1860*. Durham, 1940.

Brownstein, Rachel M. *Becoming a Heroine: Reading About Women in Novels*. New York, 1982.

Bryant, Keith L., Jr. "The Role and Status of the Female Yeomanry in the Antebellum South: The Literary View." *Southern Quarterly*, XVIII (1980), 73–87.

Calkins, Ernest Elmo. "Named for a Best Seller." *Saturday Review of Literature*, XXI (1939), 3–4, 14–17.

Callahan, Ida B. "Augusta Evans Wilson: An Analytical Study of Her Fiction." M.A. thesis, Vanderbilt University, 1943.

Carter, Maude. "A Study of Caroline Lee Hentz, Sentimentalist of the Fifties." M.A. thesis, Duke University, 1942.

Cash, Wilbur J. *The Mind of the South*. New York, 1941.

Censer, Jane Turner. *North Carolina Planters and Their Children, 1800–1860*. Baton Rouge, 1984.

Charvat, William. *Literary Publishing in America, 1790–1850*. Philadelphia, 1959.

Clinton, Catherine. "Caught in the Web of the Big House: Women and Slavery." In *The Web of Southern Social Relations: Women, Family, and Education*, edited by Walter J. Fraser, Jr., R. Frank Saunders, Jr., and Jon L. Wakelyn. Athens, Ga., 1985.

———. *The Other Civil War: American Women in the Nineteenth Century*. New York, 1984.

———. "The Plantation Mistress: Another Side of Southern Slavery, 1780–1835." Ph.D. dissertation, Princeton University, 1980.

———. *The Plantation Mistress: Woman's World in the Old South*. New York, 1982.

Cogan, Frances B. *All-American Girl: The Ideal of Real Womanhood in Mid-Nineteenth-Century America*. Athens, Ga., 1989.

Colles, Julia K. *Authors and Writers Associated with Morristown*. Morristown, N.J., 1895.

Conrad, Susan. *Perish the Thought: Intellectual Women in Romantic America, 1830–1860*. New York, 1976.

Cott, Nancy. *The Bonds of Womanhood: "Woman's Sphere" in New England, 1780–1835*. New Haven, 1977.

Cowie, Alexander. *The Rise of the American Novel*. New York, 1951.

———. "The Vogue of the Domestic Novel, 1850–1870." *South Atlantic Quarterly*, XLI (1942), 416–24.

Crofts, Daniel W. *Reluctant Confederates: Upper South Unionists in the Secession Crisis*. Chapel Hill, 1989.

Davidson, James Wood. *The Living Writers of the South.* New York, 1869.

Degler, Carl N. *At Odds: Women and the Family in America from the Revolution to the Present.* New York, 1980.

Dobson, Joanne. "The Hidden Hand: Subversion of Cultural Ideology in Three Mid-Nineteenth-Century Women's Novels." *American Quarterly,* XXXVIII (1986), 223–42.

Douglas, Ann. *The Feminization of American Culture.* New York, 1977.

Dubois, Ellen Carol. *Feminism and Suffrage: The Emergence of an Independent Women's Movement.* Ithaca, 1978.

Eaton, Clement. *The Freedom-of-Thought Struggle in the Old South.* Durham, 1964.

———. *The Growth of Southern Civilization.* New York, 1961.

———. *A History of the Old South.* New York, 1966.

———. *The Mind of the Old South.* Baton Rouge, 1964.

Ellison, Rhoda. "Caroline Lee Hentz's Alabama Diary, 1836." *Alabama Review,* IV (1951), 254–70.

———. *Early Alabama Publications: A Study in Literary Interests.* Tuscaloosa.

———. "Mrs. Hentz and the Green-eyed Monster." *American Quarterly,* XXII (1950), 345–50.

Eminent Women of the Age. Hartford, 1869.

Enloe, Harvey M. "A Criticism of Mrs. Caroline Lee Hentz." M.A. thesis, Auburn University, 1935.

Faust, Drew Gilpin. *The Creation of Confederate Nationalism: Ideology and Identity in the Civil War South.* Baton Rouge, 1989.

———. *James Henry Hammond and the Old South: A Design for Mastery.* Baton Rouge, 1982.

———. *A Sacred Circle: The Dilemma of the Intellectual in the Old South, 1840–1860.* Baltimore, 1977.

———, ed. *The Ideology of Slavery: Proslavery Thought in the Antebellum South, 1830–1860.* Baton Rouge, 1981.

Fehrenbacher, Don E. *The South and Three Sectional Crises.* Baton Rouge, 1980.

Fetterley, Judith, ed. *Provisions: A Reader from Nineteenth-Century American Women.* Bloomington, 1985.

Fidler, William P. *Augusta Evans Wilson, 1835–1909.* Tuscaloosa, 1951.

————. "Augusta Evans Wilson as Confederate Propagandist." *Alabama Review*, II (1949), 32–44.

————. "The Life and Works of Augusta Evans Wilson." Ph.D. dissertation, University of Chicago, 1947.

Fields, Barbara Jeanne. *Slavery and Freedom on the Middle Ground: Maryland During the Nineteenth Century*. New Haven, 1985.

Foster, Gaines M. *Ghosts of the Confederacy: Defeat, the Lost Cause, and the Emergence of the New South, 1865–1913*. New York, 1987.

Fox-Genovese, Elizabeth. "Scarlett O'Hara: The Southern Lady as New Woman." *American Quarterly*, XXXIII (1981), 391–411.

————. *Within the Plantation Household: Black and White Women of the Old South*. Chapel Hill, 1989.

Frederick, John T. "Hawthorne's 'Scribbling Women.'" *New England Quarterly*, XLVIII (1975), 231–40.

Fredrickson, George M. *The Black Image in the White Mind: The Debate on Afro-American Character and Destiny, 1817–1914*. New York, 1971.

Freehling, Alison Goodyear. *Drift Toward Dissolution: The Virginia Slavery Debate of 1831–1832*. Baton Rouge, 1982.

Freehling, William W. *Prelude to Civil War: The Nullification Controversy in South Carolina, 1816–1846*. New York, 1966.

Freeman, Julia Deane [Mary Forrest]. *Women of the South Distinguished in Literature*. New York, 1860.

Friedman, Jean. *The Enclosed Garden: Women and Community in the Evangelical South, 1830–1900*. Chapel Hill, 1985.

Gaines, Francis Pendleton. *The Southern Plantation: A Study in the Development and the Accuracy of a Tradition*. 1924; rpr. Gloucester, Mass., 1962.

Garrison, Dee. "Immoral Fiction in the Late Victorian Library." *American Quarterly*, XXVIII (1976), 71–89.

Geary, Susan. "The Domestic Novel as a Commercial Commodity: Making a Best Seller in the 1850s." *Papers of the Bibliographical Society of America*, LXX (1976), 365–93.

Genovese, Eugene. "Life in the Big House." In *A Heritage of Her Own: Toward a New Social History of American Women*, edited by Nancy Cott and Elizabeth Pleck. New York, 1979.

————. *Roll, Jordan, Roll: The World the Slaves Made*. New York, 1976.

————. *The World the Slaveholders Made*. New York, 1969.

Gilbert, Sandra, and Susan Gubar. *The Madwoman in the Attic: The Woman Writer and the Nineteenth-Century Literary Imagination.* New Haven, 1979.

Gossett, Thomas G. *"Uncle Tom's Cabin" and American Culture.* Dallas, 1985.

Greenberg, Kenneth S. *Masters and Statesmen: The Political Culture of American Slavery.* Baltimore, 1985.

Grimble, Ian. *The Trial of Peter Sellar: The Tragedy of Highland Evictions.* London, 1962.

Gwin, Minrose C. *Black and White Women of the Old South: The Peculiar Sisterhood in American Literature.* Knoxville, 1985.

Hagler, D. Harland. "The Ideal Woman in the Antebellum South: Lady or Farmwife?" *Journal of Southern History,* XLVI (1980), 405–17.

Hale, Sarah J. *Woman's Record; or, Sketches of All Distinguished Women from the Beginning Until A.D. 1850.* New York, 1853.

Halttunen, Karen. *Confidence Men and Painted Women: A Study of Middle-Class Culture in America, 1830–1870.* New Haven, 1982.

Hamilton, Holman. *Prologue to Conflict: The Crisis and Compromise of 1850.* Louisville, 1964.

Hardy, Evelyn. "Mrs. Caroline Lee Hentz, a Woman of Her Times" M.A. thesis, Auburn University, 1935.

Hart, James D. *The Popular Book: A History of America's Literary Taste.* New York, 1950.

Hart, John S. *The Female Prose Writers of America.* Philadelphia, 1852.

Hartman, Mary S., and Lois Banner, ed. *Clio's Consciousness Raised.* New York, 1974.

Heilbrun, Carolyn G. *Writing a Woman's Life.* New York, 1988.

Hersh, Blanche. *The Slavery of Sex: Feminist Abolitionists in Nineteenth-Century America.* Urbana, 1978.

Hilldrup, Robert. "Cold War Against the Yankees in the Antebellum Literature of Southern Women." *North Carolina Historical Review,* XXXI (1954), 370–84.

Hofstadter, Beatrice. "Popular Culture and the Romantic Heroine." *American Scholar,* XXX (1960), 98–116.

Hogeland, Ronald W. "'The Female Appendage': Feminine Life-Styles in America, 1820–1860." *Civil War History,* XVII (1971), 101–14.

Holman, C. Hugh. *The Immoderate Past: The Southern Writer and History.* Athens, Ga., 1976.

————. *The Roots of Southern Writing: Essays on the Literature of the American South.* Athens, Ga., 1971.

Hoole, William. "The Gilmans and the Southern Rose." *North Carolina Historical Review,* XI (1934), 116–28.

Hornberger, Marian. "Maria Jane McIntosh." In *Notable American Women, 1607–1950: A Biographical Dictionary,* edited by Edward James, Janet Wilson James, and Paul S. Boyer. 3 vols. Cambridge, Mass., 1971.

Howe, Daniel Walker. "A Massachusetts Yankee in Senator Calhoun's Court: Samuel Gilman in South Carolina." *New England Quarterly,* XLIV (1971), 197–220.

————, ed. *Victorian America.* Philadelphia, 1976.

James, Janet. *Changing Ideas About Women in the United States, 1776–1825.* New York, 1986.

Jeffrey, Kirk. "Marriage, Career and Feminine Ideology in Nineteenth-Century America: Reconstructing the Marital Experience of Lydia Maria Child, 1828–1874." *Feminist Studies,* II (1975), 113–30.

Jensen, Joan M. *Loosening the Bonds: Mid-Atlantic Farm Women, 1750–1850.* New Haven, 1986.

Jones, Anne Goodwyn. *Tomorrow Is Another Day: The Woman Writer in the South, 1859–1936.* Baton Rouge, 1981.

Jones, Katherine M., ed. *Heroines of Dixie: Spring of High Hopes.* New York, 1974.

Jordan, Winthrop. *White over Black: American Attitudes Toward the Negro, 1550–1812.* Chapel Hill, 1968.

Kelley, Mary. "At War with Herself: Harriet Beecher Stowe as a Woman in Conflict Within the Home." *American Studies,* XIX (1978), 23–40.

————. "The Literary Domestics: Private Woman on a Public Stage." In *Ideas in America's Culture: From Republic to Mass Society,* edited by Hamilton Cravens. Ames, 1982.

————. *Private Woman, Private Stage: Literary Domesticity in Nineteenth-Century America.* New York, 1984.

————. "The Sentimentalists: Promise and Betrayal in the Home." *Signs,* IV (1979), 434–46.

————. "The Unconscious Rebel: Studies in Feminine Fiction, 1820–1880." Ph.D. dissertation, University of Iowa, 1974.

————. "A Woman Alone: Catharine Maria Sedgewick's Sisterhood in Nineteenth-Century America." *New England Quarterly*, LI (1978), 209–25.

————, ed. *Woman's Being, Woman's Place: Female Identity and Vocation in American History*. Boston, 1979.

Kennedy, Fronde. "The Southern Rose-Bud and the Southern Rose," *South Atlantic Quarterly*, XXIV (1924), 10–19.

Kerber, Linda. "Daughters of Columbia: Educating Women for the Republic, 1787–1805." In *The Hofstadter Aegis: A Memorial*, edited by Stanley Elkins and Eric L. McKitrick. New York, 1974.

————. "The Republican Mother: Women and the Enlightenment—An American Perspective." *American Quarterly*, XXVIII (1976), 187–205.

————. *Women of the Republic: Intellectual Ideology in Revolutionary America*. Chapel Hill, 1980.

King, Richard. *A Southern Renaissance: The Cultural Awakening of the American South, 1930–1955*. New York, 1980.

Kirkham, E. Bruce. *The Building of "Uncle Tom's Cabin."* Knoxville, 1977.

Lant, Kathleen. "Behind a Mask: A Study of Nineteenth-Century American Fiction by Women." Ph.D. dissertation, University of Oregon, 1982.

Lebsock, Suzanne. *The Free Women of Petersburg: Status and Culture in a Southern Town, 1764–1860*. New York, 1984.

Lehman-Haupt, Hellmut, with Lawrence C. Wroth and Rollo Silver. *The Book in America: A History of the Making and Selling of Books in the United States*. New York, 1951.

Lerner, Gerda. *The Grimké Sisters from South Carolina: Pioneers for Women's Rights and Abolitionism*. New York, 1967.

————. *The Majority Finds Its Past: Placing Women in History*. New York, 1979.

Leslie, Kent Anderson. "A Myth of the Southern Lady: Antebellum Pro-slavery Rhetoric and the Proper Place of Woman." *Sociological Spectrum*, VI (1986), 31–49.

Lewis, Jan. *The Pursuit of Happiness: Family and Values in Jefferson's Virginia*. New York, 1983.

Lively, Robert. *Fiction Fights the Civil War: An Unfinished Chapter in the Literary History of the American People*. Chapel Hill, 1957.

Mabie, Hamilton W. "The Most Popular Novels in America." *Forum*, XVI (1893), 505–15.

McCardell, John. *The Idea of a Southern Nation: Southern Nationalists and Southern Nationalism, 1830–1860*. New York, 1979.

Mackethan, Lucinda H. "Plantation Fiction, 1865–1900." In *The History of Southern Literature*, edited by Louis Rubin, Jr., *et al*. Baton Rouge, 1985.

McKitrick, Eric L., ed. *Slavery Defended: The Views of the Old South*. Englewood Cliffs, N.J., 1963.

McMillan, Malcolm L., ed. *The Alabama Confederate Reader*. Tuscaloosa, 1963.

McMillen, Sally. *Motherhood in the Old South*. Baton Rouge, 1990.

McPherson, James M. *Ordeal by Fire: The Civil War and Reconstruction*. New York, 1982.

———. *The Battle Cry of Freedom: The Civil War Era*. New York, 1988.

Manly, Louise. "Augusta Evans Wilson." In *The Library of Southern Literature*, edited by Edwin A. Alderman, Joel Chandler Harris, and Charles William Kent. Vol. XIII of 17 vols. Atlanta, 1921.

Massey, Mary Elizabeth. *Bonnet Brigades*. New York, 1966.

Matthews, Glenna. *"Just a Housewife": The Rise and Fall of Domesticity in America*. New York, 1987.

Maurice, Arthur B. "Best Sellers of Yesterday: I: Augusta Jane Evans' *St. Elmo*." *Bookman*, XXXI (1910), 35–42.

Melder, Keith. *Beginnings of Sisterhood: The American Woman's Rights Movement, 1800–1850*. New York, 1977.

Moers, Ellen. *Literary Women: The Great Writers*. New York, 1976.

Montejano, David. *Anglos and Mexicans in the Making of Texas, 1836–1986*. Austin, 1987.

Moran, Neva R. "Caroline Lee Hentz, an Early Southern Novelist: A Study of the Life and Works of Mrs. Caroline Lee Hentz." M.A. thesis, Birmingham-Southern College, 1937.

Morrow, Ralph E. "The Proslavery Argument Revisited." *Mississippi Valley Historical Review*, XLVII (1961), 79–94.

Mott, Frank Luther. *Golden Multitudes: The Story of Best Sellers in the United States*. New York, 1947.

Muhlenfeld, Elizabeth. "The Civil War and Authorship." In *The History of Southern Literature*, edited by Louis Rubin, Jr., *et al.* Baton Rouge, 1985.

————. *Mary Boykin Chesnut: A Biography*. Baton Rouge, 1981.

Munk, Eunice A. "The Life and Writings of Augusta Jane Evans Wilson." M.A. thesis, Emory University, 1948.

Norton, Mary Beth. "The Evolution of White Women's Experience in Early America." *American Historical Review*, XCIX (1984), 593–619.

————. *Liberty's Daughters: The Revolutionary Experience of American Women, 1750–1800*. Boston, 1980.

Nye, Russel B. *Society and Culture in America, 1830–1860*. New York, 1974.

O'Brien, Michael J. *Rethinking the South: Essays in Intellectual History*. Baltimore, 1988.

Osterweis, Rollin G. *The Myth of the Lost Cause, 1865–1900*. Hamden, Conn., 1973.

Our Famous Women. Hartford, 1884.

Papashvily, Helen. *All the Happy Endings: A Study of the Domestic Novel in America, the Women Who Wrote It, the Women Who Read It, in the Nineteenth Century*. New York, 1956.

Parks, Edd Winfield. *Ante-Bellum Southern Literary Critics*. Athens, Ga., 1962.

Pattee, Fred Lewis. *The Feminine Fifties*. New York, 1940.

Pease, William H., and Jane Pease. *The Web of Progress: Private Values and Public Styles in Boston and Charleston, 1828–1843*. New York, 1985.

Perry, Lewis, and Michael Fellman, eds. *Antislavery Reconsidered: New Perspectives on the Abolitionists*. Baton Rouge, 1979.

Phillips, Sidney. "The Life and Works of Augusta Evans Wilson." M.A. thesis, Alabama Polytechnic Institute, 1937.

Potter, David M. *The Impending Crisis, 1848–1861*. New York, 1976.

Pryor, Elizabeth Brown. *Clara Barton: Professional Angel*. Philadelphia, 1987.

Pugh, Evelyn L. "Women and Slavery: Julia Gardener Tyler and the Duchess of Sutherland." *Virginia Magazine of History and Biography*, LXXXVIII (1980), 186–202.

Rable, George C. *Civil Wars: Women and the Crisis of Southern Nationalism*. Urbana, 1989.

Radway, Janice A. *Reading the Romance: Women, Patriarchy, and Popular Literature*. Chapel Hill, 1984.

Reynolds, David S. *Beneath the American Renaissance: The Subversive Imagination in the Age of Emerson and Melville*. New York, 1988.

Riley, Glenda Gates. "From Chattel to Challenger: The Changing Image of the American Woman." Ph.D. dissertation, University of Ohio, 1967.

————. "The Subtle Subversion: Changes in the Traditionalist Image of the American Woman." *Historian*, XXXII (1970), 210–27.

Rubin, Louis, Jr., *et al.*, eds. *The History of Southern Literature*. Baton Rouge, 1985.

Ruoff, John C. "Frivolity to Consumption; or, Southern Womanhood in Antebellum Literature." *Civil War History*, XVIII (1972), 213–30.

————. "Southern Womanhood, 1865–1920: An Intellectual and Cultural Study." Ph.D. dissertation, University of Illinois at Champaign-Urbana, 1976.

Ruthven, K. K. *Feminist Literary Studies: An Introduction*. Cambridge, 1984.

Ryan, Mary. "American Society and the Cult of Domesticity, 1830–1860." Ph.D. dissertation, University of California at Santa Barbara, 1971.

————. *Cradle of the Middle Class: The Family in Oneida County, N.Y., 1790–1865*. New York, 1981.

————. *The Empire of the Mother: American Writing About Domesticity, 1830–1860*. New York, 1982.

Saint-Amand, Mary Scott. *A Balcony in Charleston*. Richmond, 1941.

Sanborn, Kate. "Mary Virginia Terhune." In *Our Famous Women*. Hartford, 1894.

Scott, Anne Firor. *The Southern Lady: From Pedestal to Politics, 1830–1930*. Chicago, 1970.

————. "Women's Perspective on the Patriarchy." *Journal of American History*, LXI (1974), 52–64.

Seidel, Kathryn Lee. "The Southern Belle as an Antebellum Ideal." *Southern Quarterly*, XV (1977), 387–401.

————. *The Southern Belle in the American Novel*. Tampa, 1985.

Showalter, Elaine. *A Literature of Their Own: British Women Novelists from Brontë to Lessing*. Princeton, 1977.

————. *The New Feminist Criticism: Essays on Women, Literature, and Theory*. New York, 1985.

————. "Women Writers and the Female Experience." In *Radical Feminism*, edited by Anne Koedt, Ellen Levine, and Anita Rapone. New York, 1973.

Sklar, Kathryn Kish. *Catharine Beecher: A Study in American Domesticity*. New Haven, 1973.

Smith, Daniel Blake. *Inside the Great House: Planter Family Life in Eighteenth-Century Chesapeake Society*. Ithaca, 1980.

Smith, Henry Nash. "The Scribbling Women and the Cosmic Success Story." *Critical Inquiry*, I (1974), 47–70.

Smith-Rosenberg, Carroll. "The Hysterical Woman: Sex Roles and Role Conflict in Nineteenth-Century America." *Social Research*, XLIX (1971), 652–78.

Smith-Rosenberg, Carroll, and Charles Smith-Rosenberg. "The Female Animal: Medical and Biological Views of Woman and Her Role in Nineteenth-Century America." *Journal of American History*, LX (September, 1973), 332–56.

Spacks, Patricia Meyer. *The Female Imagination*. New York, 1976.

Stowe, Steven. "City, Country, and the Feminine Voice." In *Intellectual Life in Antebellum Charleston*, edited by Michael O'Brien and David Moltke-Hansen. Knoxville, 1986.

————. *Intimacy and Power in the Old South: Ritual in the Lives of the Planters*. Baltimore, 1987.

Strouse, Jean. *Alice James: A Biography*. Boston, 1980.

Tandy, Jeanette. "Pro-Slavery Propaganda in American Fiction of the Fifties." *South Atlantic Quarterly*, XXI (1922), 41–50, 170–78.

Tardy, Mary. *Southland Writers: Biographical and Critical Sketches of the Living Female Writers of the South*. 2 vols. Philadelphia, 1870.

Taylor, Rosser Howard. *Ante-bellum South Carolina: A Social and Cultural History*. Chapel Hill, 1942.

Taylor, William R. *Cavalier and Yankee: The Old South and American National Character*. New York, 1961.

Taylor, William R., and Christopher Lasch. "Two 'Kindred Spirits': Sorority and Family in New England, 1839–1846." *New England Quar-terly*, XXXVI (1963), 23–41.

Thomas, John L., ed. *Slavery Attacked: The Abolitionist Crusade*. Englewood Cliffs, N.J., 1965.

Ticknor, Caroline. *Hawthorne and His Publisher*. Boston, 1913.

Tise, Larry E. *Proslavery: A History of the Defense of Slavery in America, 1701–1840*. Athens, Ga., 1987.

Tompkins, Jane. *Sensational Designs: The Cultural Work of American Fiction, 1790–1860*. New York, 1985.

———. "Sentimental Power: *Uncle Tom's Cabin* and the Politics of Literary History." In *The New Feminist Criticism: Essays on Women, Literature, and Theory*, edited by Elaine Showalter. New York, 1985.

———, ed. *Reader-Response Criticism: From Formalism to Post-Structuralism*. Baltimore, 1980.

Tyler-McGraw, Marie. "Richmond Free Blacks and African Colonization, 1816–1832." *Journal of American Studies*, XXI (1987), 207–24.

Ulrich, Laurel Thatcher. *Goodwives: Image and Reality in the Lives of Women in Northern New England, 1650–1750*. New York, 1982.

Vinovskis, Maris, and Richard Bernard. "Beyond Catharine Beecher: Female Education in the Antebellum Period." *Signs*, III (1978), 857–69.

Voloshin, Beverly R. "A Historical Note on Women's Fiction: A Reply to Annette Kolodny." *Critical Inquiry*, II (1976), 817–20.

———. "The Limits of Domesticity: The Female *Bildungsroman* in America, 1820–1870." *Women's Studies*, X (1984), 283–302.

Walsh, Mary K. "Caroline Howard Gilman." M.A. thesis, Duke University, 1941.

Walters, Ronald. *American Reformers, 1815–1860*. New York, 1978.

Warren, Joyce W. *The American Narcissus: Individualism and Women in Nineteenth-Century American Fiction*. New Brunswick, N.J., 1984.

Wasserstrom, William. *Heiress of All the Ages: Sex and Sentiment in the Genteel Tradition*. Minneapolis, 1959.

Watson, Ritchie D., Jr. *The Cavalier in Virginia Fiction*. Baton Rouge, 1985.

Wauchope, George A. *Writers of South Carolina*. Columbia, S.C., 1910.

Welter, Barbara. "The Cult of True Womanhood, 1820–1860." In Welter, *Dimity Convictions: The American Woman in the Nineteenth Century*. Athens, Ohio, 1976.

Welter, Rush. *Popular Education and Democratic Thought in America.* New York, 1962.

Whichard, Lindsey. "Caroline Lee Hentz, Pro-Slavery Propagandist." M.A. thesis, University of North Carolina, 1951.

Wiley, Bell Irwin. *Confederate Women.* Westport, Conn., 1975.

Williams, Benjamin B. *A Literary History of Alabama: The Nineteenth Century.* Cranbury, N.J., 1979.

Wilson, Edmund. *Patriotic Gore: Studies in the Literature of the American Civil War.* 1962; rpr. Boston, 1984.

Wimsatt, Mary Ann. "Antebellum Fiction." In *The History of Southern Literature*, edited by Louis Rubin, Jr., et al. Baton Rouge, 1985.

Wish, Harvey, ed. *Antebellum.* New York, 1960.

Wood, Ann Douglas. "The 'Scribbling Women' and Fanny Fern: Why Women Wrote." *American Quarterly*, XXIII (1971), 3–24.

Wright, Mary Hudson. "Mary Virginia Terhune ('Marion Harland'): Her Life and Works." Ph.D. dissertation, George Peabody College for Teachers, 1934.

Wyatt-Brown, Bertram. "The Evolution of Heroes' Honor in the Southern Literary Tradition." In *The Evolution of Southern Culture*, edited by Numan V. Bartley. Athens, Ga., 1988.

———. "Honor and Secession." In Wyatt-Brown, *Yankee Saints and Southern Sinners.* Baton Rouge, 1985.

———. *Southern Honor: Ethics and Behavior in the Old South.* New York, 1982.

Zimmerman, John J. "The Novels of Caroline Lee Hentz." M.A. thesis, University of Florida, 1949.

Index